Thank you for returning
your books on time.

GAYLORD

The History of Christian Europe

LION

G. R. EVANS

THE HISTORY OF CHRISTIAN EUROPE

Copyright © 2008 G. R. Evans
This edition copyright © 2008 Lion Hudson

The author asserts the moral right
to be identified as the author of this work

A Lion Book
an imprint of
Lion Hudson plc
Wilkinson House, Jordan Hill Road,
Oxford OX2 8DR, England
www.lionhudson.com
ISBN 978 0 7459 5265 9

First edition 2008
10 9 8 7 6 5 4 3 2 1 0

Text Acknowledgments

Scripture quotations taken from the New English Bible
copyright © 1961, 1970 by Oxford University Press and
Cambridge University Press.

A catalogue record for this book is available
from the British Library

Typeset in 12.25/15 Bembo
Printed and bound in Hong Kong

Contents

Introduction

'Why write history?' was a simpler question in pre-Christian Europe. The answer which tended to be given was in terms of recording heroic achievements. Herodotus, the historian of ancient Greece (b. c. 484 BC), says at the opening of his histories that his purpose is to ensure that the great deeds of men are not lost to memory. The Roman historian Livy (59 BC–AD 17) had no such difficulty. He says in the Preface to his history of Rome that he is setting out simply to record the achievements of the Roman people from the foundation of their city.

This approach did not die away altogether with the advent of Christianity. It still appeared in the writing of the lives of saints, who were held up as examples for imitation. But a grander conspectus opened up, in which history merged with philosophy and theology. Questions had also been asked by ancient philosophers about the purpose of the world and whether anyone was in control of the final outcome of world events, but for Christian thinkers those questions were most naturally answered in terms of the providential plan of an omnipotent and wholly good God.

The church had a written history quite early on. Eusebius of Caesarea (c. AD 260–340, bishop of Caesarea from at least AD 315) conceived the idea of writing a history of the church, mainly in the East and mainly in the form of a compilation of extracts from the writings of others, but others took up the idea and began to create a historiographical tradition. The first Christian historians thought of themselves as continuing 'salvation history', the narrative of God's dealings with humankind as set out in the Bible. This had begun before time and would continue after the end of time, into eternity. This was the approach Augustine of Hippo (AD 354–430) took in his *City of God*, completed early in the fifth century, in which he was faced with the embarrassing task of explaining to articulate, well-educated pagan refugees from Italy, who had arrived in north Africa in flight from the barbarian invaders, how God could possibly have intended the fall of a Christian empire. The answer he gave was that Christians needed to take the long view: in God's plan for the world the fall of the Roman empire was a comparatively minor moment.

The same approach of looking at the story on a grand scale, which went beyond history in time and included eternity, was worked out with particular enthusiasm in the twelfth century by Rupert of Deutz (d. 1129), Anselm of Havelberg (c. 1100–1158) and especially Joachim of Fiore (c. 1135–1202), whose prophetic writings sought to put a date on the end of the world. They all read the Bible as a story told in three ages, of the Father, Son and Holy Spirit respectively. The secular context faded behind this Christianized account of not only what had happened in the history of the world but also the reasons why it had happened.

In the early modern world Christian writing about the past began to mutate into a more human-centred view of historical progress. Europeans 'discovered' the New World and new ways of studying new topics became fashionable. It was difficult for Europeans not to see themselves as advancing. In England the 'Whig' view of history thought of human civilization as progressive (with Whig politics at the apex of the development).

Auguste Comte (1798–1857) wrote a *Cours de Philosophie Positive* (1830) in which he postulated that humanity had experienced three ages of development. The first had been the theological, which he regarded as 'fictitious'. The second had been the age of metaphysical or rational and philosophical thinking. The present age was the age of science. This became a fashionable subject.

Yet the notion that 'modern science' must somehow supersede an earlier approach to life in which religion forms a significant strand was not new. The battle for dominance between 'science' or 'philosophy' (which used reason alone) and 'religion' (which involved faith) and the vexed question of how they are to coexist is to be observed in Europe in every Christian century.

Literature and the arts come into it too. This is an aspect of the problem with which Jerome (c. AD 345–420) was wrestling in the fourth century, when he felt that the temptation to read the secular classics was a dangerous distraction from his concentration on studies connected with the Christian faith. When Guibert of Nogent (1053–1124) guiltily read secular poetry under the bedclothes in the late eleventh century he was grappling with the same problem.

Our story in this book concerns the way Christian Europe came to have its extraordinary influence upon the world. The teaching of Jesus, which he never wrote down himself, survived and was carried throughout the Roman world, transforming not only the thinking but also the structures of society, in a Christendom which was, until relatively modern times, essentially a 'European' phenomenon. It was a phenomenon which helped to define Europe itself and to drive its civilization and its activities in the directions which have stamped it with its Christian shape. One of the questions which this book seeks to answer is how this happened, and what it has meant for the peoples of Europe and the wider world; for, since the sixteenth century, Europe has been increasingly engaged with a world much bigger geographically than the range of its own small territories.

1 Christianity and Europe's Sense of Identity

Although the European Community is still growing, Europe is physically very small in proportion to its historical importance and its influence in the modern world. On the map of the world, as a modern geographer sees it, Europe occupies a tiny corner of the Eurasian land mass, naturally bounded by the sea on every side except to the East, where the boundary with the continent of Asia has been the subject of political and religious dispute. The British Isles are separated by sea from the European mainland by twenty miles or so at the narrowest point. Iceland is often included in Europe, though it is remote from its main territories.

The problem of determining the boundary between Europe and Asia presented itself quite forcefully to early Christians. Orosius (c. AD 385–420) discusses it in his book *Against the Pagans*. Russia reaches far into Asia, but European Russia begins at the Ural mountains. The border runs south a little uncertainly, down to the Caspian Sea, along the mountains of the Caucasus or perhaps the Kura River, and on to the Black Sea, where it runs though the Dardanelles. Then the sea provides a continuing natural boundary to the Middle East down to the Suez Canal and the beginning of Africa. The exact point where Europe becomes Asia is viewed differently by geographers of different nationalities, the Russian view, for example, tending to put the Caucasus in Asia. The dual-continent aspect of Russia was still a point of interest in the seventeenth century, when 'Europian Tartars' are mentioned (1603).

Looked at from outside the 'world' of Europe, it is not obvious that Europe is entitled to be considered a continent at all. Sometimes it has been called a peninsula of Eurasia, and some of the migrant Indo-European peoples who moved west into Europe treated it as though that was exactly what it was. There are important – and topical – questions today about the influence Asian civilizations had upon the

RIGHT: This map of the world was drawn at the end of the Middle Ages based on the ideas of the first-century Greek thinker Ptolemy. It shows how closely the geography depended on the detailed contemporary knowledge of some parts of the world and how vague everything else was.

formation of Europe at this early stage and later; why 'Europe' ended geographically where it did; and how far there was an interpenetration of cultures between the civilizations of the East and those of the European West. In other words, what does it mean, culturally and geographically, to talk of 'East' and 'West'? The answers began to change, first with the coming of Christianity and secondly with the rise of Islam in the seventh century AD.

THE IDEA OF EUROPE

Europe has not always been seen in the way it is on a modern map, as a distinctively shaped tract of territory with the physical and human geography in position. Throughout most of the history of Europe, the exact lie of the land could be mapped only roughly by the standards of

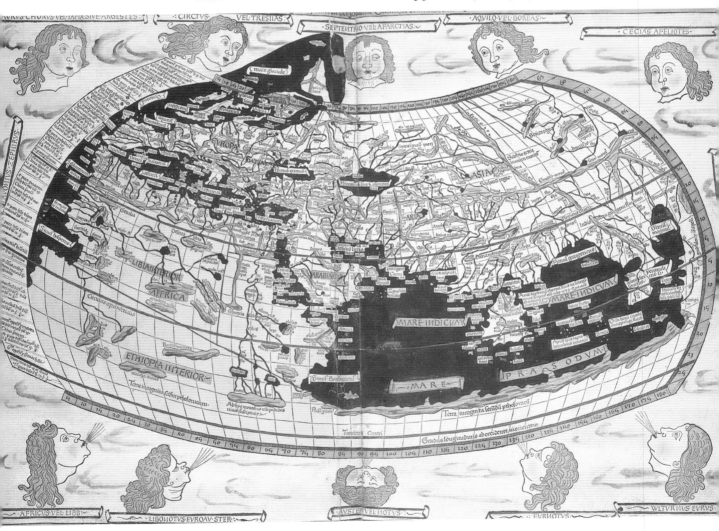

modern cartography. More importantly, Europe has been an idea, part of an explanation of the world, and Christian apologists have entered enthusiastically into that process. So before we begin on the story of the way Christianity emerged in Europe and the effect it has had, we need to explore this ancient 'theory' of Europe.

The word 'Europe' probably derives from the name of Europa. In one of the Greek myths she was a Phoenician princess, carried off by Zeus the king of the Gods, who had turned himself into a bull for the purpose; in the story he took her to Crete, where she bore the child who became its king, Minos. The Greek poet Homer describes her as queen of Crete. By about 500 BC 'Europe' was being used by the Greeks to describe first the Greek mainland and then more northerly parts of the modern European land mass.

The Classical Idea of Europe

The ancient convention was to divide the world into Europe, Asia and Africa (sometimes called Libya). The way classical authors write about this is a reminder of the heavy colouration of the politics and social structures which determined the angle from which they looked upon the world, and also the extremely limited geographical knowledge they had beyond the territory occupied by the Romans at the height of their imperial power.

The Greek historian Polybius (born c. 208 BC) pressed for Greek acceptance of Roman supremacy in Greek lands, while hoping the Greeks would quietly preserve as far as possible the autonomy of the city states, for the city state, with its modest size and opportunities for active participation in affairs, was the preferred government arrangement of the ancient Greeks. His descriptions of the lands of Europe is heavily geared to considerations of advantage in military and naval warfare. He notes the location of advantageous promontories from which to see the enemy coming, for example, and good launching points for ships to stop them.

For the duration of Rome as republic and empire, the centre of the world was Rome. The Romans fell into the habit of seeing themselves as looking out from the centre of the world, and that made it easy to leave the remoter fringes of the known world a little vague. Polybius is inclined not to bother in his main account with the lands 'densely inhabited by barbarous tribes' such as lie along the Iberian coast of the Atlantic and have only recently come to notice, or the northern parts which are 'up to now unknown to us, and will remain so unless the curiosity of explorers lead to some discoveries in the future'. To the south, too, beyond what is known of 'Asia and Africa where they meet in Aethiopia', 'no one up to the present has been able to say with certainty whether the southern extension of them is continuous land or is bounded by a sea'.

Strabo, a Greek geographer (64/3 BC–AD 24) who sees himself as a Roman citizen, is also clear that the geography of the world can best be interpreted with reference to the hegemony of Rome. Rome began with only one city. The Romans 'acquired the whole of Italy through warfare and statesmanlike rulership', and then, 'by exercising the same superior qualities, they also acquired the regions round about Italy'.

It is true that the sea bounds modern Europe on most of its sides, but for the Romans the northern extremities lay on the edge of empire, at the great rivers not the ocean. As Strabo describes it, the Rhine and the Danube were natural boundaries for the Romans:

Of the continents, being three in number, they hold almost the whole of Europe, except that part of it which lies outside the [Danube] river and the parts along the ocean which lies between the [Rhine] and the [Don]. Of Libya, the whole of the coast on Our Sea [the Mediterranean] is subject to them; and the rest of the country is uninhabited or else inhabited only in a wretched or nomadic fashion. In like manner, of Asia also, the whole of the coast on Our Sea is subject to them, unless one takes into account the regions of [those] who live a piratical and nomadic life in narrow and sterile districts; and of the interior and the country deep inland, one part is held by the Romans themselves and another by the Parthians and the barbarians beyond them; and on the east and north live Indians and Bactrians and Scythians, and then Arabians and Aethiopians; but some further portion is constantly being taken from these peoples and added to the possessions of the Romans.

Both Alexander the Great's (356–323 BC) wars with Persia in the fourth century BC and the well-established trading links had long made it apparent that there was business to be done there with advanced and civilized peoples, and peoples who might be ambitious to move into Europe. The term 'Asia' seems to have been used first by the Greek historian Herodotus about 440 BC, though he used it primarily for Asia Minor, an area familiar to the Greeks. By the time of Pliny the Elder (AD 23–79) writing his *Natural History*, it was possible to devote several books of the work to a detailed description of the lands of the world, with details of their population and history and a sprinkling of gossip to enliven the texture. These authors were writing in the period when the

Roman empire still controlled most of the lands which now form Europe, north Africa and the near part of Asia and was actively engaged in trade with India, thus reaching far into east Asia, and they saw the extent of the world accordingly. Pliny discusses a good deal of Asia, including the 'Arabs'.

The Roman notion of 'Africa' tended to be confined to the strip along the Mediterraean coast and to Egypt and Ethiopia, with vague notions of what might lie beyond. The ancient idea of the three continents being surrounded by an ocean still seemed probable for a long time, as late as Bede (c. AD 672/3–735), for example. This notion discouraged the conception of an Africa stretching unimaginably far south.

Classical authors had an assumption that if a place was uncivilized (by which they really meant not under Roman control) it was not really a 'place' at all. It needed to be inhabited in a way which would give it shape and character; to have a particular kind of human geography. The

THE ORIGINS OF THE BIBLE

The Bible did not arrive ready-made with its content agreed. It was the creation of several centuries of discussion about what should be accepted as constituting God's Word and in what sense the writings of human authors could be taken to be of 'divine' authorship.

It was not until about the fourth century that it was more or less agreed which books should be included in the Bible. Several candidates were eventually excluded. Clement of Alexandria thought the *Didache* (first to second centuries) was part of Scripture. The *Didache* gives a picture of the church life of the first Christians, the way they thought baptism should be administered (by total immersion), the way they conducted celebrations of the Eucharist and the way they fasted on Wednesdays and Fridays. Another candidate for inclusion was the *Teachings of the Apostles*, which was probably written in Syria in the early third century. Then there were the Apostolic Canons, which date from about AD 350–380. They list the books of Scripture in the last of the canons, including among them the canons themselves. Scripture was most commonly copied, studied and commented on in the form of separate books.

Jerome, who made the Vulgate Latin translation of the Bible, was then still actively discussing which books were part of the Bible and which were not. What is sometimes called the 'canon' was probably defined only about AD 382, and there was still room for dispute about the inclusion of the Apocrypha, a cluster of books which the Roman Catholic Church prints in the middle of the Bible and Protestants usually leave out. Exactly which books constitute Scripture was still being disputed in the sixteenth century. The fourth session of the Council of Trent (1546) produced a list of the Apocrypha, which the reformers did not count as

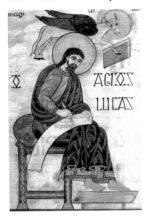

Luke the Evangelist writing his Gospel in the Lindisfarne Gospels.

classical world thus fades into a vague blur at the edges, partly because no one who matters is living there.

The Christian Idea of Europe: Europe as 'Christendom'

With the coming of Christianity the central vantage point moved for a time from Rome to Jerusalem and the world acquired new dimensions. Augustine's contemporary Jerome offers a new view of the location of the centre of the world. Referring in his commentary on Ezekiel to the statement that Jerusalem is positioned 'in the midst of the nations', he shows how the three continents are deployed around Jerusalem. That is not by any means the same as suggesting that the world began to be run from Jerusalem in a practical or commercial sense. It was all a matter of perception: primitive Christianity was a circle which had Jerusalem at its centre. This was an important shift because Christianity, like Judaism, was by origin an Eastern religion. It began in Asia, in what is now the Middle

Scripture, considering them 'false' or 'spurious' and not properly part of the Word of God.

The idea that there were certain texts which God had inspired so directly that he dictated the very words into the ears of the human authors who wrote them down is made visible in medieval pictures of the four evangelists busy writing, with the Holy Spirit in the form of a dove dictating into each one's ear. Jerome had been conscious of the importance of this idea and was careful to insist that he did not regard his translation as itself inspired. That did not prevent Western scholars of later generations treating it as though it was, analysing every word as closely as if the Holy Spirit had dictated it in Latin.

The natural mode of Bible study in the early church was for the bishop to preach lengthy exegetical sermons, working his way through whole books of the Bible. Such preaching was done from the bishop's seat in the cathedral and formed part of the liturgy. In the West this happened in Latin, but as this was still the vernacular the congregation would have had no difficulty in understanding what was read to them and what the bishop said about it. In the East, where Greek went on being spoken, the Greek text of the Old Testament, known as the Septuagint because it was believed to be the work of a team of seventy, and the Greek text of the New Testament never ceased to be available for direct study, and the Vulgate had no place in the tradition of reading, preaching and exegesis.

EUROPE BETWEEN HEAVEN AND HELL

Dante stands outside his beloved city of Florence, holding a copy of his *Divine Comedy*, with hell underneath his feet and people trying to ascend the levels of the heavens in the background behind him.

Christians from an early stage believed that this world stands between heaven and hell. The world of the classical geographers, containing Europe as one of the three linked continents of the physical world, was gradually positioned by the Christian tradition in a hierarchical universe with a heaven or the heavens (the sky and the supernatural stratum in which an eternal life was lived) above and a hell below. In due course there was also to be a purgatory, though that was not to be properly defined until the twelfth century in the West. This was a place 'between' heaven and hell, where the souls of those who were on their way to heaven could spend as much time as was necessary for them to discharge the penances for their sins which they had not completed before they died. In the Greek world this development did not take place and the Orthodox envisage something rather different, a place like the Hades of the ancient world, in which the dead await the end of the world. There those who are to go to hell have a foretaste of what awaits them and those who are to go to heaven have glimpses of the bliss to come.

East. Believers in Jesus Christ were apparently first called 'Christians' at Antioch (Acts 11:26).

However, Jerusalem did not remain central for long. The first epistle of Clement of Alexandria (c. AD 150–215) to the Corinthians suggests that the Christians in Rome were taking it for granted as early as the end of the first century that Rome should lead the church, pointing to the fact that the Apostles Peter and Paul had been martyred in their city. The great change was the decision to move away from expecting Christians to continue to observe the law of Moses. One of the defining moments was the Apostle Peter's vision of a sheet let down from heaven, containing creatures he as a Jew would have considered unclean. In the vision he was told not to consider anything 'unclean and therefore not to be eaten which God considers to be clean' (Acts 10:9–16). Another defining moment is recorded in Acts 15, when the church at Jerusalem decided that Christians who had not formerly been Jews did not need to be circumcised. Once that had happened Christianity became identified with a world outside Judaism which embraced the 'Gentiles', or non-Jewish peoples.

EARLY CHRISTIAN EUROPE

The classical division of the physical world into three continents was adopted by early Christian writers. Augustine uses it, but he also explores its geographical implications a little for himself: 'The part of the world which is called Asia stretches from the middle to the east and north; Europe from the north to the west; and Africa from the west to the south.' Cassiodorus (c. AD 490–585) in the sixth century uses it as the obvious illustration for the concept of 'where': '"Where" is as in Asia, Europe, Lybia'. Isidore, bishop of Seville (c. AD 560–636), discusses the great rivers of Europe in their relation to Germany.

It is not surprising that the early Christian authors should take over the classical writers' notions of Europe's position in the world, but the transmission continues into the Middle Ages, with no grounds apparent to authors for questioning seriously the basic geographical framework. For example at the beginning of the twelfth century, the Benedictine monk Rupert of Deutz urges that there should be preaching in Africa and Europe as well as Asia, not because that seemed a serious possibility for anyone to organize from a German monastery, but because it was still a natural way of saying 'all over the world'. The Victorine canon Andrew of St Victor (c. 1110–1175) in the mid-twelfth century links the divisions of the earth to the divisions of language.

Among the offspring of Noah's sons, the sons of Japheth have the northern part of Asia and the whole of Europe; those of Cham or Ham have the southern part of Asia and the whole of Africa; and the 'middle' of Asia, 'which is bigger than Europe and Africa', belongs to the children of Sem or Shem. This reflects an awareness (not new) that the traditional divisions of the earth did not portion it equally, some being considerably bigger than others.

2 How Europe Became Christian

MISSION AND MEMBERSHIP

Jesus sent out his disciples two by two, to preach wherever they found themselves and move on. 'So they set out and called publicly for repentance' (Mark 6:12) and healed the sick. It was in this way that they were to 'bear fruit' (John 15:8–9). Matthew's Gospel records how, after the crucifixion, when Jesus was seen by his disciples in Galilee, he said to them: 'Go forth therefore and make all nations my disciples' (Matthew 28:19).

In the story of what happened after Jesus' death, the Acts of the Apostles describes a community clinging together at first for mutual support, with reason, because it was in danger of persecution (Acts 8:1). But soon it began to grow as 'the word of God now spread more and more widely' (Acts 6:7). When 'the Apostles in Jerusalem heard that Samaria had accepted the word of God' (Acts 8:14) they sent Peter and John, who travelled there 'giving their testimony and speaking the word of God' and back to Jerusalem 'bringing the good news to many Samaritan villages on the way' (Acts 8:25).

Some of these early missionaries saw themselves as being 'sent' by the Holy Spirit. For example, Barnabas and Paul, having received the blessing of the community at Antioch, set off for Seleucia and then sailed to Cyprus (Acts 13:4). The New Testament includes letters, mainly from Paul, to communities of Christians by then established widely in Greece and Asia Minor: Corinthians, Galatians, Ephesians, Philippians, Thessalonians. The early church was concentrated in the Greek-speaking half of the Roman empire. Ephesus is in modern Asia Minor; Thessalonica (Thessaloniki) in modern Greece.

But Paul also wrote a letter to the Christians in Rome. From Christ, says Paul, 'I received the privilege of a commission in his name to lead to faith and obedience men in all nations, yourselves among them' (Romans 1:5–6). 'I have often planned to come,' he continues, 'though so far without success... I am under obligation to Greek and non-Greek, to learned and simple; hence my eagerness to declare the Gospel to you in Rome' (Romans 1:13–15). Paul went to Rome and spent time in prison there and he died in Rome, thus extending the Christian mission decisively into western Europe and the lands where Latin, not Greek, was the dominant language.

The enterprise was by no means confined to Europe and the nearer parts of Asia, however. Christianity was practised as far afield as China by the seventh century.

Membership

The Acts of the Apostles describes how Philip baptized a eunuch whom he found reading the book of Isaiah in his chariot (Acts 8:26–39). This baptism took place by the roadside and not in church, but it was not the act of a breakaway rebel. Philip was one of the seven men of honest

UNITY OF FAITH

The spread of the gospel was a recipe for its dilution and the introduction of potential misunderstandings and even deliberate changes. One of the first things to be recognized was the importance of preserving the 'one faith' as Jesus had taught it.

In the very early period which is described in the Acts of the Apostles, it already seems to have been agreed that the leaders of the community would take responsibility for teaching the faith. Acts 15 contains the story of a dangerous division of opinion involving those who said that the disciples of Jesus ought to go on keeping the laws of the Old Testament and observing Jewish practices such as the circumcision of male infants. Others thought this was not what Jesus had intended, for had he not come to bring freedom? This was a question of fundamental importance and the future of the church probably depended on the way it was resolved. The community at Jerusalem held a meeting and arrived at agreement through debate. Then they appointed leaders to teach on their behalf in the continuing missionary work of the community. This episode brought together the concept that there could be only one faith with the idea that trusted leaders ought to be responsible for spreading it.

Probably quite early a declaration of faith came into being, of which we have an example in the text of what is now known as the Apostle's Creed. This seems to have developed from the worship of the early church, although its present form was fixed only in about the Carolingian period (the eighth or ninth century) in the West. It was then perhaps that the legend grew up that it was the work of the apostles. The word for 'creed' in Greek was *symbolon*, which prompted the idea that the apostles had actually sat together round a table and put it together by contributing a clause each:

reputation who were given special responsibility for making sure that the practical requirements of the widows and the needy were not neglected by the community of believers (Acts 6:5).

This episode is a reminder that the first Christians had to make important and far-reaching decisions about a number of basic questions. Could anyone be a 'Christian' who said he was? Was being a Christian a matter solely between the believer and God? Was some ceremony or act of admission to the community helpful, or perhaps even necessary, so that other Christians could know that the new Christian was really one of them? Who could perform such a ceremony and on what authority? There were self-appointed 'Christians' willing to take considerable powers to themselves, not least in what they taught, so these questions mattered.

Some 'charismatics' or 'spirit-led' Christians believed the Holy Spirit spoke to them directly. Such independently-minded individuals prompted

I believe in one God, the Father Almighty, maker of heaven and earth, and in one Lord Jesus Christ, his only-begotten Son, who was conceived by the Holy Ghost, born of the Virgin Mary, suffered under Pontius Pilate, was crucified, dead and buried. He descended into Hell. The third day he rose again from the dead. He ascended into heaven, and sitteth on the right hand of God the Father. From thence he shall come again to judge the quick and the dead. I believe in the Holy Ghost, the Holy Catholic Church, the communion of saints, the remission of sins, the resurrection of the body, and the life everlasting.

To a degree which is surprising in the circumstances, certain fundamentals remained consistent throughout the old Roman empire. One was the very rule that there should be agreement in one faith. Variation in forms of worship was one thing, but diversity was not to be allowed in matters of faith. Vincent of Lérins (d. before AD 450) proposes a test in his *Commonitorium*, written about AD 434: the church should believe what has been held 'everywhere, always and by everyone', he says. In that way, the church will remain 'catholic' or 'universal' (these being terms for the same idea, derived respectively from Greek and Latin).

Nevertheless, there were topics not covered by the creed. Much was left to be decided about the nature of the church, its visible forms, the ministry and its duties and the administration of the sacraments, which was to lead to debate in the Middle Ages.

A seventeenth-century drawing of Philip baptizing the Eunuch, who has climbed out of a lavishly appointed chariot, which indicates his social status, and kneels down humbly while his servant holds the horses.

the crisis which is recorded in Acts 15:1. They were travelling about, teaching Christians that they would have to be circumcised as Moses had instructed or they could not be saved. Acts 15:2–27 describes a meeting of the community of Christians in Jerusalem, at which various opinions were put to the whole community for discussion. When agreement was reached that circumcision was not necessary, it was decided that this was to be disseminated by chosen and trusted individuals and was to carry the authority of the apostles and elders at Jerusalem, on behalf of 'the whole Church'.

All this was of huge importance. It underlined the community and consensual character of the little band of Christians; it encouraged them to identify their faith and practices as distinct from those of Judaism; it made them realize that they were going to need to agree about organization and the apportioning of roles within the community, and who was to be authorized to do what. They were going to have to decide what was central to being a Christian and would require unity, and what could vary from place to place.

Decisions were also going to have to be taken about lingering pagan beliefs, for the populations of the Roman empire were used to the idea that many gods could coexist comfortably together and that they could choose their favourites for the need of the moment. This was an early manifestation of the problem of 'multiculturalism'. The church learnt to be cautious and not well disposed to toleration when it came to allowing its own members to pick and choose.

Visible or Invisible?

Not all the points which emerged so urgently could be resolved once and for all, as long as some believers preached that the church was not necessarily going to be visible. If it was up to God to decide whom he accepted, as Paul had said in his letter to the Romans (Romans 1:5; 12:6–8), there could be no guarantees that everyone the church baptized and called a 'member' was really a member in God's eyes. The Holy Spirit was believed to act in the entrusting of ministerial duties through the laying on of hands (compare Acts 13:3). Yet under persecution many who had been 'ordained' in this manner fled from their pastoral duties or reneged on their faith, handing over copies of the scriptures. Had they really been God's ministers at all? Only God knew. So from the beginning there ran deep in Christianity a tension or fault line between the visible church, made up of the people one might meet at church on Sundays, and that great cloud of witnesses who were Christians in the sight of God, but whose identity might turn out to be surprising.

A CARING COMMUNITY

Were Christians going to be a 'caring community'? Jesus had been clear enough that the right thing to do if someone asked you for your shirt because he was cold was to give him your cloak at once (Matthew 5:40). Jesus expected his disciples to do good quietly and not so that all the world could see how charitably they were behaving (Matthew 6:1). In the early church it was keenly felt that the Christian community should ensure that those who were in need among them should be supported and kept from want. Widows and orphans of members of the church were seen in this category. There was not the same sense at the beginning that Christians had a general duty to support the poor and mount what would now be called welfare programmes, or to campaign for social change to bring about more equal treatment for everyone. They concentrated on their own members and their families and encouraged Christians to accept social disadvantage patiently and wait for a better life to come, after death.

Even Augustine of Hippo, who thought that 'there was no salvation outside the church', reserved his position on whether this necessarily meant that the visible sacramental acts of a visible community whose members could be clearly identified were necessary or efficacious for salvation. In his book *The City of God*, Augustine insisted that the church is invisible, made up of those God chose before the world began and even before they were created (Romans 8:29). The chosen have no say in his choice and he will never change his mind. Augustine says this means that the visible church is a mixed community, in which the wheat and the weeds grow together until the harvest (compare Matthew 13:28–30). Only at the Last Judgment (Matthew 25:32) will it be revealed who belongs to the church and who is a member of the other 'city', of the damned.

Yet ironically, it was in Augustine's day that the practice of infant baptism became usual in the West. A complex system of public penance had already evolved to enable the restoration of adults who committed serious sins after their baptism. Both developments rested on the emergence of a doctrine of 'original sin', the belief that every human being born since Adam and Eve sinned had inherited the taint of their sinfulness and was guilty in God's eyes just as much as they were; and had moreover also inherited a tendency to commit actual sins, something everyone would inevitably do from earliest childhood, adding to their unacceptability to God.

This made the visible church important as the agent and instrument of God's forgiveness of sin, and as a monitor of the good standing of its members. It created an essential place in the lives of ordinary people for the institutional church. The key text supporting the view that it had these responsibilities was the promise of Jesus that those whose sins were 'retained' by the disciples would remain sinners and those whose sins they remitted would be free of their sins and the consequences (compare Matthew 16:19).

There were several reasons why baptism had tended to be delayed at first until as near death as possible. The most important of these was the belief that it could not be repeated. Jesus had said that someone who put his hand to the plough and then turned back was not fit for the kingdom of God (Luke 9:62). So a person who was baptized too young was in great danger of sinning afterwards. It was sensible, though risky, to wait until old age. It also became important for the would-be Christian to take systematic instruction.

The process of instruction evolved into a progression, in which a person interested in becoming a Christian would begin among the 'hearers' and then move on to be a catechumen, and begin serious instruction in the faith. Canon 14 of the Council of Nicaea (AD 325) sets out rules about what is to happen if a hearer loses interest part of the way through and then changes his mind and wants to continue (he is to go back and serve part of the time of preparation again).

This was not for children. It was not like the simple catechisms of later ages, in which the catechumen simply learned a series of answers to standard questions. The process of learning about the faith could take a considerable time, a period of years. Augustine's *On Catechizing Simple People* gives a lively picture of the difficulties of teaching adults in the north Africa of his day. Adults could, as Augustine complains, prove reluctant to begin on amendment of life until they had completed their classes and perhaps even until they had actually been baptized. He tried to chivvy his readers into matching their behaviour with their growing faith. Indeed, it was this problem which formed the background to his writings on faith and works, which were quoted by both sides in the Reformation of the sixteenth century, though the dispute was then about something quite different: the question of whether it was having faith or living virtuously which fitted a person for heaven.

Catechumens joined in the worship of the church but sat apart. They left before the celebration of the Eucharist began. As Easter approached each year those who were to be baptized formed a special group in which they would receive final instruction. All this may have helped to emphasize to those who were thinking of joining the huge significance which came to be attached to becoming a full member of the church at one's baptism.

But conversely, the more importance baptism had, not only as the rite which admitted a person to full membership but also as the sacrament which remitted all their sins and made them clean in the sight of God, the more parents began to want it for their infants. Infant mortality was high. If the unbaptized could not go to heaven, as Augustine and others taught, Christian parents wanted their babies to be protected. Even the followers of Pelagius (c. AD 354–420/440), a Roman society preacher from Britain who believed that there was no such thing as original sin and anyone could be good by trying hard enough, secretly brought their babies to be baptized just in case original sin was a reality after all, so great was this anxiety.

It will be clear by now that becoming (and remaining) a Christian and an accepted member of a local church community was not turning out to be a simple matter in these first centuries.

From Persecution to Official Religion

Jesus was acclaimed as a Messiah by some of his popular following but he made it plain by his behaviour that the civil authorities need not fear that

RIGORISM

Infant baptism probably exacerbated what had already become quite a problem for the church and had caused rifts in the third century between the 'rigorists' and those who thought that although rebaptism was not possible, penitence might work to restore a sinner who was truly sorry. The problem was that baptized people misbehaved. Those baptized as infants had longer to commit more sins. If being purged of all one's sins was a once-in-a-lifetime chance, there was an obvious need for a means of dealing with these episodes.

The early church concentrated on its disapproval of three especially serious sins: murder, adultery and apostasy. These it might indeed be possible to avoid for a lifetime, and those who were caught, and who repented, were faced, at best, with a process of public penitence as protracted as the preparation for baptism in maturity, but with a less happy ending. Such sinners were to be excommunicated (not allowed to join with others in the Eucharist), cut off from normal participation in the life of the community and dressed in special penitential garments.

The period of penance could be very lengthy. Canon 11 of the Council of Nicaea deals with those who have betrayed the faith even though no one has threatened them with persecution. They are to go back to the beginning and spend a decade progressing towards readmission as though they were new hearers, and they can never be restored to the fullness of their original post-baptismal membership, or if someone had formerly been a priest, to his full priestly role and tasks. No one was to be left in any doubt of the seriousness of the repentance and the penitent's desire to be readmitted. The absolution eventually given was an act of the bishop, in front of the whole congregation.

One of the writers who had an influence in shaping the church's policy about all this was a north African bishop. Cyprian, who was bishop of Carthage from AD 248 and died in AD 258, was himself a late-life Christian convert, becoming a Christian only in AD 246. Soon after he was made a bishop a period of persecution of Christians began (the 'Decian' persecution, started by the emperor Decius) and he went into exile. When it was safe to return, in AD 251, he came back to find than many of his Christian flock including the clergy had abandoned the faith in fright. Some had obtained certificates declaring that they had sacrificed to idols to prove they were not Christians and save their skins, although he would be a revolutionary in the way they thought. He rode into Jerusalem not in triumph but on an ass (Matthew 21:2). Pay Caesar what you owe him, and render to God what you owe to him, said Jesus (Matthew 22:21; Mark 12:17). Paul took a similar line when he taught that slaves should obey their masters (Colossians 3:22). All this encouraged Christians in the early generations to be quiet, responsible members of

A medieval picture, by a fourteenth-century Spanish book illustrator, of the bishop of Carthage being brought before the Emperor Valerian, who ordered the execution of Christian clergy and was responsible for Cyprian's martyrdom.

in fact many of them had not really gone back to pagan practices. Those who hid behind these certificates were known as the *libellatici.*

The problem was that if people like these cowards were forgiven, those who had been brave and risked their lives for the faith might feel they had had their courage trivialized. And next time there was a persecution, Christians might believe it was acceptable to go back to paganism until it was safe to emerge again as Christians. Novatian (c. AD 200–258), a priest in Rome, strongly disapproved of that. It contradicted Jesus' condemnation of those who put their hands to the plough and then turned back (Luke 9:62). His followers, known as the Novatianists, favoured a rigorist approach. This was in line with the teaching of Tertullian, another influential theologian from north Africa (c. AD 160–225). There could be no restoration of such sinners, said the rigorists.

Yet it was impractical to be rigorous to the point where every little misdemeanour would exclude a Christian from membership of the church for ever. And where was the line to be drawn?

A picture of Christ teaching his disciples from the Domitilla catacombs in Rome, the earliest surviving catacombs, where Christians buried their dead, including some of the martyrs, until the period of persecution came to an end. This depiction of Christ as a teacher was the usual way of portraying him in the first centuries.

RIGHT: This picture of the catacombs of St Sebastian in Rome shows the funerary jars that were used.

society and not refuse to pay their taxes. But in reality it raised complex questions, questions which would shift over time with changes in secular government structures and practices, about what fell into God's province and what into that of the secular state.

The first stage of the story saw Christianity establishing a place in contemporary society. The process showed that the secular authorities were far from considering Christianity to be harmless, at least at first. Christianity had begun under the shadow of the trial of its leader for allegedly fomenting civil unrest and even revolution. Christianity was some centuries in finding social and political acceptance and proving itself not to be dangerous. One of the ways in which Rome dealt with the challenge of the invading tribes which were arriving enquiringly in Roman lands on the fringes of an empire which had grown too big to control, to see whether they could safely take them over, was to invite them into the local society, allowing a role in government and administration to the leaders of the invaders. Jews and Christians would not accept the pervasive syncretism which had served Rome well as it extended its rule and took in new lands inhabited by a variety of polytheists. The Jews and the Christians insisted on monotheism and would not allow their God to be identified with the Roman Jupiter or the Greek Zeus in a unified pantheon. This led to the episodes of state persecution.

These periodic bursts of official, state-sponsored attacks on Christians went on for some centuries, beginning with the persecutions of AD 64–68 under the emperor Nero (r. AD 54–68). In AD 249–250 the

emperor Decius (r. AD 249–251) issued an edict in which he ordered all his subjects to sacrifice to the pagan gods.

Christians were sometimes terrorized into apostasy, handing over their copies of the scriptures to the state bullies. The English word 'traitors' derives from these *traditores* or 'handers-over'. Bishops were required to sacrifice publicly to the emperor and public inquiries were set in train, which issued certificates to those who had complied.

After the death of Decius in AD 251, his successor the emperor Valerian (r. AD 253–260) began fresh persecutions in AD 257–258. The death penalty was imposed on Christian clergy who would not sacrifice to the gods. Diocletian (r. AD 284–305) began yet another period of persecution in AD 303, ordering church buildings to be burned and copies of the Christian scriptures to be seized. Christians were not allowed to meet for worship. They were to enjoy the privileges of citizenship only if they agreed to sacrifice to the pagan gods.

CIVIC RELIGION

Relations between church and state were not all plain sailing from the point when Constantine decided to become a Christian emperor. The emperor Julian (r. AD 361–363) took the empire temporarily back to official paganism. He had a taste for Neoplatonic thought and he set about suppressing the Christian 'mysteries', earning the title of 'Apostate' for himself because he was thought to have turned his back on the Christian faith. The mystery religions of Asia Minor, such as Mithraism, included practices which seemed to some akin to those of the Christians, especially the worship of a god who died and rose again and the celebration of rites from which initiates were excluded. There was still a risk of contamination of the faith with 'cognate' systems of belief. Whether a citizen would be willing to show a reverence to the emperor amounting to worship remained a useful test of citizenly good behaviour, and it lent itself to use as a instrument of state control in the Roman empire. Augustine speaks of this 'civic religion' in *The City of God*. So although from the time of Constantine Christianity became the official religion of Europe, its position was not yet politically secure.

Becoming 'official' and 'recognized' created new problems for the Christian community. A balance of power now had to be established between church and state, even if the Christian church was now the state church. That did not mean that it wanted the state to run it. On the other hand, the state was soon going to find the ecclesiastical authorities an important source of reliable administration in an empire under severe strain. The church in the West had means of operating a supply network which held up even after the secular structures began to collapse with the barbarian invasions.

Rome fell in AD 410. Wealthy pagans, educated and articulate, began to flee

The Emperor Constantine.

This sort of thing went on longer in the Eastern half of the Empire than it did in the West, where Constantine (c. AD 280–337) became Emperor in AD 306. He declared for Christianity in AD 312–313, for pragmatic reasons. He had been persuaded that the Christian God was a more powerful ally than any pagan god or gods, and his conversion was announced. He had had a vision in which he was told that 'in this sign' (the sign of the cross) he would be victorious in battle, and so it proved

from Italy to the fringes of empire, including north Africa. Augustine as bishop of Hippo encountered them in his congregation. He wrote *The City of God* partly to answer their indignant questions about the vulnerability of a Christian empire to overthrow by non-Christian and heretical invaders. Surely this demonstrated that Constantine had been in error in believing that the Christian God was the strongest? Augustine's answer was that we must not imagine that we can see and understand the whole of God's plan. Within that plan the fall of the Roman empire was a minor matter. It certainly did not suggest any weakness on the part of the God of the Christians, or that he was less than omnipotent.

The empire did not collapse once and for all in the early fifth century. Pope Gregory the Great (c. AD 540–604) was preaching on Ezekiel in AD 593 when Rome was under threat again, this time from the Arian Lombards. He explains in the surviving text of his sermons that it has taken him eight years to get them ready to be published because of the sheer weight of worries which have got in the way. Gregory had plenty of other matters to concern him (the distribution of grain throughout the empire, for one). But some of Gregory's correspondence shows that he was right to be worried about the Lombards in particular, for a threatening letter arrived from their leader in mid-AD 592, followed not long after by the armies in person.

at the Battle of the Milvian Bridge, where his army, whose soldiers bore crosses on their shields with the Chi-Rho symbol (the first two Greek letters of 'Christ'), defeated a much larger army and enabled him to enter Rome. In AD 313, he issued the Edict of Milan. This removed the sanctions against those who publicly practised Christianity or professed it openly, which had allowed periods of persecution in the past.

The Arians

According to legend, Constantine was baptized by Pope Sylvester (r. AD 314–335). He was probably really baptized by Eusebius of Nicomedia, the Patriarch of Constantinople (d. AD 341), but Eusebius was an 'Arian' or follower of Arius, and that became an embarrassment. Arius (d. AD 336), a priest in Alexandria in Egypt, had stirred up a great controversy about the doctrine of the Trinity and the nature of the incarnate Christ.

The doctrine of the Trinity is of central importance to the Christian faith. Getting it right was essential if Christianity was to be a truly monotheistic religion while preserving the belief that Jesus Christ was truly God. It would not do to let unorthodoxy on the subject spread. On the other hand – and this is an example of a problem which has often cropped up in the history of Christianity – until someone asked an awkward question, kept asking it persistently and made everyone really think, it might not be obvious what the church thought. An 'orthodox' view might have to be agreed to meet the challenge. Arius created such a dramatic challenge that he won a considerable popular following and thus came to seem a dangerous threat to the church in Alexandria. He was condemned by the bishops at a local synod in AD 320.

Arius had, it seems, been saying that the Son was a creation of God the Father and not himself God, and that God had merely used him as an instrument when he created the world. This was one of the options which had been canvassed in the early Christian period as philosophers struggled with the paradoxes of Trinitarian doctrine and tried to understand what a 'person' of the Trinity could be. English now uses the word 'person', which derives from the Latin term for a character in a play, and suggests something like the mask such a character would wear in a classical theatrical performance. The Greek vocabulary which could be used was more subtle and complex in its connotations, and allowed those trying to think about this to move in and out of the idea of divine and human 'natures' also. And how could three persons really be one God?

The Ecumenical Councils and Deciding About the Faith

Defining what the church considered to be 'orthodox' came to be the function of a council of the whole church, a universal or 'ecumenical' council, of which the one Constantine called at Nicaea was afterwards regarded as the first. So the second result of the Arian upheaval was the idea that the best way for the church to make up its mind when there were disagreements was for it to meet, or at least for the bishops to meet as the representatives of the local communities or churches. The model of a 'council' (from the Latin) or 'synod' (from the Greek) was already well understood, but hitherto councils had been chiefly concerned with disciplinary matters and questions of liturgical practice such as rites, and they had been relatively local, involving a meeting of bishops from a comparatively limited area of Europe, usually in the East or in north Africa. There the holding of such meetings was encouraged. The theory was that they articulated the 'mind of the church'; rather than giving orders to the faithful, they were to reflect what the faithful believed under the guidance of the Holy Spirit.

This method of making joint or collective decisions was now to be mapped with some thoroughness in a series of councils. They were all held in the Eastern part of the Roman empire, and some outside modern Europe altogether, but they proved to be of fundamental importance to the future of the whole church. The first five came to be known as 'ecumenical' (universal) councils because they were taken to

LEFT: In this French twelfth-century Bible, the eagle, symbol of John the Evangelist, is silencing the heretic Arius. John was the appropriate choice because his Gospel begins with the description of Christ as the Word of God, so he could be considered the expert evangelist when it came to Christology.

HERESY

The upheaval Arius began resulted in a clarification in the church of the nature of heresy. 'Heresy' comes from the Greek word for 'choice' (*haeresis*). Just being unsure what to believe is not heresy. Nor is having doubts. Heresy involves persistence in the choice of a particular view. But that is still not heresy until it has been defined as going against the faith of the church. How is that definition arrived at? Who has authority to declare what it is 'Christian' to believe and what not? How are the consensus of the community and the wishes of the Holy Spirit made clear? The church was facing, for the first time on such a grand scale, the difficulty of defining heresy as a concept, and then defining what particular beliefs should be deemed to be heretical.

have made decisions binding on everyone. The fundamental difference in holding a 'universal' council was that because its decisions were taken on behalf of the whole church they could also embrace matters of faith. Unity in the faith was held to be inseparable from unity of the church itself. If there was to continue to be only one faith, it could not be

THE NICENE CREED

The Council of Nicaea produced a creed. It was carefully worded to clarify the points which Arius had made controversial, stressing that God in three persons is a single divine substance, and therefore indisputably one God, while the three persons are equally and fully God.

I believe in one God the Father Almighty, Maker of heaven and earth, and of all things visible and invisible:

And in one Lord Jesus Christ, the only-begotten Son of God, begotten of his Father before all worlds,

God of God, Light of Light, very God of very God, begotten not made,

Being of one substance with the Father, by whom all things were made;

Who for us men and for our salvation came down from heaven;

And was incarnate by the Holy Ghost of the Virgin Mary,

And was made man;

And was crucified also for us under Pontius Pilate.

He suffered and was buried,

And the third day he rose again according to the Scriptures,

And ascended into heaven,

And sits on the right hand of the Father.

And he shall come again with glory to judge both the quick and the dead:

'Whose kingdom shall have no end.

And I believe in the Holy Ghost,

The Lord and giver of life,

Who proceeds from the Father and the Son,

Who with the Father and the Son together is worshipped and glorified,

Who spoke by the prophets.

And I believe in one catholic and apostolic Church.

I acknowledge one baptism for the remission of sins.

And I look for the resurrection of the dead and the life of the world to come.

decided upon piecemeal. Lucifer Calaritanus, bishop of Cagliari (d. c. AD 370/1), argued that there must be no associating with heretics, in particular with the Arians. Schism is division of the church. But to the minds of early Christians, schism and heresy overlapped. A little later, Augustine of Hippo would take the essential unity of the church to be a point of faith in itself.

The church continued to hold ecumenical councils for a century and a half. These were mainly still preoccupied with the fundamental questions which had been raised by Arius about 'Christology', Christ's relationship to the other two persons of the Trinity and the way in which he became man.

THE COUNCIL OF NICAEA AND THE FIRST COUNCIL OF CONSTANTINOPLE

The emperor called a council at Nicaea in AD 325 to deal with the increasingly divisive difference of opinion between the Arians and the Catholics about the nature of Christ. This had been the first time a Christian emperor was in a position to perform this service for the Christian church, and it raised at once a number of questions about his proper role. It was agreed after some discussion that it was acceptable for him as a lay ruler to convene and dismiss such a council, but not to involve himself in its discussions or decision-making. Only the bishops assembled at the council truly 'represented' the church and only they could be trusted to have the guidance of the Holy Spirit to ensure that they came to the right conclusions.

This attitude is reflected in the repeated statement in the formal declarations which the councils made, that it is the 'bishops assembled' who are speaking, with no mention of any lay authority. They always speak as though 'with one voice' in the early councils, and are stated not only to be unanimous in their conclusions but to agree unanimously with what was agreed in previous councils. The idea was that this was a sign that the Holy Spirit had been the guide of their own deliberations. It helped to confirm the authority of the letters and decrees a council sent out.

The underlying idea continued to be that councils (or 'synods', the equivalent Greek term) were a practical way of ensuring that the 'mind' of the Church, the 'consent of the faithful', could be articulated, so that the faithful could be clear what was the right thing to believe and to do as Christians. This was a way of making decisions together which reduced any claim by an individual patriarch or archbishop to have personal authority to make such rulings. It was 'collegial'.

How Christian Europe Nearly Became Arian

Whole populations remained divided on 'Arian' and 'non-Arian' lines, even after the Council of Nicaea had made its definitive credal formulation of the 'right' answer in AD 325. Ulfilas (c. AD 310–388), who was descended from Christian captives who had lived among the Goths beyond the Danube for several generations, held Arian beliefs, and when he was made a bishop in AD 341 and was sent to exercise his ministry among the Goths, the Goths too became Arians. Arian ideas spread to the East, where they were found among the Visigoths, and to the West, where they appeared among the Ostrogoths, the Burgundians and the Vandals. The Bible was translated into the Gothic language. These tribes were significant among the invaders of the empire, and it seemed possible that their influence might make Arianism the orthodoxy in the end, for political reasons if not theological ones.

During the latter part of this period of Roman rule the barbarian threat, heightened where the 'barbarians' were identified, rightly or wrongly, as 'Arians', was felt as much in Spain as in other areas of the empire. The decisive period at the western end of Europe was the first decade or so of the fifth century, although Frankish peoples and some of the Alemanni tribes had made damaging raids into Spain in AD 264 and created immense pressures on the economy there, if adequate defences were to be mounted.

When the Arian Visigoths moved south over the Pyrenees in AD 412 to establish a capital in Barcelona and later in Toledo, the Catholic Christians found themselves in a subordinate position. Granada and areas to the south were lost to Christian (which by this stage in the decline of the empire really meant Byzantine) influence for a period, though in the mid-sixth century the formerly Arian Visigothic leadership became Catholic for a time.

The Romans had brought Christianity with their conquest to the regions of Austria and Hungary south of the Danube. From the first century the region had bishops and a series of stories of martyrs bear witness to a living Christian tradition when the power of Rome began to fail. Severinus (d. AD 482) had a pupil, Eugippius (c. AD 465–after 533), who wrote a biography of his master in which he describes how Severinus set up a community with his companions near modern Vienna and set an example of ascetic self-discipline. He would walk on the frozen Danube in the winter in bare feet, on errands of mercy and support to the local people who were frightened by the incursions of barbarians who made raids to rob and intimidate them. The story goes that Severinus went as far as modern Salzburg and Passau on these expeditions.

This was a period of transition, in which the decay of Roman strength was leaving a dangerous power vacuum, and Severinus seems to have thought it was important that the new authorities should take control without destroying the lives of local peoples. When the king, Odoacer (AD 435–493), went to fight the Romans he asked Severinus for a blessing. He was successful in gaining control of

In this twelfth-century picture, St Severinus is curing the Emperor Clovis of the illness that none of his doctors had been able to ease.

Italy. But the ruler of the Alemanni tribe was exhorted by Severinus to refrain from ravaging the lands under Roman control.

Hungary had been 'infected' by Arianism at an early date; the emperor Valens, who was himself an Arian, sent missionaries there. The Arian Goths dominated the area in the third and fourth centuries. Ulfilas was unable to accept the decision of the Council of Nicaea in AD 325 against Arianism. Yet his translation of the New Testament into Gothic was important and influential among the peoples who spoke the language. The last Arian Visigothic king conquered most of the north between AD 574 and AD 585 and reconquered parts of the south.

This is one of the parts of Europe which spent a period under 'Arian' domination at a crucial time, where it might perhaps have been possible for Arian Christianity to remain the norm. However, this state of affairs proved unstable. Gradually the Catholics won back their dominance. The invaders became assimilated and inculturated. They learned Latin. The Catholic Franks conquered the Arian Burgundians, and the former Arians in that region became officially Catholic in AD 517. In AD 589 the Visigoths became Catholics, too. The Vandals of north Africa gave in in AD 534 and the Italian Ostrogoths in AD 554.

The first Council of Constantinople (AD 381) made some adjustments to the wording of the Nicene Creed, resulting in the text still accepted today.

THE COUNCIL OF EPHESUS

In AD 431 another ecumenical council was held in Ephesus, still preoccupied with dealing with the cluster of potential heresies surrounding the incarnate Christ. Were there two natures, divine and human, in one person, the Christ, or were there also two persons, a man as well as God? How could he have been fully man if there was no human person?

The two leaders of heretical opinion (or 'heresiarchs') who had become important here were Nestorius (c. AD 386–451) and Eutyches (c. AD 380–456). Nestorius claimed that Christ was two persons not one. Eutyches said that there was only one nature in Christ, as well as one person. The council repudiated Nestorianism and also resolved a related current controversy concerning the Virgin Mary. Was it acceptable to describe her as the 'God-bearer'? Nestorius said no, because that would make the human infant Jesus a divine person. The council affirmed that it was.

THE COUNCIL OF CHALCEDON

A council that was important in its consequences for the long-term division of the Christian world was the one held at Chalcedon in AD 451. This ruled out the doctrine of Eutyches, which became known as Monophysitism because it insisted that there was only one nature in the incarnate Christ. The council decreed that true Christians must accept that the incarnate Christ was one person with two natures, divine and human. This seemed to make non-Christians of the 'non-Chalcedonian' churches, the Nestorians, Armenians, Copts and Ethiopians, and the Syriac Christians of the Middle East and Egypt, who would not accept this doctrinal position. These are now known as the 'Oriental Orthodox' churches, in contrast with the Eastern Orthodox churches, which are descended from the Greek-speaking churches that accepted the ruling of Chalcedon.

This first great church-dividing issue has come to seem less important in modern ecumenical dialogue. A common declaration was made by Pope John Paul II and the head of the Oriental Orthodox church in 1984, declaring the differences to be no more than matters of terminology and cultural difference, and not church-dividing at all.

There were also persecutions of those who presented a challenge from within Christianity. Spain became Christian under the Romans. But in Spain as everywhere else people questioned aspects of the new faith, and some of them were natural leaders who started movements and trends. The official church drove Priscillian of Avila, one of the first of these to appear in Spain, to martyrdom in AD 385. Priscillian's offence was to preach an asceticism so extreme as to be declared a heresy. A council at Saragossa condemned his teachings in AD 380. But this was a mode of Christian living which had a powerful appeal in the climate of thought of the time. Priscillianist heretics proved obstinate and difficult to root out and were persecuted by the Catholic bishops for generations. Priscillianist bishops objected to attempts to remove them from their sees. The bishop of Astorga in Galicia wrote to Pope Leo I in the 440s AD to ask for support from the Roman see in completing their eradication. This is an important early example of a Christian 'witch-hunt', and perhaps the first that led to the actual death of the offending heresiarch.

THE SECOND COUNCIL OF CONSTANTINOPLE

Another Council of Constantinople was held in AD 553 to reaffirm what previous councils had said and to condemn new heretical writings which had appeared, considered to be of an Arian, Nestorian or Monophysite character, so evidently these opinions still needed stamping out. It began to be suggested that perhaps a solution to the problem of getting all Christians to accept that the incarnate Christ had one person and two natures was to say that he had one will. This theory (known as Monothelitism) was rejected by a sixth ecumenical council in AD 680–681.

A COUNCIL ABOUT THE USE OF IMAGES

The last of the councils which the Christians of Eastern Europe include in the first definitive decision-making councils of the whole church was the second Council of Nicaea. This was held in AD 787 at the height of a controversy of the Eastern church about iconoclasm. Those who were against pictures and statues were afraid that, far from being used as aids to the worship of the true God, they would lead people astray into idolatry, and they would worship the pictures and statues as people in pagan times had done. A council had been held at Constantinople in AD 754 to condemn the veneration of icons. The second Council of Nicaea, however, decided the other way. It permitted the veneration of icons and brought the iconoclastic controversy to an uneasy end, at least in the east of Europe. This was an immensely important decision because from it has proceeded the whole emphasis and visual culture of the Orthodox churches.

Though there was no equivalent iconoclastic controversy in the West at this period, Western Christians were to be far from uniform in their opinions about the way this danger was to be avoided. Theophilus, the Western author of the book *On Diverse Arts*, was evidently aware that some disputed strongly the place of decoration in the house of God and thought it either a distraction or an invitation to idolatry, and for that reason he is careful to defend it. 'It is certain,' he argues, that King David 'desired the embellishment of the material house of God, which is the place of prayer.' The concern reappeared in the West in the sixteenth-century Reformation and after, when Puritan reformers insisted that the insides of places of worship should be simple and stripped of decoration which might itself become a focus of worship.

Islam forbade outright the creation of images which might become objects of veneration. Here, too, the belief affected the visual culture of the religion and shaped the development of its artistic expression, with an emphasis on the design of lettering taken from the wording of the Koran.

A Territorial Religion

Practical Church Government on the Ground

The Christian church was about to embed itself into the soil of Europe in a way which left an imprint, not only in the form of some of the most beautiful and impressive buildings of the European heritage but also by dividing the land into local ecclesiastical areas. These could easily outlast change in political structures, kings and emperors.

The New Testament has a good deal to say about 'church' and 'churches' but it is not very consistent about their relationship. A 'church' seems to have a geographical location and a territorial identity. There is 'the Church of the Thessalonians' (1 Thessalonians 1:1), and the community at Colosse, 'the saints and faithful brothers and sisters' there (Colossians 1:2). Paul writes to some of these local churches, calling them 'the Church' in a particular place, for example 'the Church of God that is in Corinth' (1 Corinthians 1:2, Revised Standard Version; compare 2 Corinthians 1:1). There may not be two churches in one place.

There appears to have been a good deal of quarrelling in some of these communities. Paul writes to the church at Corinth (1 Corinthians 1:10) begging the Christians there to avoid division and try to arrive at

ICONS

An Orthodox church has an iconostasis or screen separating the nave where the congregation sits from the sanctuary, on which a series of icons are displayed. This example is from the Panagia Angeloktisti Church in Cyprus, which dates from the fifth century, but was rebuilt in the twelfth. Its name refers to the story that it was built by angels. Various scenes appear in the lower row. The baptism of Christ, with the Holy Spirit descending in the form of a dove, can be seen in the central picture. Above, note the use of writing as well as the visual coding of iconography to identify the figures.

A significant shift of understanding was needed before Christians could begin to use icons as aids to worship. They had to be understood not as objects of worship, holy in themselves, but as images of holy things. This is a sophisticated distinction and one which the ordinary faithful never wholly mastered, for popular trust in icons has remained close to worship in every century. The Greek church made a decision to restrict representations of Christ and the saints to two-dimensional pictures because statues were more likely to be treated as gods. The belief that Luke the Evangelist had painted pictures of Jesus and Mary encouraged the view that such pictures were acceptable. But the most important feature of the icon is probably the way its imagery contains a code, carrying a theology within it just as the liturgy does. For example, in depictions of the Resurrection of Christ he bursts from the tomb in a shower of symbols, such as burst locks and flying keys.

Since the period of the iconoclastic controversy Eastern Christianity has made extensive use of icons, which are still produced in great numbers and may be bought even in tourist shops. The piety of the ordinary faithful is strongly focused on icons. There are icons in every Orthodox home, treated somewhat like the domestic gods of the Romans. Orthodox churches contain many icons and each church has a screen, dividing the priests from the people, hung with icons and known as an iconostasis.

the same mind and the same purpose. Local churches were from the first not merely local church buildings or places of worship, and indeed the early communities tended to meet in someone's house and not have a special building for the congregation to worship in. They were communities or fellowships.

One answer to the question of how the multitude of local communities could still be one 'church' was to think structurally, and to work out the relationship of local churches to one another. Solving this problem was regarded as extremely important from a very early stage. Hints of it are noticeable in the debates recorded in the Acts of the Apostles. The first Christians were quite clear that they must hold together somehow when it came to matters of faith, and that meant that there must always be 'one church', one faith and one baptism. The church could not be holy, catholic and apostolic unless it was also 'one'. These four marks of the church went together.

The answers eventually arrived at were conceptually different in East and West, and reflected the contrasting mindsets of the two cultures. The West tended to think in terms of parts and wholes, so that each local church could be seen as a section of the one church. Ambrose of Milan (c. AD 339–397), for example, saw schism and heresy in terms of a fragmentation of Christ's body into broken pieces. This went with the view regularly taken by councils that those present at a council, or meeting of the churches, represented the relevant local churches, and only those churches could subsequently be bound by what had been agreed to within their own territories. A group of bishops representing local churches at a council would agree disciplinary rules on the understanding that these would apply in the places where the participating churches held territorial sway. If it was a matter of faith which was being discussed (and that was comparatively unusual) it required the whole church (that is, bishops representing all churches everywhere) to be invited to meet, since decisions of that kind could not be taken except 'universally', though they kept to the same rules about decisions of local councils.

The Greek-speaking part of Europe, thinking more 'Platonically', preferred the notion of microcosm and macrocosm. Here each local church was thought of as the whole church in microcosm; 'the church' in each place rather than a part of the church. Theodoret (c. AD 393–460) saw the many geographically distinct churches as 'one church', spiritually speaking.

The urge to spread the faith, frequently lent wings by a sense of trusting the Holy Spirit to lead the mission, created from the first the need to set up reliable structures for running the new churches. The conviction that the Holy Spirit was directing the Christian communities by grace ('charism') could be strong but (from the point of view of those keen to set up reliable structures) dangerously difficult to control and monitor.

Order – in the sense of a set of more or less institutional requirements – had to be introduced to create a balance and provide a way of testing what the wilder figures on the scene were preaching. It was this orderliness which perhaps did more than anything else to ensure that Europe was planted with churches in the physical sense and which has left such a rich heritage of ecclesiastical buildings throughout the continent.

THE BISHOP AS A FOCUS OF UNITY

Augustine, himself a bishop at Hippo in north Africa for most of his life, stressed that this supreme ministerial office ought not to be treated as a form of 'lordship'. The bishop should think of himself 'with and among' his people, as their servant. By contrast, Gregory the Great, who was to be almost as influential as Augustine on the thinking of the West for the next thousand years, encouraged the view that a bishop is primarily an overseer and a ruler. However, it seems to have been generally agreed that the bishop was the natural representative of his people, and the right person to go on their behalf to any meetings of the churches in councils or synods and to speak for them. 'The bishops assembled at Nicaea... constitute the great and holy synod,' say the records of the Council of Nicaea. When bishops met in councils and synods they took collective decisions on one 'plane' of the church's life, that is, the church of their own lifetimes. They articulated and approved the view of their generation.

But councils also expressed the idea that the church had a historical continuity which formed a second 'plane', of continuity over time. Tertullian taught that the true church is to be identified in the visible succession of bishops, and that the stewardship of the faith is entrusted to them. It began to be thought that the bishops carried in their persons the apostolic succession. Before the end of the first century Clement of Rome (bishop of Rome, c. AD 88–98) emphasized the importance of the line of succession of ministry from the apostles and of the apostles from Christ; the consecrated laying hands on the next to be consecrated.

The local community was the third 'plane'. Three planes intersect at a point, and by analogy the three planes of the church's life were seen to intersect in the person of a bishop. He was thus immensely important to the structural integrity of the church and made sense of the way in which the local church could also be the universal church.

Making the Church into an Institution

The structures for running the church were partly institutional, but above all practical, to do with the details of the way a new community should be run. First, there was the question of leadership. The New Testament is as various in its thinking about leadership in the church as it is in its ideas about the nature of the church itself. It speaks of 'elders' and 'bishops' as well as 'deacons'. Acts 20:17 speaks of the elders of the church. In Acts 20:28 Paul bids farewell to the elders at Ephesus and expresses the view that the Holy Spirit has made them 'overseers' of the flock there. It is impossible to say whether the elders of the New Testament (for example, Acts 14:23; Titus 1:5; James 5:14) were priests (from the Greek *presbyteroi*) or bishops (from *episkopoi*) in anything like the way which would be recognized now. Nor is it clear whether priests and bishops were thought of as two distinct orders or just different words for the same thing.

The job of the deacons as described in the New Testament, on the other hand, seems fairly clear. They were to look after the practical charitable activities of the local community, and make sure the widows and orphans were not in want. The word *diaconos* is not used in the Acts of the Apostles where this special commissioning is described (Acts 6:5), but it appears elsewhere (Philippians 1:1 and 1 Timothy 3:8).

RITES: DIFFERENT WAYS OF DOING THINGS

Paul says that women should learn in silence in church (1 Timothy 2:11). Is this a matter of faith (which cannot change) or of order (which may)? The practices most familiar to the Christian faithful are those they encounter in regular worship in their own churches. A great deal of Christian practice in Europe has been taken to be open to variation, and some of the most heated moments of controversy have involved disagreements about exactly what is open and what is not. The Council of Nicaea (AD 325), Canon 1, sets out the rules for priests who become eunuchs in the expectation that they will embody the general principles appropriate to the decrees of a universal council. Someone who has been castrated for medical reasons or 'by barbarians' may remain a priest, but if someone voluntarily castrates himself he is to be suspended. The 'human impositions' cries of the fifteenth-century Lollards and sixteenth-century reformers were in effect accusations that the institutional church in the West was trying to make requirements of matters which were not absolute requirements at all.

It was not long before, in both East and West, there emerged a career ladder of ministry with distinction of functions, the most important being reserved for those at the top of the ladder. The deacons were the bottom rung of the ladder by the time Ignatius of Antioch (c. AD 35–107) was writing his letters. Canon 18 of the Council of Nicaea stresses that deacons do not have authority to 'offer', that is to celebrate the memorial of Jesus' last supper with his disciples, presiding at the Eucharist (Holy Communion or Mass) and saying the words of Jesus which consecrated the bread and the wine (Luke 22:17–19). The second step on the ladder was the priesthood. Priests could preside at the Eucharist and also say the words of absolution when people confessed their sins. The final stage in the progression up the ladder of ordained ministry was to become a bishop. This went with the leadership of a local church and authority to ordain priests, as well as to readmit the excommunicated who had committed serious sins and repented and done their (at first very public) penance.

The Bishop at Home in His Diocese

Local loyalties could be strong. In AD 373–374 the people of Milan clamoured for Ambrose to be made their bishop. Yet although he had been brought up in a Christian family, he was not yet baptized, let alone ordained into the priesthood. That should have ruled him out. In 1 Timothy 3:6–7 Paul had expressed the concern that the rapid promotion of a recent convert was likely to expose him to temptation. The Apostolic Canons (eighty in number) include the rule that no one should be made a priest or a bishop as soon as he has been baptized. Canon 2 of the Council of Nicaea (AD 325) reinforces this rule, noting that 'a catechumen needs time and further probation after baptism'. Ambrose was made bishop of Milan just the same.

An *ecclesia* (Greek *ekklesia*) seems quite early on in the emergence of episcopal church government to have been a territory in which a single leader or *episcopus* (Greek *episkopos*) had pastoral responsibilities. He could not interfere beyond the boundaries of his diocese. Canon 2 of the Council of Constantinople (AD 381), for example, says that 'Diocesan bishops are not to intrude in churches beyond their own boundaries.' Normally, when there were too many congregations for him to minister to them all personally, the bishop would ordain priests to act on his behalf within the diocese. If for some reason a priest wanted to move to another diocese his bishop would write a letter for him to take with him, introducing him to his new bishop and testifying to the fact that he was genuinely a priest and in good standing, and the second bishop would decide whether to admit him to work in his own diocese. The etiquette was strict. It was also designed to discourage 'wandering' by priests, some of whom might turn out to be disreputable. Canons 15 and 16 of the Council of Nicaea stress that clergy ought to remain in the diocese where they were ordained, and require them to be sent back if they try to move elsewhere without permission.

The natural place for the 'seat' of a bishop in the late Roman empire was a major city which was also an administrative centre. The word *paroikia*, from which 'parish' eventually derived, was used in the East and 'diocese' in the West, and by the fourth century in Africa too; *diocesis* is used in the published proceedings of the Council of Carthage (AD 411). In a large purpose-built or dedicated building stood the bishop's *cathedra* or throne, and from there he taught the people by preaching, usually in the form of homilies on the scriptures. These could last an hour or more, and some of the most important and influential of those that survive consist of long series in which the bishop would expound a whole book of the Bible bit by bit. Augustine's sermons on John's Gospel and on the Psalms and Gregory the Great's sermons on Ezekiel and the First Book of Kings are examples. The congregation would not necessarily sit quietly and listen. There might be a good deal of walking about and gossip during the service. But when they appreciated a sermon they might applaud.

As the faith spread, more and more Christians were living in rural areas and this rather urban and metropolitan approach to organizing the church had to be adapted. It was necessary to make provision for the pastoral care and teaching of small worshipping communities in places which might be quite remote from the city with its cathedral. In the Eastern church this led to the creation of 'country bishops' as extensions of the bishop himself, to act on his behalf in rural areas (*chorepiscopoi*); in the West the problem tended to be solved with parishes whose vicars were the bishops' deputies, though they were merely priests, not bishops in their own right, as the *chorepiscopoi* possibly were (though this is not quite clear).

This development emphasized another key role of a bishop, which was to be pastor or shepherd of the flock. Isidore of Seville describes it in this way in his *Sentences*: 'Just as the shepherd stays awake to guard his sheep against attack (by wolves), so the priest of God is careful to ensure that Christ's flock is not laid waste by the Enemy.'

Rulers of synagogues in the Roman period held office for a period, not for life, and they had a practical rather than a teaching authority. They were supposed to ensure that local worship was conducted in a proper, orderly and dignified way. But in second-century Palestine a 'patriarchal' office emerged, in which the patriarch was the head of the academy which trained rabbis, recognized by the Romans as having authority to collect taxes and appoint judges. Something of this polarity in the conception of the role of the ministry found its way into the history of the Christian tradition. There were times and places in which the ordained ministry was there mainly to 'keep order' in the church in a benign and pastoral way, and times when it was thought of as a locus of power, spiritual and sometimes even temporal.

There was also a changing sense of what a local church was, which went with the development of Christianity as a world faith for 'all who call in the name of Jesus Christ in every place' (1 Corinthians 1:2). Paul called a local community or assembly an *ekklesia* ('church'), but that did not then carry all the associations it does now. In 1 Corinthians 16:19–21 Paul sends greetings from one *ekklesia* to another in a network. That of Aquila and Prisca is in a private house, but it still counts as one of the churches of 'Asia'. For most of the centuries of Christianity in Europe, for most people 'going to church' has meant going to a particular building to worship, and even where the principle has remained strong, as it has in many places, that the 'local church' is the diocese, for the local worshipper the parish church is a much stronger natural focus.

Provinces

In a fundamental sense the diocese continued to be thought of as the 'local' church, even when it had developed into a more diffuse area, no longer a city, and containing rural residents. It was administratively the basic ecclesial unit. But the spread of Christianity created another need. Geographically adjacent dioceses began to form into groups making up provinces, whose divisions more or less mapped onto the administrative divisions of the Roman state.

The bishop of the most important city would tend to become the 'metropolitan' ('mother-city') bishop, recognized as the natural leader by the other bishops in the province because his see happened to be in the leading city of the region (though sometimes in the north African provinces pre-eminence went to the bishop who had been a bishop longer than the others). The Council of Nicaea of AD 325 was the first council to use the term 'metropolitan'.

The relationship of the other bishops to their metropolitan also had to be settled. Were they to be regarded as suffragans, as assistants, or as equals in a collegial relationship in which all dioceses were ultimately on the same level as local churches? In modern episcopal church structures a suffragan is usually understood to be an assistant bishop within a diocese. One thing seems to have been consistent in both East and West: the metropolitan bishop did not hold a higher order. He remained still a mere bishop. Even today when an archbishop or pope retires (which a pope is allowed to do, though most die in office) he reverts to being just a bishop, although he remains a bishop as long as he lives. That is considered to be an 'order', a kind of 'character' stamped upon him at his ordination, and not merely a post he has held, like that of archbishop or pope.

The five patriarchs were higher up the pyramid still. They exercised authority over the metropolitans, with judicial authority to hear disciplinary accusations against them. They could also act as a court of appeal against judgments the metropolitans arrived at in their own courts.

The great patriarchates of the ancient world were only three at first, identified at the Council of Nicaea in AD 325 as Antioch, Alexandria and Rome. Constantinople was added in AD 381, as was felt to be appropriate in view of Constantine's creation of his 'new Rome'. Canon 3 of the first Council of Constantinople in AD 381 expressly decreed that 'because it is new Rome, the bishop of Constantinople is to enjoy the privilege of honour after the bishop of Rome'. Jerusalem was added to make up five at the Council of Chalcedon in AD 451. Moscow and others were added to the list much later.

A Universal Primacy?

A patriarch was primate or 'chief bishop' of a large and significant area. But which primate was Primate of all? Gregory the Great, relying on Jesus' words to Peter, first bishop of Rome, when he told him that he was the rock on which the church was to be built (Matthew 16:18), said that the Primate of the whole church must be the bishop of Rome. Naturally the patriarchs of the East had other views, and we shall see that towards the end of the Middle Ages and in the Reformation and after, some of those in the West did too, challenging the very idea of a 'primacy of jurisdiction' which gave real power, as distinct from a 'primacy of honour' which conferred only respect.

It was one thing for other patriarchs to accord to the bishop of Rome a primacy of honour, as the successor of Peter; it was quite another

A fifteenth-century statue of Pope Gregory the Great shows him wearing the triple papal crown, which evolved as the official headgear for popes long after his lifetime.

THE HISTORY OF CHRISTIAN EUROPE

for them to accept that he could have personal jurisdiction to make decisions which would be binding in other places, as though he stood at the peak of a pyramid of power in the church. Leo I (r. AD 440–461) wrote on the subject in AD 446 to Anastasius, the bishop of Thessalonica. He explained that not only was Peter, the first bishop of Rome, the same Peter to whom Jesus gave supreme authority in the church; he handed on that authority to his successors. Gregory the Great went even further when he refused to accept the claim of the Patriarch of Constantinople to call himself an 'ecumenical patriarch'.

In the West, though not in the East, this potential conflict between a monarchical and a collegial authority became an issue of some importance. As early as the late fourth and fifth centuries it was suggested that if there was an important question, whether of faith or of order, it should be referred to the bishop of Rome to decide. Augustine of Hippo seems to have thought much the same.

CHURCH BUILDINGS AS ANCHORS FOR THE GROWING CHURCH

The interior of the Ayios Minas Church at Iraklion in Crete illustrates the density of the illustration and decoration of the interior with holy pictures and scenes.

The church as New Jerusalem, the City of God (Revelation 21:10), comes down from heaven. There is no temple here because God dwells in it directly and does not need a building erected where he can be worshipped.

The word 'church' in English has come to mean both the building and the community of believers. In the first generations the contrast was blurred by the tendency for Christians to meet for worship in the houses of their members. The structures of the growing church became, increasingly, actual physical buildings which could provide a home for local worshipping communities or religious communities of monks. Among the first dedicated Christian buildings were the catacombs in which Christians were buried.

The idea of building a church for regular meetings emerged, and in due course the idea of building a cathedral, a great church in which a bishop's *cathedra* or throne could be placed, was being made a reality. The building of a great church such as a cathedral, where the bishop has his see or seat, could become vainglorious. Orthodox Christians do not use the word 'cathedral' but 'great church' for the bishop's see or seat. 'Minster' comes from *monasterium*, because a community of canons served a cathedral. Cathedrals need not necessarily be physically very large; early Celtic and Saxon cathedrals were quite modest in size, although they were important. Nor did the idea that God should have a house quite die away. In some European languages the words for cathedral (Italian *duomo* and German *Dom*) come from *domus dei*, 'house of God'.

Then there was the question of design. A difficult decision for Christians was what to do about the pagan temples which still stood in Christian cities and towns. Should they take them over and use them for Christian worship, or would that lead to confusion in the minds of the faithful? A Christian church ought perhaps to look different from a pagan temple; it should have a shape which symbolically represented Christian beliefs.

The characteristic design features of East and West developed differently. In the East the decoration and symbolism is inward-looking, and the outside of the church rather plain. In the West, after a period of solid construction styles ending with the Normans, the soaring pinnacles, arches, towers and spires which tested construction skills to the limit (and sometimes beyond, when the buildings fell down) made the outsides as visually compelling as the insides, particularly in the period known as Gothic.

In the late Roman period churches began to acquire the status of property. The earliest Christian communities were gatherings of people who met for worship in private houses and

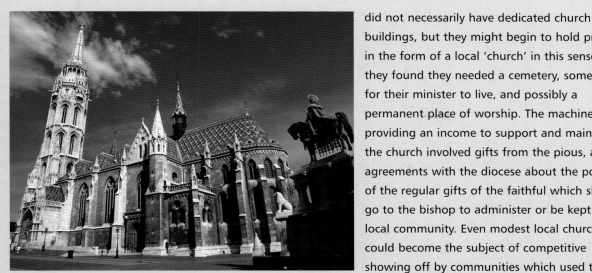

St Matthias Church in Budapest, built in the thirteenth century, is a lively example of Gothic design.

did not necessarily have dedicated church buildings, but they might begin to hold property in the form of a local 'church' in this sense when they found they needed a cemetery, somewhere for their minister to live, and possibly a permanent place of worship. The machinery of providing an income to support and maintain the church involved gifts from the pious, and agreements with the diocese about the portions of the regular gifts of the faithful which should go to the bishop to administer or be kept by the local community. Even modest local churches could become the subject of competitive showing off by communities which used them to display their wealth and importance.

As feudalism emerged as the system of land tenure in northern Europe, 'holding', as a form of tenant to the owner, became more common than owning. If a lay lord owned a church he was not free to do with it whatever he chose. He could not go and live in the building or otherwise change its use; he could not treat its lands or its serfs as his to do with as he pleased; he was not supposed to take the revenues for his own use (though kings frequently did that for a time with the revenues of vacant bishoprics); he could not decide independently who should serve as priest or bishop in the church.

The church building itself became the vehicle of narrative, with stories from the Bible painted as frescoes, inserted into the windows in coloured glass pictures, or, in Byzantine churches, made into mosaics on the walls. The ceiling is heaven, with angels in the roof, or, even as late as the Baroque period in the West, with cherubs flying against a backdrop of clouds. In many Byzantine churches, Christ in majesty presides in the apse. Tombs in Western churches and plaques and statues commemorating the dead are not far in conception from the pictures of saints in the West and icons of saints in Eastern churches.

'Stained' glass appears in churches and cathedrals in the West from about 1100. As the buildings of Western cathedrals grew more ambitious, flights of stone fancy potentially full of light, stained glass made them darker. Once this was realized, attempts were made to adjust the design so as to include areas of clear glass which would let in white light.

3 East and West Draw Apart

A Two-headed Empire

Christianity began within a political and social framework ruled from Rome, in an empire at the height of its power. The might of the imperial state looms behind the story told in the gospels. Jesus was born while his mother was obeying instructions from Rome. 'There went out a decree from Caesar Augustus' (Luke 2:1), and Mary and Joseph obediently set off to be 'counted'.

The death of Jesus also took place under this political power structure. He was arrested by the Roman authorities as a danger to the state and possible terrorist. He was brought for trial before the Roman authorities. He was sent for execution by the same authorities. At this stage Rome was still a unified great power, though somewhat stretched militarily speaking to make sure its orders were obeyed and potential rebellions were put down throughout the empire. Yet the events of Jesus' life took place far from Rome, in what was soon to become the Eastern empire.

At the end of the third century, Roman rule became overstretched by the sheer extent of the territories it had to control. The emperor Diocletian divided the empire into an Eastern part and a Western part for administrative purposes. A permanent division of the empire into these two halves was made in AD 395 at the end of the reign of Theodosius (AD 347–395), with the Eastern half of the 'bipolar' empire being ruled from Ravenna in southern Italy from AD 402. When Constantine established his new imperial city of Constantinople in AD 330 he provided the Eastern empire with a fitting place from which to rule and a plausible rival to Rome. He put in place a division which was inadvertently to shape the church in Europe down the centuries. From AD 476, after the last emperor of the West (Romulus Augustus, AD 463–476) was made to abdicate, the only imperial authority which could claim continuity with the Roman empire lay in Constantinople, which gets its modern name of

'Istanbul' from the attempt of the later Islamic conquerors to pronounce the name.

An extreme conservatism of theology became a distinctive feature of the Greek 'end' of early Christian Europe. By the end of the period of the ecumenical councils, probably as early as the fifth century, the faith was considered a fixed quantity, especially in the East. There was no scope for the rewording and debate about the finer points which has taken place in the West throughout the centuries up to the present day. The theologians of the Greek church became adamant in insisting that there should be neither change nor development. It was not an abrupt or decisive division at first. Between AD 687 and AD 751 eleven popes out of thirteen came from the Eastern empire or from Sicily. These were Greek-speakers, and Pope Theodore I (AD 642–649) was a Greek who came from Jerusalem. But as the centuries passed the 'static' approach of the Greek-speaking Christians contrasted more and more obviously with the exploratory and argumentative approach of much Western theology.

Two Languages, Two Worlds of Thought

It is appropriate that the word for Europe should come from Greece, because many of the features of 'European' civilization which now seem distinctive took their first recognizable form in ancient Greece. Politically, Greece was overtaken by Rome, as the north Italian city first became a republic in the sixth century BC, and then won itself an empire. Yet Roman imperialism was marked by a common-sense readiness to assimilate the cultures of the lands it conquered, and it particularly respected that of Greece. Young Romans of good birth were often sent to Athens to finish their studies. Rome added features of its own to the evolving civilization, particularly ideals of good citizenship and a government free from corruption. So the cultural and intellectual foundations of Europe were in the end laid jointly by Greece and Rome in a fusion of their respective contributions.

Despite this attempt to unite the best of the cultural heritage of the eastern and western Mediterranean under Rome, the eastern end of the Roman empire had begun to develop as a separate locus of government, partly because of the problem of the dual-language inheritance. Although educated Romans learned Greek the two language communities had remained fundamentally distinct and only a limited proportion of mostly technical and special terms from the Greek entered into the Latin and thence into the Romance languages of Europe. When the empire grew too big to control and evolved into a bipolar shape the two ends of the empire divided naturally into the Greek and the Latin. Greeks at one end of the empire spoke Greek, and Latins at the other end spoke Latin. The administrative division of the empire into two further encouraged the separate development of two styles or flavours of Christianity associated respectively with these two language communities.

Important though this underlying duality was, the complexity of the situation in the borderlands should never be underestimated. The collapse of the Roman empire left the Balkans, the uncertain eastern boundary of Europe, open to invasions and disturbance for centuries. They were always to be the subject of some claim, controversy or tribal warfare, the place where Christian East met Christian West, and later the boundary between Moslem and Christian imperial ambitions. As a consequence the inter-relationships of the peoples of the area and their religious affiliations have become immensely complex. The Christianization of the area was not straightforward either. 'Bogomil' Gnostic or dualist sects and Photinians had a strong presence in the Balkans and also had followers in Hungary and Transylvania.

Ways with Words

The citizens of Rome had taken education seriously (though they had not considered it essential for the whole population). A young man of the late empire was expected to attain a reasonable proficiency with words. He was going to have to be able to argue a case in court if any member of his household, including any of his slaves, got into trouble with the law, or if the family's lands or possessions became the subject of litigation. He might well find himself in public office for a time and having to make political speeches. He might even find himself writing a panegyric to flatter the emperor. These were the three practical purposes to which a late classical rhetorical education was directed, and all other studies were subordinate to the purpose of making a boy into an orator.

In this world of education for public life, knowledge was useful primarily because it furnished material for use in argument and to illustrate points in speeches. The study of philosophy added a top-dressing of high ideals to one's speeches. So pragmatic was this approach that a whole branch of the syllabus, 'topics', was concerned with the collection and arrangement of such materials in one's memory, and with the training of the memory to ensure that they could be sorted and retrieved at will.

An orator did not read out a finished text. He had to be able to be persuasive off the cuff. Nevertheless, the performance was expected to be shapely and polished and orators sometimes practised with friends if they had an important speech to make. Indeed, the importance placed on skill with words in education in late antiquity meant that educated people were much concerned with the beauty and elegance of what was said. This respect for language had a strong influence on the syllabus. A boy from the Roman empire first studied grammar (including some Greek if he came from the Latin end of Europe). Then he learned logic, so that he could argue convincingly as well as persuasively, and if he used fallacious arguments, he would not do so because he did not know what he was doing, but to gain an effect.

No Western author was more acutely aware of all this than Augustine of Hippo, who had been a professor of rhetoric first at Carthage and then at Milan before he became a Christian and shortly after that a bishop at Hippo Regius in north Africa. There he found himself confronted with awkward questions about the way a Christian should use such skills. Did they have a place in the composition of sermons? Did they have their uses in the critical analysis of the text of the Bible? Was it appropriate to identify the rhetorical images the Bible uses? Augustine himself had been put off the Bible as a schoolboy by his perception then that it was crudely written and not at all up to the standards of elegance a Roman intellectual would expect.

It was to address this set of questions that Augustine wrote his enormously influential book *On Christian Education*. In the preface he addresses those who are not sure that the rules of rhetoric, or any other systematic method of critical study, is necessary or appropriate in reading the Bible and who want to rely directly on the guidance of the Holy Spirit:

Now for those who exult in their divine gift and boast that they understand and interpret the sacred books without rules of the kind that I now plan to give, and so consider superfluous what I have chosen to say. Their elation must be checked by the recollection that although they have a perfect right to rejoice in their great gift from God they nevertheless learned even the alphabet with human help.

With the end of empire the school system which had produced such highly educated and textually sophisticated Christians collapsed. It is difficult now to get a sense of what that meant. We have libraries and internet resources; a determined enquirer can probably 'rediscover' knowledge which has dropped off the school syllabus, as so much did when the Roman schools decayed. There was no infrastructure of this kind. Learning was inside people's heads and libraries were relatively few.

An early fresco showing Augustine of Hippo, on the wall of the Lateran Palace in Rome, which was once the papal palace.

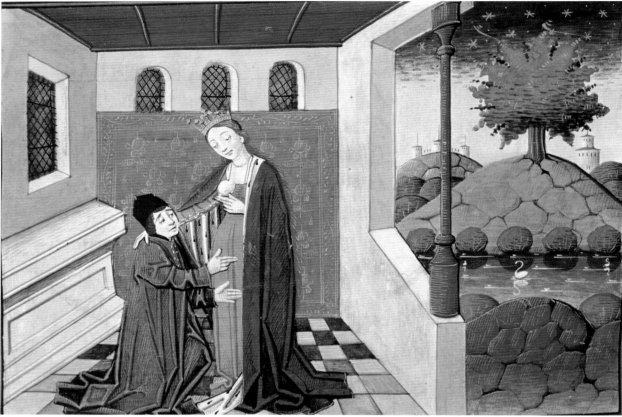

In this fifteenth-century French translation of Boethius' *The Consolation of Philosophy* by Jean de Meung, a distressed Boethius under house arrest is shown in conversation with a reassuring goddess Philosophy.

So precarious was the survival of knowledge that some books which we know once existed in the ancient world are lost and others survive through one chance copy, or in fragments. An example is the *Hortensius*, a book by Cicero (106–43 BC) which Augustine says he found particularly helpful when he was trying to learn philosophy.

As the empire collapsed, some individuals in the West were well aware of the danger that civilization as they knew it would disappear. Whereas in Jesus' lifetime and for some time afterwards educated Romans learnt Greek and often spent time in Athens polishing their knowledge of philosophy, by the fourth century, a real working knowledge of Greek was less common. Augustine of Hippo bewailed the fact that he found it hard to achieve a fluency in Greek to match his ease in Latin, and Gregory the Great probably never mastered Greek at all, although he lived in Constantinople for a time.

Moreover, the Latin language has a different style from the Greek. It is much more concrete and although Cicero, Boethius (AD 480–524/5) and others after them tried to expand its capacities so that it would be able to express abstractions better, it was never going to be

able to lend itself to the subtleties of Greek or match Greek's capacity for expressing mysteries mysteriously. It was better for the framing of crisp adversarial arguments which became the style of Western Christian theology.

Boethius, a controversial figure in the early sixth-century West, was soon to be executed after a period under house arrest. He believed it would be important to make Latin translations of the works of Aristotle and Plato. He had completed no more than some preliminary works of Aristotle on logic before he died. Boethius had been enough of a Christian to write some short works on current theological controversies, but it was to philosophy that he turned for consolation when he was arrested and waiting to be executed.

Boethius' contemporary Cassiodorus, formerly a senior civil servant, took early retirement and set up a Christian community on the family estates, where study could continue. He put together for its use an encyclopedia of basic knowledge for Christians.

Gregory the Great was an efficient popularizer of knowledge and a most competent preserver of Roman administrative arrangements. That enabled the church to make a major contribution to ensuring that the grain trade went on and Europe continued to be fed before and during the period of his papacy. Nevertheless, his own knowledge of Greek seems to have been slight and his education patchy.

Naturally the Greek-speaking world still had direct and easy access to the writings of the ancient Greeks (though the language was beginning to fracture into demotic and bastardized and educated forms). The philosophical systems of Plato, Aristotle, Epicurus and the Stoics still had their adherents, but most importantly for Christianity some of the philosophical ideas had been drawn into the Christian tradition as the early Christian apologists, predominantly writers of Greek, tried to make the faith intelligible to the educated and the leaders of society.

In the Greek world, the Neoplatonic and late Platonic traditions of thought placed an increasing emphasis on a mystical form of Platonism, which has given a lasting and characteristic flavour to Greek Orthodox Christianity. This somewhat abstracted mode of its highest intellectual life helped to take attention away from the practicalities of Western intellectual problem-solving. The philosopher Plotinus (c. AD 205–270) favoured an obscure literary style. He thought it right and proper that readers should have to make an effort to get access to ideas. In his view, the ideas were more important than their expression and he believed they might usefully be allowed to flow as he wrote, in an 'inspired' way without

THE BEGINNINGS OF MONASTIC LIFE

Monastic or 'religious' life developed on different models in East and West. In the East the ideal was represented by the lives of the 'desert fathers'. These were individuals who practised extreme asceticism and lived as hermits, remote from human habitations. They were admired for their holiness and the faithful would travel to gaze at them and be edified and benefit from the rich fund of spiritual power they were believed to represent. Hermits sometimes lived in loose communities, following their personal timetables of prayer and self-denial and only occasionally meeting for meals or worship.

Augustine of Hippo had experimented with something rather different. As a young man he had had an ambition to retire to live in intellectual and spiritual 'leisure', conversing with like-minded friends, thinking and writing. This was not unlike the retirement Cicero had long contemplated and eventually achieved; it was not new and not essentially Christian. After his conversion to Christianity and before he returned to north Africa and became a bishop, Augustine had spent a period at Cassiciacum on Lake Como in Italy with his friends and his mother, discussing such themes as 'blessedness' and 'order', which were both philosophical and of practical interest to educated Christians of the day. In north Africa he is thought to have established a fresh community in which to live. From this proceeds the Rule of Augustine, which was revived in the twelfth century for use by canons, people who wanted to live the committed lives of members of a religious order, but not in the way the Benedictines did.

For the definitive form of Western monastic life had been established in the sixth century by Benedict of Nursia (c. AD 480–543). He founded a monastery at Monte Cassino. He adapted the existing manual from the early sixth century for those wishing to live in this way, which is known as the Rule of the Master. The resulting Rule, known as the Rule of St Benedict, became the standard guide for the religious life in the West until the twelfth century.

As a result, in the West the typical pattern was of a community life in which monks lived as one, offering unquestioning obedience to an abbot. They took vows of poverty and chastity as well as of obedience and they were expected to practise 'stability', which meant not wandering the world, but remaining in the house where they were 'professed' or took their vows.

Benedict is shown in this picture giving the Rule to a community
of monks dressed in Benedictine habits. The scribe who wrote it is
humbly kneeling at the saint's feet. A hand comes down from
heaven apparently giving God's authority to the Rule.

any revision. Student philosophers were sometimes even encouraged not to write, but above all to think.

This process of absorbing the classical tradition affected the Judaic tradition too. Philo of Alexandria (20 BC–AD 50), for example, begins his book on creation by trying to show that Moses was consciously attempting to bring together the Judaic law and the law of nature, aspects of which had been of interest to Plato. Philo knew that there were philosophers who thought it beneath the divine dignity to have any active involvement with the world as its creator. He supports Moses' account, with its picture of an active God working in an orderly way to bring the world into being and all that is in it, working so hard in fact that on the seventh day he rested.

Some of the important names in the early period who left writings later regarded as 'patristic' (that is, works of the 'Fathers of the church') wrote in Greek and some in Latin. The influence of the Latin authors (especially Jerome, Augustine of Hippo, Gregory the Great and Bede) was much greater in the West for a thousand years, until the knowledge of Greek crept back into Western Europe and the Greek 'Fathers' came back into fashion there as an exciting rediscovery.

CHRISTIANITY CONQUERS EUROPE: THE SECOND PHASE FROM THE END OF EMPIRE

At the end of the Roman empire the lands which are now Europe experienced a huge shake-up of civilization. The upheavals of the fall of the empire brought new rulers to territories formerly confidently Roman, and, perhaps paradoxically, a strengthened sense of identity for 'Europe'. A civilization as well as a political and social structure died away, but slowly and unevenly. Roman power was ebbing from at least the late fourth century but it was the end of the sixth century or beyond before it could be said to have failed altogether, and even then the picture in the East was very different from that in the West.

The English ecclesiastical historian Bede (AD 672/3–735) describes how Attila the Hun laid waste almost the whole of Europe. Even when they were won over to the Christian faith, it was not to be expected that the seething tribes disrupting the empire would be converted or approach baptism with an educated awareness of the complicated questions about sin and repentance which had so exercised Cyprian and Augustine. Roman soldiers took their faith with them in their postings to the edges of empire, and archaeological remains indicate that some Christians were to be found in Britain.

Celtic Christians, members of tribes which had settled at the very edge of Europe, especially in Ireland, proved to be keen missionaries. They favoured the approach of relying on God to send them where he chose and would set off trustingly in coracles to see where they would be carried by the tides. For example, Columba (AD 521–597) came from Ireland and converted the Picts (that is, the people of modern Scotland) to the faith of Christ, and they gave him the island of Iona so that he could build a monastery there. From Iona went forth Aidan (d. AD 651) to instruct the English people, as Bede describes:

He left a most salutary example of abstinence and self-control; and the best recommendation of his teaching to all was that he taught them no other way of life than that which he himself practised among his fellows. For he neither sought after nor cared for worldly possessions but he rejoiced to hand over at once, to any poor man he met, the gifts he had received from kings or rich men of the world.

The emphasis here is on transformation of life and simple goodness. Bede describes the missionary activity of such figures. They were of special interest to him from his vantage point in northern England because their missionaries had been successful there, creating a certain amount of conflict with the traditions deriving from the Roman mission of the late sixth century, the tradition within which he himself had always lived and worked as a monk of the twin monasteries of Wearmouth and Jarrow.

Bede also tells the contrasting story of the official Roman mission to Canterbury of Augustine of Canterbury (d. AD 604), sent by Pope Gregory I (Gregory the Great) in AD 597. It is almost certain that there had been Roman Christians in the British Isles before, while the Roman armies were an occupying force, but Christian worship seems to have died away when they left. Indeed, Bede relates how the British Saint Alban died a martyr near Verulamium, rather than return to the pagan faith in a time of persecution. (The city is now known as St Albans, after him.) Bede describes how 'when the storm of persecution had ceased, the faithful Christians who in the time of danger had hidden themselves in woods and deserts and secret caverns came out of hiding. They rebuilt the churches which had been razed to the ground; they endowed and built shrines to the holy martyrs.'

The churches of Britain went quietly on until 'the time of the Arian madness', the heresy which had threatened to spilt the empire until the Council of Nicaea was held in AD 325 and produced a creed to resolve the matter. This heresy, Bede claims, 'even infected this island'. He goes on to describe various encounters with Roman affairs as the empire collapsed and in time the British Isles were invaded by Angles, Saxons and Jutes, three Germanic tribes who stood in need of conversion to Christianity.

Augustine of Canterbury's mission adopted a different style from that of the Celts. He went to the top. He landed in Kent in southern England with forty companions, equipped himself with translators, and sent a message to King Aethelberht (d. AD 616) 'that he had come from Rome bearing the best of news, namely the sure and certain promise of eternal joys in heaven and an endless kingdom with the living and true

SALVAGING EUROPEAN CULTURE: BEDE

Bede is shown in this twelfth-century picture writing his *Life of St Cuthbert*.

Christian culture proved indispensable in salvaging the culture of the ancient world, particularly in the West, mainly through the influence of Benedictine monasticism, with its emphasis on periods of reading as a regular part of the monastic routine.

The historian Bede had been a monk from childhood in the north of England, in the sister monasteries of Wearmouth and Jarrow. Wearmouth had been founded by a local figure, Benedict Biscop (c. AD 628–690) , who was a great traveller. He was anxious to ensure that his monastery and its younger sister had the resources needed for serious study and he brought back from Italy copies of a good range of materials. These enabled Bede to make a major contribution to the rescuing of classical culture for Christian use. He had to work out largely for himself what it all meant.

He invented or reinvented several areas of study. Natural science was one. This had been explored by Aristotle (384–322 BC) among the Greeks and by Pliny, Seneca the Younger (4 BC–AD 65) and Lucretius (c. 99–55 BC) among the Romans. Bede was able to read Pliny and he borrowed heavily from him in writing his own 'natural history'. There were problems of compatibility with Christian beliefs, but respect for the classical authors was strong and where possible allowances were made for the fact that it was not their fault that they had lacked the benefit of the Christian revelation. There was much discussion of the distance sheer reasoning could take them, for was not the natural world itself a revelation of the kind of God who had made it: his power, his beauty, his generosity, his goodness?

Bede also thought out a Christian 'philosophy of history' in the process of writing his ecclesiastical history of the English people. If history tells of the lives of good men, others, he believes, will be spurred to imitate them. If history recounts

God to those who received it'. This was not really news to the king, for he had a wife, Bertha, a member of the Frankish royal family, who was a Christian. She had married him on the understanding (which her parents had insisted on) that she should be allowed to continue to practise her religion.

The king asked for time to consider the matter. Then he allowed Augustine and his companions to come and preach to him, though he took the precaution of insisting that the meeting should take place in the open air, in case Augustine was planning to try any witchcraft. He gave

what bad men have done and what has happened to them, people will similarly be encouraged to avoid behaving badly. Behind this optimistic set of assumptions of the benefits of reading history lies careful thought about how to bring together the information a good history should contain, and how to ensure that sources are reliable and facts checked. He considers, too, what kinds of material ought to be included: not merely historical events of the sort to be found in a modern text, but also spiritual and supernatural 'truths' such as miracles.

He thought about the nature of time and how to measure it. This was made into an urgent question by the controversy about the date of Easter (see p. 72), to which he made important contributions to help with the way it should be calculated in a world without an agreed world-wide system for fixing the calendar.

Above all he gave his time and energy to the study of the Bible. Here we can glimpse best of all his sense of the way an understanding of a text develops with patience and re-reading, and the capacity of the texts themselves to teach someone who is prepared to allow them to do so, even if he has not had the benefit of a classical education or the stimulus of talk with a international fellowship of academics. As he says at the beginning of his commentary on Acts, he spends his days tirelessly studying the scriptures.

He was able to pick up the literary expectations of an earlier age from his quiet reading: 'I know that the outstanding doctor and bishop Augustine, when he was old, made books of "retractations" of certain things he had said in books he had written as a young man.' He recognized that Augustine did this in order that he might leave to posterity the benefits of his own growth in understanding with more mature age, and tried to do the same with his commentary on Acts.

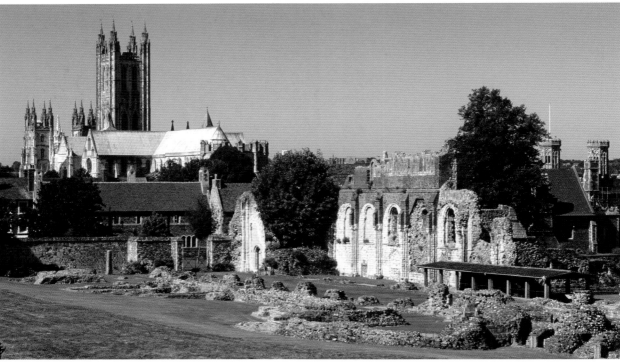

The remains of
St Augustine's Abbey just
outside the old walls of
Canterbury bear witness
to the centuries of
monastic life lived by the
community of monks
which was originally
founded by Augustine
himself.

the missionaries a place to live in Canterbury in Kent and allowed
Augustine permission to preach and see how he fared with the attempt to
convert the English. Like the Celts, they set about their task by living lives
which would show people by example what it was that Christianity could
do for them, and how it could change their lives. They were successful;
the king and others came to be baptized.

But in the mission to England, as in missions elsewhere, success
brought problems. Augustine had to go back to Arles and write to the
pope to clarify what he was to do about the practicalities of setting up
a new church structure in this new land. Augustine sent Pope Gregory
a series of questions which Bede includes in his *Ecclesiastical History of
the English People*, together with Gregory's replies. Does the new English
church have to use the same order of service (rites) as are used
elsewhere? No. Gregory's advice to Augustine is to choose from patterns
of worship he knows well and create a set of rites which suit the new
church in England. Another question is about the consecration of
bishops. Although a single bishop could ordain priests, Canon 4 of the
Council of Nicaea of AD 325 had stipulated that in normal
circumstances all the bishops of a province should come together to
ordain a new bishop. At the very least there should be three. But in a
new local church, distance might make this a practical impossibility. The

pope agrees that Augustine can hardly expect bishops to come over from Gaul to help him ordain the bishops he is going to need. But he tells him to be sensible and make sure that the bishops he will have to ordain himself in an emergency manner will be within reach when he needs them to ordain more. Another question concerns territorial jurisdiction: a bishop has authority only in his own diocese. Bede also reports how later, in the seventh century, at the Synod of Whitby in northern England in AD 664, a meeting had to be held (a local council) to try to sort out differences between the way the Celtic Christians and their northern churches did things and the customs and practice of the Roman Christians of the south.

The accounts in Bede's *Ecclesiastical History of the English People* take us closer than it is usually possible to come to the way the missionary process of the first and the medieval centuries worked 'on the ground'. There are important questions about the depth of conversion which could be achieved when 'mission' was really 'conquest'. The emperor Charlemagne (c. AD 742–814) was not above attempting forced baptisms in conquered territories. Augustine of Canterbury had been much gentler, more willing to coax and even to compromise up to a point. Gregory the Great's advice to Augustine about how to deal with paganism was not to destroy pagan shrines but turn them into churches for Christian worship. This was not the old syncretism of the Roman empire, the approach which had led to persecution of early Christians when they would not accept that their God could be regarded as just one of many. But it must have had the effect of allowing nervous peoples to accept the new religion more easily.

From England missions went out to mainland Europe in the late seventh and eighth centuries. After growing up at Ripon Abbey, to which he was given as a child oblate (that is, an infant given by a family to a monastery to become one of the monks), Willibrord (c. AD 658–739) left Northumbria for Frisia, now the Netherlands. On a second journey he was supported by Boniface (c. AD 672–754), the other leading member of this missionary thrust into the regions from which the Germanic tribes had come to England.

Scandinavia Becomes Christian

The borderlands of Europe to the north and west included the British Isles, and ultimately Iceland, but above all Scandinavia.

Norway, like England, had been made up of a number of small kingdoms in the ninth century. Harald Fairhair (c. AD 850–933) is

CHURCH AND STATE: CHARLEMAGNE AND THE HOLY ROMAN EMPIRE

One way of creating a balance between the role of the church and the role of the state was for the head of the secular structure, the emperor, and the head of the ecclesiastical structure, the pope (at least in the West), to come to terms. This was seen in the West to have been achieved up to a point when Constantine became a Christian; Sylvester I was the contemporary pope. But the needs changed with the fall of the empire because the social structures no longer extended throughout Europe. The church was a much more unified and uniform structure than the state, for now there were tribes on the move, and little by way of settled or secure arrangements.

Charlemagne was son of Pepin, a king of the Franks who had divided his kingdom between his sons. On his brother's death, Charlemagne became lord of the whole realm in AD 771. He proved an extremely energetic ruler, extending his territories by conquest, encroaching into what are now Germany, northern Spain and northern Italy. He was on the whole a benevolent ruler, setting up sound governmental structures and encouraging learning and culture. In AD 800 the pope crowned him Holy Roman Emperor.

The Holy Roman Empire was thus founded as a Frankish creation. In AD 843 Charlemagne's three grandsons agreed on a division of his empire into three. To one of them, Lothair, went the central section, between the Rhine and the Rhone, and the kingship of Italy, together with the title of Emperor. To another, Charles the Bald, went the lands which became France. To Louis fell the eastern Frankish kingdom. The Holy Roman Empire lasted for 963 years; it did not come to an end until 1806 in the period of the Napoleonic Wars, though by then it had shrunk a good deal. Voltaire (1694–1778) had cynically remarked that it was not holy, nor Roman, nor an empire any more by his time.

The first serious bid to achieve an approximation to the old overarching stability was strengthened by a bold piece of forgery. The so-called 'Donation of Constantine' came into existence in the late eighth or early ninth century, probably in the West. It purported to be a grant by the first Christian emperor, who was of course in a sense an Eastern emperor, of an upper hand to the pope in striking the balance of power between secular and spiritual authorities. (This was greater than that later enjoyed by the Eastern emperors in their relationship with the patriarchs.) The pope was to have authority to determine everything that affected the Christian faith and Christian worship; his was the Lateran Palace in Rome; the emperor had his imperial palace in Constantinople. They did not interfere with one another's jurisdiction.

Yet the purported Donation created an almost geographical division of authority which could not apply in the same terms after the fall of the empire and its division into a politically distinct East and West. Pope Sylvester I and his successors were to have dominion over Rome itself, Italy and the whole empire in the West, while Constantine was to have dominion in the East, ruling from his new imperial city of

The Emperor Charlemagne is shown here in a costume which a late medieval fresco painter thought appropriate, holding a sword and the royal orb with a Christian cross on top of it, which represents sovereignty over the world or even the universe.

Constantinople. The text says that Constantine has given supremacy in the West to Sylvester in gratitude for being given instruction in the Christian faith and baptism, and also because Sylvester has cured him of leprosy. This is crucially different from the distinction of jurisdiction between spiritual and temporal matters which was to become the real bone of contention between church and state in medieval Europe.

The emperor Otto III (r. AD 996–1002) was one of the first to say that he thought the Donation a forgery; he had aspirations to be a second Constantine. The pope whose election he fostered, the former Gerbert of Aurillac, chose the name Sylvester II (r. AD 999–1003), in the expectation which the two seem to have shared that the world would end in the year 1000. Otto made a pilgrimage to the tomb of Charlemagne at Aachen in that year and carried away some of the relics there. So he was willing to go along with the (by now accepted) view of the balance of power between church and state when it came to it.

traditionally thought to have united them in AD 872 and made himself king of a unified Norway. The 'Norsemen' made expeditions throughout Europe and beyond in small ships, from the late eighth century to the eleventh, motivated by hunger for plunder, trade and conquest. For two or three hundred years they continued to visit Greenland, Iceland, the Faroe Islands, England and Ireland, and also to cross the Atlantic to Newfoundland. Greenland, and also Newfoundland, the Vinland of the Norse saga of Eric the Red (AD 950–1003), have somehow not become attached to the idea of Europe.

The Norsemen also invaded continental lands now thought of as European. They conquered northern France, giving their name to modern Normandy. From there they began the only successful attempt to conquer the British Isles since Roman times, which resulted in the Norman Conquest of 1066. The Normans went south, too, and settled in south Italy and Sicily, where they were an important factor at the period of the First Crusade. They got as far as Constantinople for trading purposes, and also went east into Russia.

The Norsemen had no missionary purpose in making their raids. At the period when they began their expeditions, their gods were pagan, a hierarchy of mainly nature gods, such as Odin the king of the gods, Thor the god of thunder and his wife Sif, a goddess of fertility. By the time they were a serious presence in southern Europe they had become Christians. Two missionary kings, Olav Trygvason (r. AD 995–1000) and Saint Olav (r. 1015–1028), seem to deserve the main credit for spreading the faith in Norway.

A romanticized modern picture of the Vikings sailing boldly off on an adventure, illustrating the hold they still had on the nineteenth- and twentieth-century historical imagination.

The Christianization of what is now Denmark nominally took place in the mid-tenth century; it is recorded in a runic inscription on the tenth-century Jelling Stone that Harold Bluetooth (c. AD 935–986) christened the Danes. The king allowed himself to be baptized and a church was built in Jelling. Saxo Grammaticus (c. 1150–1220), who wrote the first history of Christian Denmark, explained that he had seen the creation of this record as an important task. It had not been attempted before, partly because the Christianization of Denmark was so recent ('it had but lately been admitted to the common faith'), but also because 'it still languished as strange to Latin as to religion'.

BYZANTIUM FACES A THREAT FROM ASIA

The Byzantine half of the old Roman empire faced challenge from the east during the seventh century. Arabs, full of enthusiasm for the new religion of Islam, seized former provinces to the east and south: Syria, Palestine, Egypt and the northern coast of Africa. Slavs from central Europe descended into the Balkans so that the Byzantines lost control there. The city of Constantinople itself was threatened, and Asia Minor too, by more or less yearly invasions.

The lands of the 'non-Chalcedonians', useful though they might have been to Byzantium from a geographical point of view, were no longer natural allies because they had been separated from the rest of the Christian communion at the Council of Chalcedon in the mid-fifth century. The crying need for military cooperation nevertheless encouraged attempts to splice the theological differences together. The Monothelite ('one-will') movement was in part a device to tempt the non-Chalcedonians more or less back into the fold by suggesting that, even if they could not accept that there was only one person in Christ, perhaps they could accept that there was a single 'will' (or perhaps something like a single 'driving force'). On the other hand, in order to get Western military cooperation, it was politic for the Byzantine church to reject any such solution in the end. The Moslem conquests of the seventh century got as far as Alexandria and the situation began to look more desperate still. At the sixth Council of Constantinople (AD 680–681) the emperor coaxed the bishops to reject the 'one will' formulation so that Byzantium could put itself in a position to get military aid.

This trepidation about what was happening to the east of Byzantium affected Byzantine attitudes towards the West and the Christians who looked towards Rome for leadership. Throughout the centuries, from soon after the end of the Roman empire to the end of the

THE CAROLINGIAN RENAISSANCE

The Carolingian Renaissance had different preoccupations from the 'Ottonian', twelfth-century and sixteenth-century 'renaissances', to the point where it is perhaps debatable whether they were all truly renaissances in the same sense at all, though the term has been used for each of them. 'Renaissance' means rebirth; it involves some form of 'return', and the return was usually understood to be to a classical world rather than to an early, primitive or authentically Christian one.

Among the learned men whose names are associated with the court of Charlemagne, and who seem to have been drawn in from all over Europe to strengthen its cultural claims, were Theodulf (c. AD 760–821), who came from Spain, the Frankish Angilbert (d. AD 814), and Peter of Pisa (1355–1435) and Paulinus of Aquileia (c. AD 735–802) from Lombardy. Among the most important of all was the English Alcuin of York (c. AD 740–804), a Northumbrian monk who served as head of the palace school at Aachen.

In the schools Charlemagne fostered, and which he insisted should be run in each cathedral to ensure that the cathedral canons had a reasonable level of education, there emerged a curriculum, based on that of the ancient world, but adapted to the new one and its different requirements. No longer did the educated man become a leading citizen. Now he was going to be a clerk and a cleric.

The curriculum which began to emerge in the West was based on that of the classical schools. It began with grammar, for now children needed to learn Latin as a second language, even though the Romance languages of southern Europe were still relatively close to their Latin roots. Then came logic, which was to be the most exciting area of development for some centuries, and rhetoric, which was to be taught as a mere vestige of the central subject it had once been. These three were known as the *trivium* or 'three ways'. To them were added four subjects understood as branches of mathematics (arithmetic, music, geometry and astronomy), though they do not seem to have been studied to anything like the same depth or with the same thoroughness. Boethius had invented the word *quadrivium*, 'four ways', to describe these four. These elementary subjects provided the student with tools, writing skills, powers of argument and a means of detecting fallacious arguments.

Middle Ages, the 'Greek' Christians of Europe were caught between two worlds, endangered by both.

Where Greek Christianity predominated, the Byzantine church could be as dark and complicated as the state. Photios (c. AD 820–893) had a brother who married Irene (c. AD 752–803), a sister of the empress Theodora. Theodora had taken over as empress regent when her husband Theophilus died in AD 842. Photios thus gained a place at court, first as a captain of the guard and later in a senior secretarial capacity. From this start, Photios became Patriarch of Constantinople in AD 858, although he had been no more than a cultured layman until soon before his appointment to the see. Against all the best practice and the recommendations of canon law, Photios' ordination and consecration were rushed through. The matter was urgent because the patriarch Ignatios had become involved in a family quarrel in the imperial family and was arrested and imprisoned in AD 858. He refused to resign as

This fresco of the mid-sixteenth century from a Romanian Monastery depicts the siege of Constantinople in AD 626.

Photios is condemned and his books burned, in a sketch of the sixteenth or early seventeenth century.

patriarch and was deposed. A power vacuum would be dangerous and a new patriarch had to be found at once.

This was not a restful promotion. Ignatios refused to accept that he had been deposed. When Photios began to advance patriarchal policies Ignatios' supporters appealed to the pope, who obligingly anathematized and deposed Photios in AD 863.

Photios had a number of hoops to jump through before he could get established as patriarch. His patron Bardias was murdered in AD 866 and the emperor in AD 867. Ignatios was reinstated and Photios was exiled. But he was invited back in AD 867 to educate the imperial children, and when Ignatios died in AD 877, Photios was given the patriarchate once more. His position was recognized at a council in Constantinople in AD 879, attended by legates of Pope John VIII (r. AD 872–882), who was prepared to accept him, though not without the disapproval of many in the West.

Photios was to be a significant figure in the story of the Balkans, and in the wider story of East–West relations in Christian Europe. He insisted that the West's addition of a clause to the creed (the *Filioque*; see p. 82), saying that the Holy Spirit proceeds from the Father 'and the Son', was unacceptable, and this has remained one of the justifications for the schism which formally began in 1054 and has never been mended. Photios encouraged the efforts of missionaries to convert the Slavs (who had invaded and settled the area in the sixth and seventh centuries) and the Bulgars (who became officially Christian in AD 865) to the Greek church, partly to save them from the contamination of such Western Christian ideas. The Bulgars had other ideas. They negotiated with the pope, Nicholas I (d. AD 867), because they wanted his assistance in getting the

Greek missionaries driven out of their lands. The West did not organize itself very well; Rome told the Frankish missionaries to leave so as not to interfere with the mission from Rome itself. Bulgaria returned to the Byzantine rite in AD 870, and the Western church was impotent to enforce its claims without the support of Boris I of Bulgaria (d. AD 907).

Photios was as keen to establish an authority in the West as the pope was to establish an authority in the East. As Holy Roman Emperor, Charlemagne could be seen as a rival to the emperor of the East. Photios gave him 'permission', in his capacity as Patriarch of Constantinople, to call himself King of the Romans. On the other hand, Photios seems to have proved himself a skilful diplomat as ambassador to the Arabs. His motivation was perhaps fear of the Russians, who had made raids on the empire in AD 860.

Missionary Rivalries between Eastern and Western Churches in Eastern Europe

There was often a strong link between political and personal conversion and even between mission and conquest. Clovis, king of the Franks (c. AD 466–511), for example, was baptized a Catholic instead of an Arian, and his people were deemed to have followed him. This was particularly evident in the eastern regions of Europe with their moving tides of conquering and reconquering tribes ebbing and flowing as the Roman hegemony died away. The Polish ruler Mieszko I (c. AD 935–992) was baptized in AD 966, and this was regarded as 'the baptism of Poland'. The baptism of Mieszko marked a political as well as a religious consolidation.

But although the conversion of a people often depended on perceived political needs of the moment, that did not always result in the desired period of stability. In the late Roman period there were many peoples in the territories now covered by Poland; traces of Celts, Slavs and Baltic and Germanic peoples have been found and there remained divisive loyalties. By the twelfth century the unified realm had broken up again into a series of small states which fell easy prey to the Mongol armies of the 'Golden Horde' in the thirteenth century, and it was not until the turn of the fourteenth century that Poland was unified again under a Christian monarch, Wladislaus I (1260–1333).

From the ninth century the missionary activity from East and West created painful rivalries, which helped to build the sensitivities that were to lead to the decisive breakdown of relations between East and West with the schism of 1054.

The first of the Slavs to be converted were the Croatians who, with

THE EASTER CONTROVERSY IN EAST AND WEST

The date of Easter, the great celebration of Jesus' resurrection and the day on which the newly baptized were welcomed into the community of the early church after their long period of preparation, has to be calculated each year. It is not a feast which falls on a fixed day but a 'moveable' feast. In centuries when the counting or marking of the passage of time was still evolving into a formal system it was possible for some divergence to occur in the choice of a date to celebrate Easter in different parts of the expanding Christian world, and it did.

This came to be regarded as much more important than a mere mismatch of diaries. Pope Victor (r. AD 189–198/9) declared at the end of the second century that for a local church not to accept the date the Romans had chosen was to separate itself from communion with Rome. The emperor Constantine also insisted that a difference over the choice of date divided the church and the Council of Nicaea in AD 325 (over-optimistically as it turned out) laid down a rule on that point, addressed to the Egyptians:

All the brethren in the East who have hitherto followed the Jewish practice will henceforth observe the customs of the Romans and of yourselves and of all of us who from ancient times have kept Easter together with you.

Among the Western authors writing in Latin in the century that followed, Hilary, bishop of Poitiers (d. AD 368), undoubtedly continued to see the celebration of the Eucharist as an expression of the unity of the church.

The English Benedictine monk Bede made a substantial contribution to solving the problem of agreeing dates. Britain had its own version of this difficulty because Christians who had been converted as a result of the mission of Augustine of Canterbury in AD 597 disagreed about the date of Easter with those who had become Christians as a result of Celtic missionary efforts. This was felt with particular sharpness where it caused disharmony in a royal marriage:

In these days it sometimes happened that Easter was celebrated twice in the same year, so that the King had finished the fast and was keeping Easter Sunday, while the Queen and her people were still in Lent and observing Palm Sunday.

At the Synod of Whitby in AD 664 the king opened the meeting:

declaring that it was fitting that those who served one God should observe one rule of life and not differ in the celebration of the heavenly sacraments, seeing that they all hoped for one kingdom in heaven; they ought therefore to enquire as to which was the truer tradition and then all follow it together.

The heat went out of the controversy for a time but it has remained sufficiently important for the World Council of Churches to discuss reform of the way the date of this moveable feast could be fixed as recently as 1997.

A vigorous depiction in a manuscript of about 1400 of the kind of battle fought between the Western armies and the Mongol armies of Genghis Khan. The painter has tried to represent the contrasting costumes, weapons and armour, but with mixed success.

the Serbs, had captured lands of the former Roman empire. They were won to Christianity by priests from the Roman church in the middle of the seventh century. The Bavarian peoples who had extended across upper Austria from the West were also soon converted to Roman Christianity when their duke, Theodo, was baptized at Ratisbon by Rupert, bishop of Worms (d. AD 718). Rupert pressed eastwards with his mission, settling at Salzburg, where he created a diocese and established a monastery, St Peter's.

The remaining Slavs were, for the most part, converted by a missionary movement deriving not from the West but from Eastern Christendom. Cyril and Methodius were brothers, born in the 820s AD in Thessalonica in northern Greece. They were of good birth and could have hoped for offices of state in Byzantium, but they both chose to enter the priesthood and entered a monastery on the Bosphorus. The Khazar people asked for someone to teach them about Christianity and the

Patriarch of Constantinople sent Cyril. Methodius went with him. They took the trouble to learn the language of the Khazars and were successful in converting many to the Christian faith.

Their reputation reached the people of Moravia, who had already experienced Christian mission from the West. The German missionaries who had tried to convert the Moravians had failed, possibly because they had not made sufficient effort to learn the language and study the culture of the

Cyril and Methodius shown together in an icon from Bulgaria, with their alphabet.

people. The Moravians wanted to be able to worship as Christians in their own language. Cyril and Methodius went about this new mission with equally thorough preparation, even inventing an alphabet (subsequently known as the Cyrillic alphabet) so that the gospels and forms of liturgy to be used in worship could be translated into Slavonic. In AD 863 they travelled to Moravia, where they conducted a successful mission, although under the baleful and mistrustful gaze of German critics.

Cyril and Methodius were summoned to Rome to explain themselves. Pope Nicholas I died before they arrived. But Adrian II, the next pope (r. AD 867–872), was well-disposed towards the brothers, approved of their missionary work and even gave formal approval to the use of the Slavonic liturgy. He consecrated both brothers as bishops, although Cyril did not survive to return to the East, dying in Rome in early AD 869. Adrian created an archdiocese of Moravia and Pannonia which was to be independent of the church in Germany; this he did with the support of the rulers of Moravia and Pannonia.

The German authorities were not happy about this development. King Louis and the bishops of Germany sent for Methodius in AD 870 to appear before a synod at Ratisbon. He was deposed by the synod and sent to prison. Three years later, the next pope, John VIII, insisted that he should be freed and reinstated as archbishop of Moravia. The power struggle between church and state, East and West, for control of the

Christians of these borderlands continued: Methodius was energetically spreading the faith in Bohemia and moving north among the Poles of northern Moravia and the Germans were nervous. Wiching, a German priest, made representations to Rome, claiming that Methodius was not orthodox and expressing disquiet about the use of the Slavonic liturgy.

Once again Methodius was called to Rome. Once again the papacy was broadly supportive, although a compromise was proposed: the gospel was to be read in Latin at the Eucharist before it was read in Slavonic. Wiching was made one of Methodius' suffragan or assistant bishops in the hope of appeasing his hostility. Wiching was not willing to abandon his opposition, however; he even forged papal letters.

Methodius' spiritual home continued to lie in the East. He returned to Constantinople for a time, to finish the translation of almost the whole Bible into Slavonic, and to provide the Slavs with a vernacular version of Greek canon and civil law.

The Cyrillic alphabet survived Methodius' death in AD 885. It had already won the blessing of the secular authorities in Bulgaria when Christianity became the official religion in AD 864. Bulgaria, however, looked not towards Rome but towards Constantinople for approval. The Patriarch of Constantinople recognized the Bulgarian patriarchate in AD 927, and thus added it to the five which had emerged in the first centuries. Modern Bulgaria still has an autocephalous Orthodox church, that is, one which is not under the jurisdiction of any outside bishop or metropolitan, whose members include many who live outside Bulgaria in other parts of Europe, as well as in America or Australia.

From Moravia Christianity travelled into Bohemia, where the Czechs based in Prague were driving the German tribes to the edges of the territory. Methodius baptized the Czech prince Borziwoy and his wife in AD 871. However, the pagans continued to resist Christian domination. Wenceslaus I, the 'good king' (c. AD 907–929/35), was murdered. It took some time for the area to be settled as a Christian realm. Benedictine monks were brought in in the tenth century and, after the two ruling families were united in the 960s AD by the marriage of a Czech princess and the Polish duke Mieczyslaw, their son established four bishoprics to provide institutional stability for the Christian church in the area. These – Breslau, Cracow, Kolberg and Posen – were then placed under the archbishopric of Gnesen, which dates from the year 1000.

The Hungarians or Magyars were another people whose conversion became something of a battle between Eastern and Western missionaries. They had moved west from the Urals, and Byzantium had made overtures

RIGHT: The mosque at Cordoba in southern Spain became a Christian cathedral in 1236.

to try to win them to Christianity. From the West attempts were made at the instigation of the bishop of Passau, who wanted to become metropolitan of the large area of Pannonia, by Adalbert, bishop of Prague (c. AD 957–997), and also by a monk from the monastery of Einsiedeln called Wolfgang. Once more it was the goodwill of a ruler which decided things. Stephen (later to be canonized) had been taught the faith and baptized by Adalbert and he founded an archbishopric at Gran, which was to preside over ten sees. He also fostered Benedictine monasticism in the area, and the abbot of his foundation at Martinsberg prevailed upon Pope Sylvester II to give Stephen the title of king to celebrate the year 1000.

Russian Orthodoxy claimed a very ancient beginning, through a visit by Andrew the Apostle. Legend said that he had conducted a mission on the northern shore of the Black Sea and had even got as far as the place where Kiev would one day be built. The historical record suggests that it was not until the mid-ninth century that a Christian bishop was sent to the Russians at Novgorod, possibly by Photios. In the tenth century there were Christian believers in Russia but the population was still substantially pagan. Olga, princess of Kiev (c. AD 890–969), became a Christian in the middle of the century and it was her grandson who, as ruler, made Kievan Russia officially Christian in AD 988. He adopted the Eastern Orthodox rite from Byzantium.

Southern Europe and the Boundary with Islam

The story went that the 'Moors' arrived in Spain from Morocco by invitation in the hope that they might assist the oppressed subjects of the Visigoths. A modest invasion force arrived at Gibraltar in April AD 711 and soon Moslem forces, having realized that Spain was well worth having,

THE CULTURE OF ARABIC SPAIN

The culture of Arabic Spain became a harmonious multicultural mix of Moslem, Christian, Jewish and Berber tribes and religions. This is clearly reflected in the architecture of southern Spain. Arabic learning had been ahead of that of the West for some centuries because the Arabs had translated, absorbed and added to the philosophy of ancient Greece. They had a good deal to teach Western European scholars, and it was through Arabic Spain that the first translations of much of Aristotle became available in Latin. To Spain, too, Peter the Venerable, abbot of Cluny (c. 1092–1156), looked when he needed a team of translators to make a translation of the Koran into Latin in the mid-twelfth century.

were moving northwards, capturing most of Spain in the course of the next seven years. They crossed into Gaul, taking Narbonne, and were stopped only by the Frankish army of Charles Martel (AD 686–741) in AD 732 at the battle of Poitiers. Local Christian rulers were then able to reassert their authority in the north of Spain.

The local Spanish population seems to have welcomed the Arab invaders. The Moslems were ready to promise them freedom of worship and freedom of religious conscience. Arabic cultural and social influence was generally benign and in many respects more congenial that the rule of the Romans had been, let alone that of the Visigoths. Many Jewish residents in Spain were also happy to welcome the Arabs as better protectors of their interests than the former rulers.

From AD 711 to 1492 Moslems ruled parts of the Iberian peninsula. The Umayyad dynasty, Mohammed's successors, were losing control in Damascus to the Abbasids, a rival tribe. An exile from the Ummayads became emir of Cordoba in AD 756, preserving the rule of the Ummayads into the period where the Abbasids had taken over in Baghdad.

In AD 929 the Emirate became the Caliphate of Cordoba. But from the very beginning of the eleventh century, faction fighting began to threaten the hegemony of the Moors. Christian states which had been strengthening their position in the north and west had been expanding from Galicia, Asturias, the Basque country and the Carolingian Marca Hispanica. The kingdoms of Navarre, León, Portugal, Castile and Aragon and the county of Barcelona became a political force to be reckoned with.

4 The High Middle Ages

THE SCHISM OF 1054 DIVIDES EASTERN AND WESTERN CHRISTIAN EUROPE

The potential for mutual misunderstanding between Christians in the West and Christians in the East of Europe was sharpened by the contest for the souls of the peoples of the borderlands between the two. Misunderstandings and misrepresentations abounded, strengthened by the schism which occurred in 1054. When Guibert of Nogent commented on the Eastern church when he was writing about the First Crusade, he said it was 'changeable', whereas in reality nothing could have been more conservative and resistant to change than the Eastern church. Anna Comnena (1083–1153), a Byzantine princess, described the Westerners coming through Greek territory on the same crusade as barbarians. In the mid-twelfth century Gerald of Wales (c. 1146–1223) was frank about the bad feeling between the two churches, for, as he saw it, the Greeks had deliberately seceded from Rome's legitimate jurisdiction. The Greeks, on the other hand, were saying that it was the Romans who had seceded from the shared communion and created the separation. They took to disinfecting any altar on which a Roman priest had said mass.

The schism which had given rise to these extreme polarities was as much of political as of theological origin, though there soon grew up around it a considerable body of theological detail. The Normans had by now made their way from being Viking invaders to settlers in northern France ('Normandy') and to the south of Europe, where they had invaded Sicily and south Italy. This was a part of Europe where the interface between the two languages was still alive, and where Greek and Latin Christians actually met and might compare their practices. One of the noticeable differences was that the Greeks used leavened bread in the celebration of the Eucharist and the Latins used unleavened bread, claiming that yeast represented sin and it was better to use bread which was not fermented, with the negative symbolism that called to mind.

Pope Leo IX on the right is shown excommunicating the Patriarch of Constantinople at the time of the schism of 1054, though in reality the two certainly did not meet for the purpose.

Rabanus Maurus (c. AD 776–856) had insisted in the ninth century that the bread used in the Eucharist should be unleavened, citing Leviticus 2:4 and stressing that at Passover, when the Last Supper was celebrated, there would have been no yeast in any Jewish house. In fact the West had probably gone over to the use of unleavened bread some centuries before this. The Greeks said that it was essential that real bread was used, and unleavened bread was not bread at all. A similar disagreement over yeast was complicating Greek relations with the Armenians, adding to the difference of opinion over the Chalcedonian Christology.

The Norman invaders were not finely attuned to all these sensitivities and tried to force local priests to celebrate in the Latin way they were used to. Greek priests were angry and reported their indignation to Constantinople. Cardinal Humbert (c. 1015–1061) took a strong line on behalf of Rome, writing to Constantinople to insist that the will of the bishop of Rome as Primate of the whole church should predominate. So to the conflict about the use of yeast was added a conflict about universal primacy and whether if such a primacy existed it was one of honour only, or involved an actual overarching jurisdiction.

The pope sent a legation to Constantinople, led by Cardinal Humbert and the archbishop of Amalfi. Leo IX (r. 1049–1054) died about the time it arrived there, but not before great offence had been caused by the fact that a letter had been sent first to the Eastern emperor and not to the Patriarch of Constantinople, when there was already bad blood between the two. The patriarch, Michael Cerularius (c. 1000–1059), even suggested that the emperor must have tampered with the letter, since the tone of it was so abusive that he was reluctant to believe the pope could have used such words.

The Western legation precipitated the eventual schism. On 16 July 1054, the Romans laid upon the altar in Santa Sophia in Constantinople a papal Bull of excommunication of the Patriarch of Constantinople. Both sides began to publish lists of the other's errors and to exchange anathemas.

Several early attempts were made to heal the breach. At the Council of Bari in 1098, a Western council though some Greeks were present, Pope Urban II (r. 1088–1099) called on Anselm, archbishop of Canterbury (1033–1109), who happened to be in Italy seeking the support of the pope in his own quarrel with the king of England. He asked him to explain to the Greeks why they were wrong about the procession of the Holy Spirit (they maintained that the Holy Spirit proceeds only from the Father, while the Western Christians said that he proceeds from both the Father and the Son). Anselm published a book on this, and also wrote some open letters about the use of leaven, saying that bread could be bread whether it had yeast in it or not, but neither succeeded in convincing the entrenched opposition among the Greeks.

A generation later, Anselm of Havelberg set up a dialogue in Constantinople to try to talk through these differences with leading Greek churchmen, finding translators to assist scholars busy with translation of the works of Aristotle from the Greek for use in the burgeoning schools (soon to become universities) of the West, such as Burgundius of Pisa (d. 1193), James of Venice (fl. mid-twelfth century) and Moses of Pergamum. This second Anselm wrote an account of what was said, chiefly to counter the objection of the Greeks that to say that the Holy Spirit proceeds from the Father and the Son was to suggest that there are two 'principles' or 'origins' in God, and that must be

THE *FILIOQUE*

In the Carolingian West, a phrase was added to the text of the Nicene Creed, the statement of faith agreed by the council which met at Nicaea in AD 325 in the middle of the Arian crisis. It changes what is said about the Holy Spirit so that it says 'who proceeds from the Father and the Son'. This, which became one of the key points of division between the Eastern and the Western churches, was a difference of opinion about the *Filioque* ('and the Son') clause. The question was drawn in among the issues already causing mutual offence.

There was no intention of changing the doctrine of the Trinity. This was almost certainly intended as a clarification of a point left ambiguous by the original text. The Greeks found it objectionable because it looked like an alteration. They saw the faith as something which had been deposited complete, or at any rate, had reached its final and definitive statement by the end of the period of the ecumenical councils. But in any case, the Greeks did not agree that this did not constitute an alteration to the doctrine of the Trinity. They said this addition made it seem that there were two 'origins' or first principles in the Trinity, and not only one, and that, to a Platonist way of thinking, diminished the Godhead.

In his *Mystagogia* Photios made a case along these lines against the Latins. The theologians of the West saw the force of the 'two principles' problem, up to a point. Alcuin, Charlemagne's educational adviser, mentions it in a commentary he wrote on John's Gospel. Heiric of Auxerre, a later Carolingian commentator (AD 841–876/7), tries to explain it away by saying that although both Father and Son are 'beginnings' of the Holy Spirit, they are not two beginnings but one.

The debate about the difference between Eastern and Western versions of the creed was conducted in the East, too. On the Mount of Olives stood a monastery unacceptable. However, it is clear that the arguments he and his party put were framed from the point of view of a Western understanding of the issues, as those of his namesake had been.

Eastern Europe After the Schism

The lands which had been contested between Greek and Latin Christians in the missionary period did not settle tidily into the camp of either party to the schism of 1054. King Ladislaus of Hungary (1040–1095) imposed order on the Christian church in his kingdom partly by establishing a bishopric at Grosswardein and calling a synod or 'diet' at Szabolcs. This bore the marks of the topical subjects of disciplinary crackdown currently fashionable in the Western church: the condemnation of simony (the buying and selling of preferment) and the insistence on the celibacy of the clergy. Ladislaus successfully invaded Croatia, whose ruler had sworn loyalty to the pope in 1076, in return

of Frankish monks, who offered hospitality for pilgrims from the West who were travelling to the Holy Land. Greek monks in the area were suspicious of their Frankish counterparts, and accused them of heresy. The Patriarch of Jerusalem heard of this and wrote to the pope in concern. The pope passed the matter on to Charlemagne so that he should be aware of what was happening, and he asked Alcuin to draw up a catalogue of opinions to be found in early Christian writings so that he could demonstrate that there was authority for the Western position. He sent the Eastern churches his own thoughts on the creed, which he insists is the true faith as the Roman church holds it. Western authors remained consistently firm on this point, insisting that they were adding nothing to the faith as it had been defined, merely clarifying a point. Rabanus Maurus composed a hymn (*Veni Creator Spiritus* or 'Come, Holy Ghost') which is still sung. At the end it includes the *Filioque*:

Teach us to know the Father, Son
And you of both to be but one.

The Council of Florence (1438–1445), a rare attempt of the late Middle Ages at a joint council of East and West, nearly succeeded in resolving the difference, but ultimately it failed. Even the lifting of the mutual anathemas under which East and West had placed one another in the eleventh century has not restored them to a single 'communion'.

for the title of king. The dukes of Austria, beginning with Henry Jasomirgott (1107–1177), were also Western Catholic rulers, establishing a capital at Vienna.

Estonia joined the Roman side when it was converted from paganism in the thirteenth century by German invaders known as the 'Livonian Brothers of the Sword', who regarded themselves as crusaders. From the other direction, Denmark was making a bid for the control of the land and a compromise was struck in 1227, allowing each a claim. Denmark held sovereignty over Estonia until 1346.

CHRISTIAN BOUNDARIES WITH ISLAM

In Spain, Islamic rule lasted into the thirteenth century. In Portugal a reconquest was successful in 1249, when Alfonso III (1265–1291) recaptured the Algarve. After the Christians had recaptured Granada in 1236 the Moslem rulers headed a vassal state, subject to the kingdom of Castile. The kingdoms of Aragon and Castile dominated Spain from 1284 to 1476. In 1492 Granada was finally ceded to Ferdinand (1452–1516) and Isabella (1451–1504), whose marriage united political control of Aragon and Castile from 1476 to 1516.

As in the Balkans, there were times when the reasonably comfortable and mutually tolerant arrangements which had allowed Christians and Moslems (and in Spain especially Jews too) to live together harmoniously, to the general benefit of trade, culture and intellectual life, were put under strain. The Jewish community in Spain, as elsewhere in Europe, were tolerated for their work in trade and finance. The numbers were quite substantial, with an estimated 50,000 Jews in Granada and perhaps 100,000 in the whole of Islamic Spain. In 1499 the Primate of Spain, Ximénez de Cisneros (1436–1517), arrived in Granada and began to try to force the Moslems there to become Christian, on pain of death if they refused. In 1526 the Inquisitor General went to Granada with the same purpose of forcing conversions. Some pretended to be converted and were known as Moriscos; others refused. The numbers who did so were considerable. One uprising in the mountains near Granada took Philip II of Spain (1527–1598) some time to quell by armed force, and he needed to borrow military assistance from Austria to do it. In the end, between 1609 and 1614, Spain expelled the Moriscos, allowing a very small proportion, mainly women and small children, to stay.

Spain thus settled its border problems with Islam by ejecting the Moslems from its territories. It was able to achieve this partly because of the emergence of a strong unified Christian government, and partly no doubt because the peninsula has a natural boundary on three sides in the surrounding seas. North Africa and its Moslem populations were on the other side of the water.

The situation in Eastern Europe was very different. Medieval Byzantium faced challenge from the East rather than from the West, both in military and in cultural

Finland, too, lay at the interface between the church of the Roman West and that of the Greek Orthodox East. The tradition is that King Erik of Sweden (r. c. 1150–1160) brought Christianity to the Finns in 1154, though there is archaeological evidence that Christianity had touched the region earlier, possibly through trade, both from the Roman and from the Orthodox side. In 1249 Birger Jarl (c. 1210–1266) made an expedition which resulted in Finland becoming formally part of the Swedish kingdom.

The Finns were closely linked with Sweden for nearly 700 years, possibly longer. The conquerors imposed their administrative system and

In this nineteenth-century painting the Turks are bursting into Constantinople in 1453.

terms. The Turks were originally a nomadic people from central Asia. In 1071 the Seljuk Turks conquered Anatolia, and they remained among the principal adversaries of the Western crusaders throughout the 'crusading' period of the twelfth century. The Ottoman Turks appeared in the declining Seljuk empire, settling and establishing control in Anatolia in 1227, in flight from the Tang empire of China. In 1243 the invading Mongols defeated the Seljuk Turks, and the Turkish dominance in Europe became that of the Ottomans. Ottoman Turks captured Gallipoli in 1354. The Crusade of Nicopolis was launched by the king of Hungary in 1396, and another, the Crusade of Varna (1444), was initiated by the Polish-Hungarian king. By 1362 the Ottomans had expanded across the Dardanelles. They conquered Constantinople in 1453; this was a defining moment. One more attempt at a crusade was made in 1456 to get the Ottoman siege of Belgrade lifted.

their language. That drove the use of Finnish into the lower classes and into the regions, where local court proceedings were still conducted in Finnish; Finnish was still also used to some degree by the local clergy. The subordination of the language discouraged the emergence of a literature. (Mikael Agricola, c. 1510–1557, was the first to publish his writings in Finnish, and that was not until the sixteenth century.) It remained an important question throughout the Middle Ages in the West whether a writer was going to use Latin, which would give him a potential readership all over Europe, or a local vernacular language, which would have a smaller reach and would limit him a good deal in the kinds of thing he could say because of the comparative lack of sophistication of the vernacular languages.

Poland and Lithuania also opted for the Roman, not the Orthodox, side of the debate. Lithuania is first mentioned in a historical source in 1009. Its territories were united in 1236 under King Mindaugas (c. 1203–1263), who was crowned in 1253. Lithuania was to become an extensive realm during the later Middle Ages, including modern Ukraine and Belarus and areas of Russia as well as Poland. At the end of the fourteenth century, it reached to the Baltic in one direction and the Black Sea in the other. A short-lived union of Poland and Lithuania took place in 1386, and both were ruled by the same dynasty with an acceptance of Roman Catholic Christianity. By 1401 this arrangement had broken down but the Holy Roman Emperor continued to take an active interest in the future rule of this important section of Europe.

Meanwhile in Russia the Eastern church held sway, and was politically important to helping the Russians survive the oppression of the Tatars.

CHURCH AND STATE AND THE INVESTITURE CONTEST

The Ideal of Christian Kingship

One of the new emphases to emerge with the Christianization of Europe and the end of the Roman empire was a new understanding of the nature of kingship in the West. Many of the tribes which now ruled the old territories of Rome thought in terms of a hereditary leadership drawn from a noble class. In northern Europe, where feudalism emerged as the system for land tenure, the lower orders cultivated the land either as freemen or as serfs. Serfs were in effect slaves, bound to the land and regarded as mere chattels at the disposal of their lords. The nobility came to be regarded as made of finer stuff, a superior breed of human being. The story of the princess and the pea, told by the Danish Hans Christian

The winged lion that sits on top of the famous column in Venice is a symbol of St Mark, Venice's patron saint, who is commemorated in the Basilica of St Mark in the square in which it stands.

Andersen (1805–1875), depends on this idea. The princess is able to feel a pea through many layers of feather mattresses and in this way her noble birth reveals itself.

Christian monarchy developed ideals of Christian kingship with the formalization of coronation rituals. It was always understood that coronation was not a sacrament, but kings and emperors were crowned by archbishops and popes and they were 'anointed'. A king was supposed to set an example of high-mindedness, as well as of courage and good leadership. Louis of France (1215–1270), who was king from 1226 to 1270, though he proved a strikingly unsuccessful military leader as a crusader, took holiness as far as was practical for a king. Joinville (1224/5–1317) wrote a biography which he modelled on the saints' lives of the period, emphasizing Louis' piety and his charity and support for the poor.

The real challenge to the balance of power between church and state in the Middle Ages did not come, however, from any tendency of pious monarchs to behave as though they were clergy or monks, but from a sharpening of concern about the location of the boundary between the temporal and the spiritual. A practice grew up in the eleventh century of royal or imperial interference in the appointment of bishops. There was no objection to lay choice of a candidate, although it was an abuse for royal patrons to delay making the choice for a year or so while they took the revenues from a see into the royal coffers for their own use. There was nothing wrong with the secular authority which ruled the territory in

SECULAR AND CHRISTIAN ILLUSTRATION

In Theophilus' *On Diverse Arts* there is a short analysis of the distinctiveness of the various contributions of different parts of Europe to the work of Europe's artists. Greece he links with 'kinds and blends of various colours'; Russia with enamel work; Arabia with cast work and with engravings in relief; Italy with the application of gold 'embellishments' to 'various vessels'; France with stained glass windows; Germany with 'subtle work in metals' as well as wood and stone.

The illustration of Christian and other narratives was not, however, merely a matter of technical skill. It involved all sorts of questions of design and symbolism. When a new text called for illustration, as happened with Dante's (1265–1321) epic poem the *Divine Comedy*, in which the poet travels though all the levels of

hell, purgatory and heaven, someone had to devise a picture sequence to meet the new need for a visual accompaniment to the story of the journey.

At the beginning of the *Divine Comedy* Dante meets Virgil, who explains that he is a poet too and who offers to be his guide. He is the obvious person. He is the author of the *Aeneid*, and in Book VI of the *Aeneid* Aeneas goes down into Hades, so Virgil is knowledgeable about these realms. He invites Dante: 'Follow me, and I will be your guide.'

Dante makes sure his readers understand that Virgil was not a Christian but a secular author of an earlier time. Yet he is the right guide through the realms of death to the point where St Peter stands at the gate of heaven. However, when Dante and Virgil approach heaven, Dante can enter only with a new guide: his beloved Beatrice, now dead. For Beatrice's name means 'blessed'.

A manuscript of about the 1440s contains illustrations of the *Divine Comedy*. There are Dante and Virgil standing together in a gloomy wood, just as Dante describes at the beginning of the poem, and round them, in circles of leaves, are which the lands of the see lay handing them over to the bishop as a vassal, for in that respect a bishop was merely another noble, a 'spiritual lord', and he held his lands from the king in the same way as a baron (who might well be his brother, for they might come from the same family) would hold his own lands. What the church objected to was kings or emperors trying to put the episcopal ring on the new bishop's finger or the episcopal staff in his hand, for these aspects of investiture were part of the sacramental process of making a bishop which only the spiritual authorities could complete.

four medallions containing the four Ciceronian virtues in the form of goddesslike personifications: Justice, Prudence, Temperance and Fortitude.

The depiction of the opening scene and all that follows in this manuscript – or in other manuscripts – was not the creative original work of an artist of the sort who might work as an illustrator today. Someone travelling might pass through a workshop and leave lasting changes of practice and composition behind. Someone might introduce the idea of jagged mountains, and then jagged mountains would appear as a signature in the background of picture after picture.

At the same time there were established conventions of iconography, which enabled biblical figures and saints to be portrayed with some trademark feature so that even the illiterate could look at the pictures and understand what they were. Each of the four evangelists had such a symbol: a human figure or an angel for St Matthew; a lion for St Mark; an ox for St Luke; and an eagle for St John. For different reasons St Jerome would be accompanied by a lion when his portrait was painted.

When it came to illustrating a secular story, such as the story of Lancelot, there was again an established sequence of illustrations which the artists would add, following the familiar composition for each, building up each picture in a series of stages, not necessarily all executed by the same person. An outline drawing might be followed by shading and colouring with various mixes of pigments. One person might even go through painting the red areas, followed by another painting the flesh colours. Theophilus is especially detailed about this.

LEFT: Dante is shown in this book illustration from a manuscript of his *Divine Comedy*, lost in the wood at the beginning of the story, where he meets Virgil, and Virgil is shown setting off to guide him.

The Investiture Contest

Concerns on this point led to the dispute known as the Investiture Contest. Pope Gregory VII (r. 1073–1085) was its chief protagonist. In his register of letters for the year 1075 is preserved a document containing a list of 'sayings of the pope', which push the claims of the papacy a very long way indeed. They assert: 'That the Roman church was founded by God alone'; 'That the Roman pontiff alone can with right be called universal'; 'That he alone can depose or reinstate bishops'; 'That for him alone is it lawful, according to the needs of the time, to make new laws, to assemble together new congregations, to make an abbey of a canonry; and, on the other hand, to divide a rich bishopric and unite the poor ones'; 'That he alone may use the imperial insignia'; 'That no synod shall be called a general one without his order'; 'That no chapter and no book shall be considered canonical without his authority'; 'That a sentence passed by him may be retracted by no one; and that he himself, alone of all, may retract it'; 'That he himself may be judged by no one'; 'That no one shall dare to condemn one who appeals to the apostolic chair'; 'That the Roman church has never erred; nor will it err to all eternity, the Scripture bearing witness'; 'That he who is not at peace with the Roman church shall not be considered catholic'; 'That he may absolve subjects from their fealty to wicked men'.

These claims intrude as much upon the separate jurisdictions of bishops in their dioceses as upon the powers of the secular authorities. Taken together they represent a serious bid for monarchical power on the part of the papacy, which was to have an enormous effect on the subsequent history of the church in the West, leading in the end to the Reformation.

During the next medieval centuries the personal monarchical power of the papacy grew, and with it claims to a plenitude of power. This distorted both the balance of power between church and state and the balance of power within the church. Secular powers could fight only with armies and it is a commonplace that it is easy to over-extend oneself as a monarch by trying to fight on more than one front at once. The ultimate papal weapon was excommunication, and this had the advantage that it could be imposed on any number of adversaries. The pope used it on the emperor of Germany when he considered he had been intruding on the church's role in the creation of bishops by 'investing' them with the ring and staff of their pastoral office. The pope wrote in 1076 not only to 'all the clergy and laity' but also to 'all the faithful of Germany', to lay people as well as to clerics: 'We have heard that some of your countrymen have doubts about the excommunication which we have placed upon the king: they question whether… our sentence… had the sanction of lawful authority.' At Canossa in the winter of 1077, the emperor was obliged to kiss the stirrup of the pope. That was an act which could only be demanded of a vassal. The humiliation was heightened by making him do it, and in the snow, in order to do penance so as to get the ban of excommunication lifted, for while he was excommunicated none of his subjects was required to obey him.

The dispute was brought more or less to an end by the Concordat of Worms in 1122. This was an agreement that the secular authorities would confine themselves to the 'temporalities' of the appointment of a bishop and leave the 'spiritualities' to the ecclesiastical power. But the thrust of Gregory VII's bid for supremacy now had its own momentum. Bernard of Clairvaux (1090–1153) wrote a book for Pope Eugenius III (r. 1145–1153), who had once been a Cistercian monk, in which he explored the question over whom the pope was supreme. He concluded that the pope was supreme over every power in the land, indeed over everything earthly, and that he was subject only to heaven.

The question of the Donation of Constantine (see pp. 64–65) and its implications had not entirely gone away, meanwhile. Dante had hostile things to say about it in the *Divine Comedy*. Dante also put forward in his *De Monarchia* the notion that all the troubles of the world would be resolved if only it would return to a universal empire on the model of ancient Rome. His motivation was less grandiose: he had found himself excluded from his home city of Florence by faction fighting and was living in angry exile, and naturally he favoured the largest possible power bloc to overcome such petty local squabblers. Nicholas of Cusa (1401–1464) had also argued for a single empire, claiming that such a mode of governing Europe would be the holiest as well as the highest. Christian kingship was a near miss; Christian empire was best.

John of Paris (d. 1306) wrote on royal and papal power, aiming at a compromise between extremists who would deny spiritual authorities any temporal powers at all, and those who allowed them powers over property and other secular things on the basis that all power comes from God and would naturally go first to the spiritual authorities, who might choose to lend some of it to the temporal authority. Marsilius of Padua (1270–1342) was the author of *The Defender of the Peace*, a challenging work of political theory published in 1324, in which he describes the ecclesiastical power as having a place in society primarily to ensure that the population are made quiet and biddable by religion.

The Donation itself was eventually exposed as a forgery in the fifteenth century by Lorenzo Valla (c. 1406–1457), who was able to show that the language in which it was written could not have been used in that way in the real era of Constantine.

CHRISTIANITY AND HOLY WAR

Medieval Christianity was not inclined to pacificism. The warlike conduct, first of Imperial Rome, and then of tribes invading the empire and settling throughout Europe, reflected social structures within which the leaders and nobles of society were first and foremost soldiers. Already

THE BEGINNING OF UNIVERSITIES

The schools of the twelfth century were highly stimulating places. Plato's *Timaeus* began to be studied in Latin and there was heated debate about the conflict between his idea of a God who was a mere craftsman, creating the world by assembling ready-made primal matter into ready-made primal forms, and the Christian teaching about creation based on the book of Genesis. During the twelfth century more of Aristotle's logic became available in Latin and also, by the thirteenth century, his books of natural science, philosophy and politics, already much studied by the Arabs, whose commentaries were eagerly added to the new collection of textbooks. There was challenge at every point: for example, in his theory of the soul and his view of human beings as political animals (in which he disagreed with Augustine, who said there would have been no politics if Adam had not sinned). Yet these new writings could not just be dismissed. They added significantly to the classical heritage, which had up to this point been represented in the West by a relatively modest number of mainly Latin works.

In Paris and at the cathedral schools of Laon and Chartres, in Oxford, Bologna, Montpellier and Salerno, there were growing numbers of students from the mid-twelfth century and a burgeoning 'academic' profession of teachers able to give advanced instruction and prepare students for careers in the expanding ecclesiastical civil service, in the church, in the law, and as fresh generations of academics in what were about to become universities. More universities emerged early in the next century in Cambridge, in Germany and throughout Western Europe.

It is fair to say that universities in their modern form are a Christian invention as well as a European invention. They differed from the academies of the ancient world partly in the structures of their governance, which went with a certain self-understanding. In the north of Europe, the 'Masters' who lectured saw themselves as masters of a skill, much as they would have done if they had been goldsmiths or fishmongers. They formed a guild. The students became the apprentices and the 'Bachelors of Arts' became the equivalent of the journeymen, part-qualified in the late Roman empire a well-born male had to expect to spend a portion of his adult life in fighting for his country.

Throughout European history, the church has generally supported war. This has been forced upon it, in a sense. The societies of Europe have been endlessly at war, and for nearly a millennium in the West the military life was the only career alternative to the clerical life for a boy born into the ruling classes. The church's role in this has been inextricably part of the system, for it was inseparable from the system of land tenure in much of northern Europe. In the areas of northern Europe where feudalism developed in the Middle Ages, a vassal was required to offer so many days'

This scene seems to show a lecture on a 'set book', with the students following in texts, which it was possible to hire in sections as the course of lectures progressed. These seem to be older students, possibly studying towards one of the 'higher' degrees in medicine, law or theology.

and not full members of the guild. The Masters ran the affairs of the university because it was their guild (the meaning of the word *universitas*, from which 'university' comes). In Bologna the structure was different because that was a postgraduate university, specializing in the training of lawyers. There the students hired and dismissed their lecturers. The universities were, from the outset, much aware of the need to establish a formal relationship with the ecclesiastical and secular authorities which would allow them independence while being able to rely on the protection of the powers of church and state if they needed them. So grants of privileges were actively sought alongside battles to retain control of the appointment of their own leaders.

Academic freedom meant at first the autonomy of the institutions, not freedom of speech for academics. Within the comparatively protected though highly contentious world of the new academe, a number of scholars began to make their names. Some were tried and condemned for their opinions by the ecclesiastical authorities because they were thought to be teaching heresy and misleading the faithful. Early examples, even before universities had truly emerged, were Peter Abelard (d. 1142) and Gilbert of Poitiers (1070–1154). Others, such as the Dominican Thomas Aquinas (1225–1274), were entrusted with the responsibility of producing reliable textbooks of systematic theology, such as his *Summa Theologiae*.

knight-service a year to his lord in return for the use of the lands he held. This applied equally to bishops and abbots. Even the holiest and most peaceable clerics seem to have supplied and sent off their knights without a qualm.

The church strove to ensure that battles stopped for holy days and major feasts and were not fought on Sundays. This was known as the 'Truce of God'. Between the tenth and the thirteenth centuries the ecclesiastical authorities in the West did their best to enforce this military self-discipline, with mixed success.

Yet in principle the church did not support killing, even judicially. A church court could not take life. Sentences in ecclesiastical courts stopped short of the death penalty, which was one reason why so many offenders were anxious to claim 'benefit of clergy' by endeavouring to prove that they were clergy, so that they could be tried in a church court rather than a secular one. The test was whether they could show they were literate.

The penitential system contained in its codes tables for determining the size of the penalty which must be discharged as a token of the sincerity of repentance for each sin. Such codes were clear that penance must be done if a soldier killed in battle, even if he was not sure whether he had done so or how many he might have killed or injured, as might be the case with an archer firing arrows into the enemy ranks who could not see how many he hit.

One way of dealing with the inherent paradox of Christian soldiery was to think of it metaphorically, as spiritual warfare. This fitted well enough with traditions such as that made famous by the poet Prudentius (AD 348–405/13) in his *Psychomachia*. Prudentius depicted a battle of the virtues and vices, a battle with which he himself had become familiar after he had retired from public life to live as an ascetic. From this drive to elevate the conception of 'soldiering as a Christian' came a high ideal of knighthood which tried to distinguish it from the crude violence of brute fighting.

Another important attempt to rationalize the church's attitude to war was Bernard of Clairvaux's treatise for the Knights Templar. This was an order of soldier-monks, founded earlier in the twelfth century to protect the pilgrims who visited the Holy Land but drawn into the armed combat of the times, especially in the period of the Second Crusade.

Crusading

The most compelling example of the 'Christianization of war' in Europe was the phenomenon of the crusade (from the French *croisade*). The term 'crusade' has come to have connotations it did not possess at the time of the First Crusade, such as campaigning for a cause.

As first conceived, the idea of the crusade went beyond the notion of a 'just war' which Augustine had described. Augustine said that war might be justified if it aimed simply to recapture lands or property which had been taken by violence from their rightful owners. He did not think aggressive war could be just. A crusade could be justified in similar terms, if it was argued that unbelievers had stolen the holy places from their rightful Christian holders. But the call to go on crusade was presented rather differently, as a call to do something which was not merely just but also 'holy'.

THE FIRST CRUSADE

The First Crusade (1095–1099) began because the Byzantine emperor became seriously concerned about the danger Eastern Christendom faced from the Seljuk Turks. Pope Gregory VII wrote a letter to Matilda of Tuscany (1046–1115) in 1074, proposing an expedition across the sea to 'help' the Christians in Byzantium and the Holy Land who, he asserted, were being slaughtered like cattle by the 'heathen'. He envisaged going himself, not merely encouraging an army of soldiers to go, and he reported that the empress of Germany, Agnes of Poitou, was keen to come in person herself. 'If it is noble to die for one's country, how much nobler and more praiseworthy it is to die for Christ!' he cries.

At a council at Clermont (1095) Pope Urban II called on the Christians of Europe to march east to defend the Holy Land against the Turks. In return, he promised them that anyone who either reached Jerusalem or died in the attempt would be granted a 'plenary indulgence'. That was the first time a pope had made so lavish a promise. It meant that someone who died in this way could be sure of not needing to spend time in purgatory, discharging the remaining penalties due for the sins he had committed.

The crusading armies did not get a welcome from the East when they actually approached. It will be remembered that one of the imperial family, Anna Comnena, exclaimed with alarm that they were barbarians, and from the vantage-point of both Byzantine Christianity and Islam, the Western crusading movement was negatively perceived from an early stage. These were religious wars in the long tradition of unsatisfactory attempts to claim that God was on one side or the other and actively condoned the violence and bloodshed.

Nevertheless, the first crusaders were reasonably successful. They

la cité damas. Qui la fonda. des
fruit3 et iardins a son tour. De
lordre que tirent les princes a
lassieger. Comment les iardins
furent prise. Du grant coup
que fit lempereur. Et de la con
clusion pour laquelle fut le siege
leue. la cite estant pres de pren
dre.

.xlviii.

Amas est la plus
grant Cite de
la terre de la
mendre Surie
qui par austre nom est appel
lee. La prouince de liban et a
ceste occasion dit le prophete
parlant de ceste Cite de damas
Chief de Surie. Lun des ser
uiteurs de abraham appelle da
mas la fonda ⁊ fut par ce

LEFT: This later medieval picture of the siege of Damascus of 1148 depicts it as a glorious battle showing off French military prowess.

captured Dorylaeum and Antioch, and in 1099 they took Jerusalem. Several crusader states were created, including a Kingdom of Jerusalem, and the land hunger of some of the Western European nobles who had led armies to the East was appeased.

THE SECOND CRUSADE

A second crusade followed (1145–1149). The fragile equilibrium established by the First Crusade crumbled when the Moslems took Edessa in 1144. The principal instigator of this crusade was Bernard of Clairvaux, although he had at first been unwilling to preach to encourage people to join it. In his opinion, the first priority should be the task of preaching to Christians at home to encourage them to lead better lives. But he was persuaded by Peter the Venerable, Abbot of Cluny, to throw the weight of his eloquence behind the call to crusade. So successful was he that the organizers ran out of crosses for people to take away to sew onto their clothes, and more had to be made by tearing up strips of cloth.

But Bernard proved to be right. The leadership could not have been more distinguished. A French contingent set out under the leadership of the French king Louis VII (1120–1180) and a German army left with the emperor Conrad III (1093–1152) at its head. They marched on Jerusalem in 1147 and made an abortive bid to capture Damascus, but little was accomplished and the security of the young crusader states set up after the First Crusade was endangered.

Bernard found himself writing an apologia in the second part of his book of advice to the pope, which he called *On Consideration*, and preaching to disappointed congregations who could not understand how God could have allowed the crusade to fail. This was essentially the same question as Augustine had been asked at the beginning of the fifth century by refugees from Italy who wanted to know how a Christian God could allow a Christian empire to fall, as it was faced by determined resistance. Both answered in a similar vein: one must try to see these things as God does, as a mere minor episode in his grand plan for the salvation of the world. Bernard returned to his insistence that only when the Christians of the West deserved it would God allow them to win.

THE THIRD CRUSADE AND AFTER

The Third Crusade (1189–1192) was prompted by Saladin's (c. 1138–1193) capture of Jerusalem in 1187. The pope called for a crusade and again the crowned heads of Europe set out, this time Philip II of France (1165–1223), Richard I of England (1157–1199) and Frederick I, Holy

Roman Emperor (1122–1190). Frederick was drowned in an accident on his journey and the English and French monarchs were locked in mutual mistrust over disagreements at home.

There was some initial success. Acre was recaptured. But then, in 1191, Philip of France set out for home. Richard was left to lead the crusading army onwards, and it came close to Jerusalem, but in the end Richard settled for a truce with Saladin rather than attempt to fight the matter out. The Christian army was suffering in the local conditions, and he calculated that a deal would be better than a showdown.

Richard's own journey home, in 1192, was interrupted by a shipwreck and a period of imprisonment at the hands of the Duke of Austria, whose men captured him. He handed him over to the emperor, Henry VI (r. 1190–1197), who asked for a ransom before he would release him.

As 1200 approached, Jerusalem was back in Moslem hands and Pope Innocent III (r. 1198–1216) began the Fourth Crusade (1201–1204), this time planning to approach the Holy Land by way of Egypt. But the process of getting the necessary ships entailed making deals with the Venetians, and the Venetians had objective of their own. They were willing to give the crusade their support only if the crusaders would first attack their trading rival Constantinople for them. The crusaders were successful there in 1204, and they sacked the city, but the impetus was lost and the crusade never succeeded in its real objectives.

Crusading as a 'movement' was now fading. But the idea of going on a crusade was still attractive. A Fifth Crusade was promised by the Fourth Lateran Council of 1215 and from 1217 to 1221 there was an attempt on the part of crusaders from Hungary to support the King of Jerusalem and the Prince of Antioch to try to regain Jerusalem for the Christians. Another group captured Damietta in Egypt in 1219 but overreached itself in trying to move on to Cairo. A Sixth Crusade (1228–1229), led by the emperor Frederick II (r. 1212–1250), achieved a surprising amount mainly through diplomacy and for ten years the Christians once again controlled Jerusalem, Nazareth and Bethlehem.

MEDIEVAL HERESY AND DISSENT

It is possible to list still later crusades – a seventh in 1248–1254, an eighth in 1270 and a ninth in 1271–1272 – but the only further crusading of note was the Albigensian Crusade. This was an exception to the series of crusades focused on the Holy Land. The Albigensian Crusade began in 1209 and continued for decades. It had the aim of overcoming by force

PILGRIMAGES AND SHRINES AS HOLY PLACES

The idea of sainthood had by now developed a long way from the notion which is found in the New Testament. The Latin word *sancti*, from which the word 'saint' derives, originally referred to the ordinary members of the Christian community but it had come to be used for those who were notably holy, in fact so holy that they could be used as examples to others. It was only one more step to giving them official recognition by canonization, which placed them in the official list of saints recognized by the church. This was a highly desirable status for those churches and abbeys which had the relics of a holy bishop or abbot and wanted people to visit the shrine in which they were kept. The number of saints allocated special days on which they were to be remembered was greater in Eastern Europe in the Orthodox churches, where the annual 'calendar' had few empty days.

Buildings used as churches became sacred places, formally consecrated. They might contain shrines, as Roman Catholic and Orthodox churches often still do, with relics of saints, in which a special holiness is believed to inhere. This encouraged the building of

In this modern photograph of the celebration of the Eucharist at the Orthodox shrine of Tinos with its candles in the darkness something of the atmosphere of holy mystery can be felt.

structures and the fashioning of containers for the relics (reliquaries), of great beauty and value, so that they might be appropriate to the importance and holiness of that which lay within.

In later medieval Europe the fashion for going on pilgrimage made certain shrines a great draw, such as the Holy Sepulchre in Jerusalem, the shrine of St James at Compostella in Spain and the cathedral at Canterbury in England which was the scene of the martyrdom of Thomas Becket in 1170. The pious gifts of the pilgrims made it possible to elaborate and decorate shrines even more richly. So a fine building could also be a sign of status and in part it added to the glory of those in charge of the buildings and their contents, as builders and enlargers.

In the Orthodox world the enthusiasm for sacred places and especially those connected with particular saints and their relics was even stronger. The shrine on the small island of Tinos, for example, dominates the island and makes it in the modern world, as in the past, a strong attraction for pilgrims and tourists, many of whom come in both capacities.

the obstinacy of the Albigensian heretics, who were not responding to attempts to convert them by preaching. The conception of crusading not in the Holy Land but in Christian lands began a minor trend. There were 'crusades' in central Europe and in Baltic lands in an attempt to subjugate and convert the peoples there who were not yet Christians, thus muddying the distinction between mission and conquest.

The Albigensian Crusade tested the concept of a crusade to the limit by extending the idea of 'holy war' to something which could properly be waged within Christendom itself. The Middle Ages was far from being the first time that heresies and dissenting movements had appeared in the West. The mass popular movements of the Middle Ages tended to be focused in the south of France and the strip which runs from northern Spain across Lombardy. Two main forms of heresy and dissidence flourished there, particularly in the late twelfth and early thirteenth centuries. They exemplify well the difference between 'heresy' and 'dissidence'. A heresy was still understood as it had been earlier, as a deliberate adherence to a belief which was incompatible with the Christian faith (asking a question in puzzlement is not a heresy; persisting in the 'wrong' view becomes heretical). Anti-Establishment dissidence involved protesting and pressing for reform where it seemed that something had gone askew in the way the church was run.

Dualism and the Devil

Albigensianism was certainly a heresy, because the beliefs involved could not by any stretch be held by a Christian. It was a form of dualism, an indirect descendant of the dualism of the pre-Gnostics, and perhaps also of the Manichaeism Augustine had adhered to for a decade in his youth. Augustine had had a great deal to say about the Manichees after he left their number, and that had certainly affected the future transmission of such ideas and the way educated Christians viewed them. Alan of Lille (d. 1202), for example, wrote against the dualists of his own day at the end of the twelfth century with heavy reliance on Augustine's arguments. The Albigensian heretics, like other dualists, believed in a fundamental division of the universe between two warring powers, of good and evil respectively. These were both seen as 'First Principles' in the universe, so dualist belief could not be compatible with belief in one God, and therefore no dualist could be a Christian.

Characteristically, dualist believers also held that the good is 'spiritual' and the evil 'material'. In dualist sects there tended to be a strong emphasis on ascetic practices, and a division between the 'elect', who were

In this sixteenth-century picture Adam and Eve stand under the forbidden tree, from which Eve has picked an apple, which she is giving to Adam. Satan, in the form of the seductive serpent, is coiled round a branch to watch. Around their feet lie the birds and animals whose futures will be affected, like the whole of creation, when Adam and Eve disobey their Creator and eat the apple.

thought to be sufficiently 'spiritual' to be able to transmute material things they ate into spirit, and the 'hearers' or 'followers', who humbly served the elect and provided the material goods.

These threads of asceticism and puritanism were not in themselves incompatible with Christianity. On the contrary, they had considerable importance in the ideals of the religious orders, and also in certain reforming communities of the sixteenth century. The belief that some are 'elect', specially chosen by God and perhaps predestined to heaven through no merit of their own, also found a place in reforming thinking in the sixteenth century, most notably in Calvinism. These are examples of one of the problems with maintaining a consistent Christian faith down the ages. A particular matter of emphasis or preference may appear in conjunction with a true faith or in a heretical confusion.

But these elements aside, dualism was obviously incompatible with Christianity, with its insistence that God is One and wholly good, and with its quite different explanation of the origin of evil. While dualism takes evil to be a power in its own right in the universe from the beginning, Christianity sees it as a lapse from the good which the One good God made possible when he gave his rational creatures freedom of choice.

There are hints in the Old Testament that evil might be a personal power of some sort, with malevolent intentions. Medieval Christian interpreters certainly thought so. Medieval and post-medieval Western writers were drawn to the idea of a personal Devil, and Milton's *Paradise Lost* (1667) tells the story in that way. The first and most important of these hints is the story in Genesis of the 'serpent' who tempts Adam and Eve to disobey God's instruction that they are not to eat the fruit of the forbidden tree (Genesis 2–3). The identity of this serpent was explored by early Christian commentators, for it presented problems.

SHOULD CHRISTIANS SEEK WEALTH?

The medieval Christian acceptance that some were born to be masters and some to be servants, that it was fitting for the nobility to wear finer clothes and eat better food than the poor, faded when a degree of social mobility became a real possibility for the enterprising rising bourgeoisie.

The sensitivities of the 'poverty debate' of the thirteenth century were strong at the time. They arose when the Franciscans became divided into two camps on the death of their founder, Francis of Assisi (1182–1226). One group thought the only way forward for mendicant friars such as themselves was to work within an institutional framework, and indeed they began to develop in parallel (and partly in competition) with the Dominicans, who were doing much the same thing.

But another faction within the order insisted on trying to preserve the purity of Francis' original vision. He had tried to live a life modelled on that which Jesus had prescribed for his disciples, wandering without possessions or a regular place to live, preaching the gospel, eating whatever food they were offered and accepting a night's hospitality perhaps, and moving on. This conception of the apostolic life seemed to them to be incompatible with the ownership of possessions, which would be unavoidable if the Franciscans were going to build houses to live in. The

ecclesiastical authorities became alarmed. The church was wealthy and its higher clergy inextricably involved in the property-owning and property-using of the day. There ensued a prolonged and fierce debate involving the church at the highest levels and also the universities. One side said it was possible to separate actual ownership from the use of what was actually owned by others, and that this allowed an apparently wealthy lifestyle to be perfectly compatible with a vow of poverty. The other said this was mere trickery and a betrayal of the vow of poverty.

For those Christians who had taken no special vow of poverty, ordinary business and commercial pressures applied, though for all Christians a question was bound to arise as to the appropriateness of engaging in trade at all. Jesus had taught his disciples to live simply and disdain the acquisition of possessions. Medieval Christianity in particular had to develop its attitudes to trade and to commerce. Was it acceptable to lend and borrow money if interest was involved? This was usury, which the Bible forbade. Was it acceptable to engage in the manufacture of goods beyond what people needed, and create a market for luxuries? Was it acceptable to make a profit?

These became burning questions in the Middle Ages, most noticeably from the twelfth century, when towns began to expand as trading centres and their inhabitants began to look more like the bourgeoisie of later times. They formed an anomalous class. They did not fit into the familiar hierarchy of nobility and peasantry. They did not have the education of clerics, but they were articulate, entrepreneurial and given to speaking their minds. It was from such new townspeople that the Waldensians probably came.

But others did not rock the boat. Merchants began to form associations to make travel safer and Christians began to prosper. The distances covered were considerable. Baltic regions had furs and timber to sell. In the Far East were to be found spices, silk and jewellery. Dutch merchants could trade these for salted herring; English merchants for wool; merchants from the south of Europe for wine and oil. Trade encourages travel and travel encourages trade. Both have affected Europe's sense of itself through the resulting contact with people living in other places.

LEFT: The painter Giotto depicted Francis of Assisi preaching to an interested Pope Honorius III in one of the frescoes in the great church at Assisi, which was built within a century of Francis' death. Francis, like Dominic, had to win papal support for his movement and the order of friars he was founding. Francis' call to his followers to lead lives of extreme poverty was to become highly controversial after his death because it threatened to interfere with vested interests in the wealthy church.

If God created everything and everything he created was good, where did this ill-intentioned serpent come from and how was it able to do so much damage? For after Adam and Eve ate the fruit, Genesis says that the whole cosmos was changed for the worse, with unfriendly vegetation such as thistles sprouting to prick people. One possible explanation put forward was that the serpent had originally been part of God's good creation, indeed one of the angels who came into being at the point in the Genesis story of creation where God separated the light from the darkness. But, it was suggested, he had, of his own free will, turned against or disobeyed God and the terrible consequences included the emergence of a demonic will to damage the human creation too. 'Lucifer', mentioned in Isaiah 14:12–14, became one of the accepted names of Satan, partly as a result of the way Jerome translated this passage in the Vulgate. Medieval Last Judgments zestfully portray Satan and his devils carrying off his spoils in the form of souls.

When Jerome's contemporary Augustine tackled this problem, he placed the emphasis not on a personalization of evil, but on its negativity. Evil is nothing, an absence of good. Its terrible effects are consequences of the separation of the sinful, rational creature from the God who made it.

The Waldensians

The second strand of popular challenge to manifest itself in Western Europe from the late twelfth century involved dissidence rather than heresy. It had a longer reach in terms of its direct effects. Its instigator, Waldes or Valdez (d. 1218), became the leader of a movement in Lyons. Townspeople running their own businesses, articulate and opinionated, were a relatively new European phenomenon, and they added their voices to a mounting tide of criticism heard from many quarters at the time of conspicuous excess in the dress and lifestyle of the higher clergy. In fact, they asked more radically whether a clergy with the special privileges of ordained ministers was really essential to ensuring the salvation of ordinary Christians. Could one get to heaven without the aid of the sacraments, and if not, were the sacraments efficacious only if administered by ordained ministers?

In search of authoritative guidance on such points outside the decrees and other statements of the official institutional church and the writings of the early Fathers, Waldes and his followers looked to the Bible. But the Bible in general use in the West was the Vulgate. That was in Latin, and ordinary people no longer understood Latin. Why should it not be translated so that everyone could either read it, or at least understand it when it was read out to them? The rebels seem to have become quite adept at mastering the Bible, with the help of some friendly local clergy, to the point where official apologists for the church's position complained that it was no good trying to convince the Waldensians and their like by quoting the Bible to them; they smartly quoted it back, with a surprisingly good grasp of the way one passage could be used to counter another.

And did the preaching of sermons explaining the meaning of the Bible have to be left to the ordained ministry? Why could lay preachers not preach to ordinary people in a language they could understand? There was a good deal of experimentation with this possibility in the late twelfth century and at first the official church seems to have regarded the practice as benign enough, provided the sermons confined themselves to the topic of practical morality. A preacher who simply called on the faithful to live more holy lives could not do much harm and might even do good. But when lay preachers openly criticized the official clergy or ventured into the territory of technical matters of faith, it became dangerous to allow them to continue, and there was a tightening up of the granting of licences to preach.

Dissent in England

England was a late recruit to the scene of popular heretical uprisings. Geoffrey Chaucer (c. 1343–1400) pointed a satirical finger at the failings of contemporary clergy in the Prologue to his *Canterbury Tales*, written towards the end of the fourteenth century. Chaucer's pilgrims include specimens of a number of the (by then) numerous varieties of clerics and members of religious orders. There is a nun who is a prioress, a genteel and simpering figure, drawn like many of her kind from the nobility. Her table manners are 'ladylike'. She has lapdogs of which she is excessively fond in a sentimental way. She wears a brooch with the words 'Love conquers all', and is accompanied by a household of a nun and three priests.

There is a monk, too. Far from living the life of poverty he has vowed to follow, he keeps fancy horses with jingling bridles, and also greyhounds. He goes hunting. He is fat and bald and wears fine clothes and jewellery. He is like a fish trying to live out of water, for he does not spend his time in the cloister. He sees no point in the study and manual labour which ought to be part of his calling.

Then there is a friar, wanton and merry. He is popular with women and hardly distinguishable from a pedlar at a fair, so many little gifts for ladies does he carry. He is always ready to provide a little entertainment

This is a fifteenth-century picture of the Prioress in Chaucer's *Canterbury Tales*, taken from the copy known as the 'Ellesmere Chaucer'. The artist has captured the daintiness Chaucer describes.

SACRAMENTS

In this complex symbolic picture the unique sacrifice of the Crucifixion of Christ is linked with the idea of the Eucharist as a sacrifice. The blood and water flowing from the side of the dying Christ are caught in a chalice by his Bride the Church. On the altar below stands the chalice and beside it the circular wafer representing the body of Christ. The connection of the death of Christ with the celebration of the Eucharist is shown in terms of a link from heaven to earth.

The theology of the sacraments was worked out with particular energy during the Middle Ages in the West. What was a sacrament? How many were there? What did they 'do' exactly? How? Who had authority to ensure that they did it? Did they 'work' because God was at work within them or because a minister exercised delegated powers to make them work?

In a general sense *sacramentum* simply meant 'mystery', but Augustine had been more specific in the way he used the term for certain actions in the life of the church. He had defined a sacrament as an outward and visible sign of an inward and spiritual grace. For example, in baptism there was water; in the Eucharist (Holy Communion or Mass) there was bread and wine. There were also required words and actions. In baptism there was a declaration of faith, by or on behalf of the person being baptized, the signing of the cross and the statement that the baptism was in the name of the Father, the Son and the Holy Ghost. In the Eucharist the words Jesus himself said at the Last Supper, when he took bread and said, 'This is my body' and then took wine and said 'This is my blood', must be said.

The definition of the relationship between sign and thing signified became especially controversial in the case of the Eucharist when the doctrine of transubstantiation emerged at the end of the eleventh century, reaching its full definition and acquiring its technical term during the twelfth century. Berengar of Tours (c. AD 999–1088), a grammarian of the mid-eleventh century, had started a dispute by questioning hard the way Christ's words were to be understood. When he said 'This is my body' did he mean 'This bread stands for my body'? Or did he mean that by saying those words he was making it 'really' his body? And in that context, what did 'really' mean? The official church position in the West was gradually defined to state that the consecrated bread actually became Christ's body and the wine his blood. Its very substance was changed ('transubstantiation'). The actual substance of the consecrated bread was flesh. Its 'accidents' (appearance, taste, smell) did not change; it still looked, tasted and smelt exactly like bread. The rules about substance and accidents described by Aristotle in his *Categories* were reversed, for Aristotle would have said that bread can remain bread in substance even when its accidents change, as it grows stale and then mouldy and begins to look green and smell and taste different.

The doctrine of transubstantiation was going to be extremely important because it enhanced the personal power of the priest; only the priest could 'make' the body of Christ by saying the words of consecration. The legends of the late Middle Ages in the West are full of examples of popular credulity about the 'host', such as visions of the Christ Child observed as the priest lifts the consecrated wafer up for the people to see.

It was during the medieval period that the number of the sacraments was fixed. Baptism and the Eucharist had a clear biblical origin. Jesus himself was baptized by John the Baptist, a figure who appears in all the gospels calling for repentance and acting as the forerunner to the ministry of his cousin Jesus. Jesus himself instituted the Eucharist as a memorial of the Last Supper he ate with his disciples and also of his crucifixion, with which he had linked it in his own words when he said that his body was to be 'given for' his disciples. Confirmation, confession, anointing of the sick, holy orders and matrimony were added as recognized sacraments, each with its history but also with its controversial aspects.

Which sacraments need an ordained minister? It had always been accepted that in an emergency anyone could baptize, and the baptism was agreed to be valid and efficacious (and unrepeatable), provided it was done with water and in the name of the Trinity. For the other sacraments, a minister validly ordained was held to be necessary, and it was essential that he should administer the sacrament with the intention of doing so, or it would not 'work'. For example, the laying on of a bishop's hands formed part of the ritual of confirmation and also of ordination, but a child brought to be confirmed by the bishop could not accidentally be ordained when he laid his hands on her, because he would be saying different words with a different intention. The idea was that the Holy Spirit would act by 'grace' to bring about the appropriate consequence. This sort of thinking underlay the doctrine of *ex opere operato*, the belief that when a sacramental act was properly carried out by an ordained minister with the right words and using the correct signs or symbols and with the appropriate intention, it would be both valid and efficacious.

It was decided quite early on that it could not matter whether the minister was 'worthy', or the faithful would never know where they stood. Suppose they had been baptized or married by someone who turned out to be a serious sinner and that meant they had not been baptized or married at all; it would not do. It was agreed that an ordained minister was merely a channel for the work of the Holy Spirit and his personal behaviour, however appalling, did not affect the consequences of his sacramental acts.

The most controversial area of sacramental development in the Middle Ages was the sacrament of penance. In the post-patristic period, when penance had been a public affair and had been imposed only for serious sins such as murder, adultery and apostasy, there began to emerge a more domesticated and comfortable penitential system in which a person could go to a priest privately to make a confession of the multitude of small sins which clutter daily life and receive absolution in return for doing penance. In the Bull Unigenitus (1343), Clement VI (r. 1342–1352) set forth for the first time the claim that a 'treasure' consisting of a 'heap of merits' built up by Christ and the saints had been entrusted to Peter and his successors with the power of the keys, so that they might disburse the merits to the benefit of the sinful faithful. This, it was held, could be done by remitting penances imposed, in the grant of an 'indulgence'.

with a current popular song. These are mendicants' skills gone bad. To say that he was the best beggar in his house ought to have been a compliment, because the orders of friars needed successful beggars to win the money the orders needed to run, freeing others for the work of preaching, study and teaching. But he has authority to hear confessions and grant absolutions, and that placed him in the tradition of the 'friar confessors', some of whom achieved immense influence through their privileged positions at courts, with the ears of kings and queens available to them. This friar hears confessions in a way which will cause no pain or difficulty to the person confessing. He is a familiar sight in taverns and always ready to conduct a wedding.

A similar hard-headed and ruthlessly satirical view of the shortcomings of the clergy is to be found in William Langland's (c. 1330–1387) *Piers Plowman*, the work of one of Chaucer's contemporaries.

John Wyclif and the Lollards

Many of the main threads of dissident questioning identified by the Waldensians became points of dissent in England too in the late fourteenth century, in popular movements which rode on the coat-tails of John Wyclif (c. 1320–1384). He probably never saw himself primarily as a popular preacher, for at heart he was an inveterate academic. Wyclif had become a controversial figure at Oxford and had challenged the certainties of the contemporary church to a dangerous degree. He had made powerful enemies and had eventually been condemned and exiled from the exciting world of Oxford debates, to die in lonely ill-health in a parish. He had become associated, however, with the ideas of others, people who preached political as well as theological ideas and who shared Wyclif's hostility to the religious orders and to the papacy, even if they did not keep pace with his more detailed theological arguments on a number of technical points of doctrine.

Those who earned themselves the puzzling label of 'Lollards' probably met in small local groups; there was no society for them to join and no national organization. Nevertheless, the official church was quick to attack those alleged to be Wyclif's followers, some of them scholars whose names were well known, such as Nicholas Hereford (c. 1345–after 1417), who was said to be 'notoriously under suspicion'. The church was especially worried about the impact of popular preaching, for this was taking place without licences being granted and so the church had no control over what was said to the large audiences such sermons could attract. It was also keen to ban the holding of unacceptable ideas on the Eucharist and the penitential system, and seditious claims that abuse of power should result in the powerful being stripped of their possessions, on the grounds that power, whether spiritual or temporal, could not legitimately be exercised by those in mortal sin. The chronicler Henry Knighton (d. c. 1396) comments that the talk of Lollards had a family resemblance: it was as though they had all been to the same school and been taught by the same schoolmaster. This impression is strengthened by the similarities in the lists of heretical opinions which survive in a fourteenth-century collection known as the *Bundle of Weeds*, after the mention in the gospel of the way wheat and weeds are to grow together until the harvest of the Last Judgment. The collection includes accounts of a series of trials of alleged Lollards.

For nearly a quarter of a century after Wyclif's death the most senior figures in the church were still intent on extirpating ideas associated with his name, and were prepared to take far more extreme measures. When Arundel, Archbishop of Canterbury (1397–1414), moved against those now regarded as Wyclif's followers in 1407, he first put forth Constitutions, initiating an 'inquiry', another classic method of suppression. These order all clergy of the province of Canterbury wherever they are (implicitly including the universities) to keep to the orthodox faith. Constitution I forbids anyone to preach without a licence. Constitution V stipulates that a Master of Arts shall not neglect to instruct the boys correctly about the sacraments. No one is to read any work of Wyclif before it has been examined by a committee of twelve drawn from both universities (Oxford and Cambridge), which the two universities are to choose. This committee is to examine the books and must agree unanimously that they are orthodox before they may be read. No one is to translate the Bible into English or any other language. No one is to dispute about questions which have been 'determined', that is, already been 'decided' upon by the church, except for the purpose of gaining a better understanding of them. Arundel insisted on a thorough search to find out whether any scholar or anyone living in a college, hall or academic university lodging had asserted, held or defended any conclusion, proposition or opinion about the Catholic faith or good behaviour which went against the decision of the church.

The Council of Constance, meanwhile, pronounced that:

In our times the old Enemy has stirred up new battles, of which the ringleader is a certain pseudo-Christian John Wyclif. While he lived this Wyclif asserted various

John Wyclif, looking as thin and intense as contemporaries describe him.

The appeal of the 'religious' life in the Western Middle Ages depended in part on certain social assumptions. The Benedictine monasticism (see p. 56) which had begun in the sixth century had gradually embedded itself in feudal Europe. Benedictine communities of monks and nuns became wealthy landholders in their own right, benefiting from the gifts of the pious. Local communities looked to them to provide prayer on behalf of those who were busy working, and sometimes medical help.

But wealth has its dangers for communities whose members are vowed to poverty. Cluny, which had been founded in AD 909 by William, Count of Auvergne, became a leader of reform. In the course of the eleventh century it produced new and more rigorous requirements for the daily life of its monks. But to some observers these seemed misconceived. In order to ensure that silence was observed at mealtimes a complex sign language was devised, to enable monks at table to ask for what they wanted without speaking. But that meant that they had an opportunity to be fussy and demanding. It went against the spirit of the simplicity of life and abandonment of personal will which Benedict had wanted to help his monks achieve.

From the end of the eleventh century there was a good deal of experimentation in the monastic life. Many older members of the nobility, both male and female, were drawn to it as a form of retirement after a lifetime of military service and landholding (or aristocratic wifely) duties. Instead of giving lands, the nobility began to come in person to be monks and nuns. This altered radically the normal pattern of admission to the monastic life of the very young, who had for centuries been the gift of their families.

From the eleventh century a pious nobleman might found a new monastery as a personal venture rather than joining an existing one, as Herluin (1001–1087) the founder of Bec did. The Italian scholar Lanfranc (d. 1189) came upon him building an oven with his own hands and decided to join him. Some rogue monks such as the notorious Henry left their orders altogether and became popular demagogues, while some went off to live as experimental hermits or in small groups which devised their own patterns of life.

Among these experiments was one which led to the foundation of the Cistercian order, called after the abbey of Cîteaux established by Robert, abbot of Molesme, in 1098. The Cistercians followed the Benedictine Rule, but the structure of their communities was something new. They set out to avoid the danger of becoming too wealthy and growing corrupt by building their abbeys in remote places and keeping sheep rather than farming broad acres of rich land. They had lay brothers who did some of the humbler work, as well as full members who concentrated on a life of prayer.

Among the canons of cathedrals there was a need for a good standard of education, for these were priests who had to lead lives of practical pastoral service and not merely read and pray. The emperor Charlemagne had had this need

The Benedictine abbey of Moissac was founded in the seventh century at a time when its survival was precarious because of the danger of attacks by invading Norsemen as well as Moors. It flourished in the eleventh and twelfth centuries, when it became linked with the successful reformed abbey of Cluny. Its Gothic cloister was built in a further period of success in the fifteenth century. In the seventeenth century it was eventually taken over by Augustinian canons.

pointed out to him, and he had responded by requiring each cathedral to run a school. In the twelfth century a new breed of canon began to appear: those of St Victor in Paris, known as the Victorines. Hugh of St Victor (d. 1141), Andrew of St Victor (c. 1110–1175) and Richard of St Victor (d. 1173) were three important teachers. Andrew seems to have had a special interest in Hebrew and the study of the Old Testament and Richard wrote on spirituality. The Premonstratensians, another order, were founded by the German Norbert (c. 1080–1134) in 1120, to live a strict and simple life according to the Augustinian Rule and serve local parishes.

The last invention of the Middle Ages in the living of the religious life was the founding of the orders of the friars. These, like the canons, differed from contemplative monks in their outward-facing and active mission. Francis of Assisi, founder of the Franciscan order, was a rich man who had a vision of a better way to live, which was simply to return to the simplicity of the 'apostolic life' as Jesus had taught his disciples to live it, travelling unencumbered to preach the gospel where the Holy Spirit led.

The Dominicans, like the Franciscans, were preachers, but their founder, Dominic (c. 1170–1221), had a missionary vocation. He felt called to take over the work the Cistercians had been doing (without success) in preaching against the Albigensian heretics in southern France and northern Spain. Dominic formally began his work in 1214 and the order gained papal recognition in 1216. After the deaths of their respective founders both orders became academically ambitious and began to be rivals for chairs in the leading universities of Europe.

articles [forty-five of which are listed]. He also wrote books, which are condemned by the Council, the Dialogus *and* Trialogus *and many other treatises, books and short works. These books he made available for the public to read and many ills have followed, especially in the kingdoms of England and Bohemia.*

The council made a point of the fact that the Masters and Doctors of the universities of Oxford and Prague had long disapproved of Wyclif's work. It noted that 260 of his articles have been further condemned by Oxford. The council accordingly forbade the reading, study, exposition or citation of Wyclif's books except for the purpose of refuting what they contain, some of which is heretical, some merely erroneous and some simply offensive to right-minded ears. Wyclif was declared to have died a heretic and the council anathematized him; it condemned errors from Wyclif's works and ordered his works to be burned and his bones dug up (which was done in 1428).

John Hus and the Hussites in Bohemia

John Hus was born in about 1369 and was executed in 1415 at the Council of Constance. He developed views which lay within the traditions which were becoming familiar through the teaching of Waldensians and Wycliffites.

The general shape of Wyclif's ecclesiology is echoed in John Hus' *On the Church*, a book which shows a considerable debt to Wyclif but puts together the framework more tidily. Copies of Wyclif's writings had been taken to Prague and had been immensely influential there. In this present world Hus finds the word 'church' being used in at least three senses. The first is simply to refer to a building, for example 'the church' in a particular village. So long as this is not confused with the local community of the faithful, that usage raises no particular difficulties, though in the sixteenth century the role of the 'gathered congregation' and its relation to the universal church was to become a matter of heated debate.

The second meaning takes the church to include the priesthood alone. There were theologians and canonists who would separate the clergy from the laity by reason of their ordination, and even went so far as to regard the clergy alone as forming the church. On this model, the laity are merely the object of priestly ministry rather than a constitutive part of the *laos* or 'people' of God. Wyclif decided in favour of a concept of the people of God as a whole which included both the clergy and the laity. Every person can receive the gift of grace; it does not come only with ordination.

In this picture John Hus is being executed by being burned at the stake, the usual method for those condemned as heretics.

The third sense of 'church' Hus identifies includes all people who can be said to be 'under the rule of Christ'. Here Hus makes a distinction between those members of the church who are predestined to heaven – some in the church triumphant (in heaven), some in the church militant (on earth) and some in the church dormient (in the place of waiting and purification after death, known as purgatory) – and those 'foreknown' by God to be among the damned.

Hus offended the ecclesiastical authorities chiefly by his insistence that the ordinary faithful should be allowed to receive both the bread and the wine at the Eucharist. The custom had grown up of giving them only the bread and reserving the wine for the priests present. When attempts were made to suppress this movement he responded by bending the rules for ordaining priests so as to ensure a supply of ministers for the congregations which wanted to join his 'Utraquist' ('both kinds') movement. This put him still further beyond the pale because it began to look like schism.

When in 1415 the Council of Constance condemned Hus to death, a type of sanction with a long ancestry was being applied. The Council was asserting an authority to define heresy. The early Councils of the Church are surprisingly infrequently concerned with doctrine, but they certainly considered themselves competent to pronounce upon it. It was the Council of Nicaea of AD 325 and the Council of Constantinople of AD 381 which produced what is still known and used as the Nicene Creed.

The pretexts given for the witch-hunting which happened next were nothing new. Souls were in danger; disorder threatened in church and state and within the university. Justice required strong action. Inquisition involved bringing suspected or accused individuals before inquisitors and requiring them to answer for their opinions, often opinions the inquisitors had put into their mouths. But persecution may have the effect of clarifying, focusing and strengthening the very trends it seeks to reverse. Some were undoubtedly hardened in their views by persecution. An unwillingness to swear, for example, was taken to be an indication of heretical tendencies and it was easy enough for inquisitors to trip someone up and make it look as though he held such unsafe views.

5 The Reformation in the West

Byzantium did not have a 'Reformation'. The upheaval which reshaped the Christian geography of Europe from the sixteenth century was confined to the heirs of the church of the Latin West, which remained under the jurisdiction of the ancient Roman patriarchate. Byzantium's contact with what was happening in the West was restricted to receiving puzzling overtures, for example from the Lutherans, who were anxious to make common cause with Christians who they thought might agree with them in their criticism of Rome. The chief driving forces of what happened in Western Europe have already been glimpsed. There was a build-up of resentments against what was perceived to be an increasingly autocratic clerical hierarchy, making ever greater claims for their own powers and imposing on the faithful 'requirements' which did not come from God but were their own human invention. Criticisms of that sort were already to be found in Wyclif.

The Reformation of the sixteenth century altered the political and social shape – and the style of living – of much of Western Christian Europe. After the sixteenth century, the visible church at least could no longer be thought of as 'one' in quite the old way, where for more than a thousand years the Western church had been organizationally unified. The new religious divisions tended to be associated with political divisions, with a strong predominance of one branch or 'face' of the now fragmented Body of Christ in each, though few if any of the fragments saw itself as a piece of a broken whole. Each of the resulting pieces was more inclined to see itself as alone preserving 'the true church'. Spain, France and Italy were to remain 'Catholic' and much of Germany and Scandinavia were to become Lutheran. In France and parts of Switzerland, Calvinism predominated. England struck a balance in defining the faith of the Church of England. Each affiliation went with a characteristic pattern of life. Calvinists, for example, favoured a puritan and hard-working style of life.

Martin Luther (1483–1546) in the course of his elementary education spent some time in 1497 at a school run by the Brethren of the Common Life, a community of the 'confraternity' type. This had been founded in the Netherlands by Geert Groote (1340–1384) in the fourteenth century, to make it possible to live a life of devotion to Christ in the utmost simplicity. The Brethren constituted a body of the sort to which the

At Bruges, pictured here, is one of the most important surviving houses built for the Beguines. This one dates from the thirteenth century.

Beguines (for women) and Beghards (for men) had also belonged some centuries earlier. They offered a way of life for ordinary lay people who were not called to enter the traditional forms of the religious life, and for those who might not be acceptable in some houses because they were not of noble birth. Members of such confraternities did not take vows or beg for alms. They earned their livings in order to free themselves for a life of interior spirituality and prayer.

When he was seventeen Luther began to study at the University of Erfurt. His father had wanted him to become a lawyer and that would normally require him to get a degree and then a higher degree, for law was one of the three higher degree subjects in medieval universities.

The course of his life was changed when he was nearly struck by a thunderbolt and in fright he promised to join a religious order if he survived the storm. In 1505 he kept his promise and joined the

Augustinians at Erfurt. The Augustinians were canons, not monks, which meant that they did not aim to lead an enclosed life but a life which included practical work in the world. He was not half-hearted about this decision. This was a genuine conversion, in the sense in which the term was understood in the medieval West; that is, a decision to make a commitment to a life of poverty, self-denial and prayer. He worked hard at the required observances, at prayer and at confession, but he found that it did not ease his sense of his own sinfulness.

This worried state was diagnosed by senior figures in the order as the result of not having enough to do, so he was sent back to university to become an academic, but in theology, not law. From 1508 he was lecturing in theology at Wittenberg. He achieved his doctorate in 1512 and spent the rest of his career, against the background of the controversy he was to raise, teaching in the university.

He lectured on the Bible, as all young theologians were routinely expected to do. He began to believe, as he did so, that the only thing that matters is faith. It is faith in Christ which 'justifies' (makes a person seem 'just' or 'righteous' in the eyes of God), not anything the believer does to earn God's good opinion. This was a challenge to the whole penitential system, which had grown elaborate in the later Middle Ages, for that taught that sins must be paid for and that, to be free of the consequences of sin, the individual must not only repent and confess but make reparation.

His starting-point for protest was the perception that the system of 'indulgences' had become corrupt. An indulgence was a remission by the church of the temporal penalty it imposed when sin was forgiven in the penitential process. This took place outside the penitential system where the penalty had been imposed, because it remitted that penalty. The underlying theory was that the basic authority to do this had been granted by Jesus when he told the disciples that he was entrusting them with the keys of heaven. Those sins they 'retained' would continue to be held against the sinner and those they remitted would not.

But the working of the system of indulgences, as it had evolved by the end of the Middle Ages, depended on additional assumptions, some added under the pressures of pastoral expectation (by popular demand) and others driven by the church's need for money. One was that the temporal penalties remained to be discharged when a person died with them uncompleted, and would have to be served like a prison sentence in purgatory before the forgiven sinner could enter heaven. Another was that the church had the disposal of a 'treasury' of merits left over from the

Holbein's woodcut of the 1520s shows the contemporary selling of indulgences in progress.

amount the saints had needed to secure their own places in heaven and the immeasurable riches of the merits of Christ himself. Another was that the church's senior ministers could make these available. Yet another was that it was possible for them to be substituted for the actual discharge of penitential tasks by the sinners on whom they had been imposed. Another was that 'vicarious satisfaction' was possible; in other words, a person could obtain such aids on behalf of someone else. People were very glad to accept this if they thought it could help a member of the family who died (or even themselves) get out of purgatory sooner.

Luther was indignant at what he saw as the abuse of the church's claims to have authority to grant indulgences and the general muddle about the theology of the way indulgences were related to the sacrament of penance (in which he was quite right). In the course of the later Middle Ages it had become acceptable to sell indulgences. The faithful now paid to buy 'time off' for dead relatives or for themselves, with the expectation that this would shorten their time in purgatory and speed them on their way to heaven. The need to raise money for the building of St Peter's basilica in Rome was one of the prompters to this excess. It was a sensitive moment, because Johann Tetzel (1465–1519), the papal commissioner for indulgences in Germany, was busy raising funds to pay for the building work on St Peter's.

Luther is shown in this nineteenth-century painting, hammer in hand, nailing his ninety-five theses to the door in person.

It was with a wish to get behind the by now immensely complicated apparatus of the penitential system on which the additional theory of indulgences rested that Luther proposed his great simplification. To counter all this he taught that 'faith alone' would 'justify' a believer and make him or her righteous in God's sight, and that getting to heaven had nothing to do with behaving well.

His first, and as it turned out decisive, public move was the posting (though this was apparently done by his students rather than himself) of ninety-five 'theses' on the church door at Wittenberg, with a copy being sent to the archbishop of Mainz. These theses consist of a jumble of assertions on aspects of the question of indulgences and other matters. The format itself was nothing new. Medieval university teaching involved a mixture of lecturing on set texts and the holding of formal 'disputations' on propositions such as these. Luther was simply throwing down an academic gauntlet, a challenge that these matters ought to be discussed. He was not at first saying that the pope had no right to pardon people so that they did not have to complete penances the church had imposed. It seemed to him that if the church could impose such penances it could certainly remit them. It was the rest he objected to; the buying and selling and the laying of burdens of expectation on the people.

A disputation was held at Leipzig in 1519 in late June and early July. Johann Eck (1486–1543), a pugnacious defender of the official church position who was to put in many official appearances in the debates which were now beginning, confronted Luther. Such public disputations were popular entertainment, even though they were held in Latin, and it may have been because the populace were aware of them that popular interest in the kind of thing Luther was saying began to grow. For if he was right, ordinary people did not have to go on labouring under the burden of what reformers had been calling 'human impositions' for a century or two. They could just have faith in God and all would be well.

By the time the disputation took place, things had already moved on. New aspects and topics were emerging. Luther began to insist that the power of the 'keys' had been entrusted not to the pope alone as head of the church, but to the whole church, which was the congregation of the faithful. This disputation also brought about a new set of contacts for Luther: with Philip Melanchthon (1497–1560), who was to work with him at Wittenburg, and with Erasmus (see later).

It made Luther's name. His writings began to circulate outside Germany, and in a surprisingly short time they were being read in England, Italy and France. Of the Reformation books held in the library of Emmanuel College, Cambridge, in the late sixteenth century, two thirds were of Lutheran and only one third of Reformed (Calvinist) origin. Wittenberg became a great attraction to students, who wanted to hear Luther lecture in person. More senior figures came to see him to discuss his ideas. The heirs of John Hus in Bohemia, the 'Utraquists', who were still pressing for ordinary people to receive communion in both kinds (that is, wine as well as bread) approached him. Among the local rulers one or two began to think it might be in their interests to offer him protection.

This last development was to become important. The long-running story of the uneasy balance of power between church and state in the Middle Ages was now going to enter a new phase. Reformers were so hostile to monarchical control of the church by the pope that they were even prepared to allow secular rulers or 'magistrates' to take it over. It is on that basis that English monarchs since Elizabeth I (1533–1603) have been heads of the Church of England, although they are not ordained, merely crowned.

Luther spoke of certain princes as 'these lay theologians' in a prefatory letter to his commentary on Galatians, published in 1518. In 1520 he wrote in German 'to the Christian nobility of the German nation', urging the laity to take it upon themselves to instigate reform. He wanted to embolden them to sweep away all the claims of the institutional church to a clerical monopoly of the way of salvation, which had been built in recent generations into a towering edifice. He pressed them to take control for themselves:

If a little company of pious Christian laymen were taken prisoners and carried away to a desert, and had not among them a priest consecrated by a bishop, and were there to agree to elect one of them… and were to order him to baptize, to celebrate the mass, to absolve and to preach, this man would as truly be a priest, as if all the bishops and popes had consecrated him.

Luther was a prolific writer; three of his works were published in 1520 alone. *To the Christian Nobility of the German Nation* claims that the laity are members of the priesthood of all believers, and that this creates a duty for them to work for the reform of the church. The *Prelude on the Babylonian Captivity of the Church* seeks to restrict the number of the sacraments to the two (baptism and the Eucharist) which were instituted by Christ and argues that the papacy has taken even these into a 'Babylonian' captivity. Then there was *Freedom of a Christian*, primarily a devotional work setting out the freedom of the Christian, but coupling it with a duty to spend life in the service of others.

But he was not going to be allowed to present such a challenge for long without some comeback. The procedure his enemies used was one which had been familiar for some centuries and which had also been used in bringing about the condemnation of Wyclif. A list of offending opinions is prepared. Their author is invited to recant. Often he responds by denying he ever said the things he is accused of. In Luther's case the response was to challenge the very authority of the Bishop of Rome to call him to account. He responded: 'The die is cast.' He said he despised Rome and did not seek its favour. He wished to have nothing to do with Rome. Let Rome burn his books; he did not care.

In 1520 Luther was excommunicated. This was a very serious sanction. The excommunicated person was shut out of the communion of the church, was not allowed to take part in any sacrament and, it was believed, faced condemnation to hell if he or she died in that state. In addition, where the excommunicated person held any position of authority, those subordinate to him no longer had any duty to obey. The papal Bull of excommunication of 15 June 1520 begins: 'Rise up, O Lord… rise up, Peter', and calls upon Christ and St Peter to 'act' in defence of the Holy Roman Church, which is 'mother of all churches and teacher of the faith'. It calls upon St Paul, too, because he 'illuminated' the

'SCRIPTURE ALONE'

One of the most important consequences of Luther's developing ideas about the claims of the institutional church in the West to have special authority from God, to establish what was the true faith and to tell believers what they must do to please God, was the new light in which he began to see the Bible. Alongside 'faith alone' he set 'Scripture alone'. Yet when Luther and his followers embraced the claim that 'Scripture alone' was to be relied on, they were misunderstanding the historical reality of the way the early church had decided which texts the Bible was to contain. To take away everything but the encounter between the individual and the Word of God with no guidance could be dangerous, for people could persuade themselves that almost any interpretation came from the Holy Spirit's direct guidance.

The 'licence to preach' which a bishop gave in the medieval West constituted official approval of the preacher by the church; it helped to ensure that the preacher had a sound theological grounding and was orthodox in his beliefs. Untrained preachers and private reading by individuals could, and did, lead to dangerous ideas, as was recognized from the end of the twelfth century, when popular, even demagogue, preachers began heretical and dissident movements. Allowing anyone to preach who felt like it was a recipe for misleading the faithful.

Part of the problem with the attempt to exclude everything except the text of the Bible itself was that this also removed a vast apparatus of commentary and explanation which had been built up over the centuries in the West. That apparatus had its uses. For example, it had tackled the problem that the gospels do not all agree. The *Diatessaron* of the late second century (attributed to Tatian, d. c. 185) had made a first attempt. Augustine of Hippo had written *On the Harmony of the Gospels* to try to make sense of the discrepancies and apparent contradictions. Deciding to dispense with everything except the Bible left that problem still to be addressed, and indeed Calvin wrote a *Harmony of the Gospels* to try to deal with it.

Another practice of earlier centuries some of the reformers thought it would be desirable to dispense with was the use of more than one level of interpretation. Some passages of the Bible can be read as plain historical narrative or straightforward statement, but others clearly cannot. The Song of Songs is apparently a mass of imagery. When Jesus himself told a parable he did not expect his listeners to think that the sower who went out to sow (Luke 8:4–8) or the man who threw a great feast and had to call in the homeless from the streets because his chosen guests would not come (Luke 14:16–23) were actual people. Everyone understood that these church with his teaching. 'Let the whole Church arise,' the Bull cries, as one with these apostles, and remove errors so that peace and unity may be preserved.

Luther was now exposed to political sanctions. The Holy Roman Emperor Charles V (1500–1558) had been crowned at Aachen in

were metaphors, stories with morals or lessons.

It took some centuries in the West for an agreed system of distinguishing between different kinds of figurative meaning to be arrived at. Tichonius the Donatist in the late fourth and early fifth centuries provided a set of seven different kinds which Augustine of Hippo used in his book *On Christian Doctrine*, recognizing its value, even though he strongly disapproved of the Donatists (schismatics who claimed no ministry could be valid if it descended from bishops who had turned traitor in times of persecution) and campaigned against them tirelessly.

It was Gregory the Great who settled on the most useful system, subsequently adopted in the West. This was limited to four kinds of interpretation. The first was the literal or 'historical' meaning; the three 'figurative' meanings were 'moral', 'prophetic', and a general 'allegorical' one. A text might be taken to teach the reader how to live; to point forward to the future; or to provide a simile. (For example, to say that Jesus was the 'Lion of Judah' was not to suggest that he was actually a lion.)

This critical technique was disapproved of by some reformers, though others used it, including Calvin. The strict alternative was to insist on the literal truth of everything the Bible said, the 'fundamentalist' position. Nor did the reformers refrain from making new commentaries of their own, for they were great preachers.

Without an adjudicator in the form of a church which could be the repository of agreement about what was orthodox and what was not, it became possible for individual readers exercising their private judgment to come to unorthodox conclusions. The idea was that the Holy Spirit would guide them; that the Word of God would speak to each reader directly, with the Spirit's aid for their understanding always available. But without a common external point of reference there was no way of distinguishing between those of whom this might be true and those who might seem to be in more than one sense on the lunatic fringe. This became a matter of considerable concern in the sixteenth-century debates.

So when Luther cried 'Scripture alone' as a challenge to the church's claims to authority, he was creating a hornets' nest of difficulties.

October 1520 in a tradition of imperial coronations going back to Charlemagne. He summoned a 'diet' or congress at Worms. Luther appeared before it in April 1521. Once again the protagonist of the official church position was to be Johann Eck. Luther was brought before a table containing copies of his works. He was asked if he had written these things and if he still held the opinions expressed in them. Luther took time to consider his response overnight. The next day he told the Diet that he could not retract what he had said, for it could never be right to act against one's conscience.

It was not easy for the emperor and his Diet to decide what to do, but in the end it was decided that Luther must be banned, and his writings too, and that he should be arrested and punished as a heretic. The emperor wrote to the princes of the empire to give reasons for the Diet's condemnation of Luther. He has allowed himself to adopt independent views:

A single monk, led astray by private judgment, has set himself against the faith held by all Christians for a thousand years and more, and impudently concludes that all Christians up till now have erred.

Luther is shown in this contemporary woodcut explaining himself at the Diet of Worms of 1521, in front of the Emperor Charles V.

Moreover, Luther is 'stiff-necked', obstinate in his opinions, as he had make plain the previous day at the meeting of the Diet. The emperor calls on the princes to stand with him against this threat: 'For myself and you, sprung from the holy German nation, appointed by peculiar privilege defenders of the faith, it would be a grievous disgrace, an eternal stain upon ourselves and our posterity' to let this pass so that heresy could succeed in capturing the minds of the faithful.

Luther went into exile at Eisenach, where he remained for a year, quietly working at a German translation of the New Testament which was published in 1522 and thinking out his position. Luther now consolidated his thinking on the doctrine of 'justification by faith'.

The ferment Luther had already occasioned did not die away in his absence. Melanchthon had begun to attack the very idea of monastic vows. This was not a new attitude among dissenters. Wyclif too had vigorously disapproved of the monastic orders of his day more than a century earlier, calling them 'sects' and criticizing what he perceived as a claim to be a superior kind of Christian. Monastic vows could not, he pointed out, be a second baptism. What advantage could they possibly confer? There were also pressures to 'liberate' nuns. Nuns, more perhaps than male members of religious orders in the late Middle Ages, were likely to have been given to the religious life by their families rather than conceiving any special vocation for themselves.

Alongside the rejection of duties for 'special' Christians to which they bound themselves by vows, such as celibacy, went a movement, in which some clerics of Saxony were prominent, to reject the requirement that the ordinary clergy should be celibate. The revolt against clerical celibacy which took place among the reformers of the sixteenth century was not driven by any wish to return to the practice of buying office for one's children. It reflected, rather, the desire to normalize the lives of those engaged in ministry in the church, to diminish the degree to which they were perceived as set apart and possessed of spiritual powers which ordinary Christians did not have.

The new 'normality' and the chance to lead a family life appealed to nuns as well as priests and monks. In April 1523 nine nuns from one convent presented themselves to Luther at Wittenberg, and three others who had escaped with them from their convent in herring barrels with the help of a friendly burgher returned to live with their relatives. Among

LITURGY AND MUSIC

Where there is a formal liturgy, the language of worship becomes important, and for centuries the patterns of worship or rites had been formalized in detail, although they were allowed to vary somewhat between one place and another.

In a Western monastic community, the Bible remained central to the *Opus Dei*, the 'work of God', which took up much of the day, as monks took part in the daily Mass and the round of 'offices' or hours of worship. The Psalms were sung round and round in an everlasting sequence until the familiar words would have run in every head. The Cistercian abbot Bernard of Clairvaux could not write a sentence which did not contain some internal reference to the words of Scripture in the Vulgate version. The medieval universities placed theology at the head of all possible studies, and made the study of the Bible fundamental.

Medieval Christians in the West could not help being aware that when they went to church the worship was in Latin and not in the local vernacular, and they had only a limited idea what was going on. The move to the vernacular was a strong call of the late medieval dissidents and the sixteenth-century reformers in the West, and for many reforming communities it was accompanied by an abandonment of the old liturgical forms. The result was a freeform pattern of worship in which Bible readings, sermons, prayers and hymns formed a multi-layered sandwich. Important in this mix was the wish to restore the Ministry of the Word to a place in worship which the reformers claimed it had lost. This, they insisted, had come about with the trend towards the saying of private Masses and the diminution of the participation of the congregation in worship, together with the use of Latin when the population now spoke a vernacular which had departed so far from Latin that they could no longer understand it.

Church music had always been important, but there had been a recurring difficulty in preventing it turning from an aid to worship into purely popular musical enjoyment. Various efforts were made to discourage this over the centuries. Sometimes the use of musical instruments was forbidden in church; sometimes the only singing allowed was settings of the Psalms.

In the medieval centuries in both East and West, the words of the liturgy were chanted. Different forms of plainchant emerged in Armenia and among the Copts, the Ethiopians, the Syrians, the Latins and the Byzantines, which allowed solo performers or the congregation to sing rather than say their part in the service. This evolved, especially in the West, into polyphony. By the fifteenth and sixteenth centuries, Western composers such as Josquin (1440–1521) and Palestrina (c. 1525–1594) had developed this into high art.

Lutherans enjoyed hymns and approved of music in worship. J. S. Bach (1685–1750) was a Lutheran; under his influence church music in the West attempted something which went beyond even the glorious polyphonic music of the Roman Catholic Renaissance.

The Lutheran composer Johann Sebastian Bach.

Zwingli (see p. 138) banned the use of instruments in worship, though not music altogether. Many Reformed were particularly hostile to organs, which they associated with Roman Catholic cathedrals with their great decorated arrays of organ pipes and their dominant musical traditions. Calvinists favoured severe limitations on the aesthetic aspects of music in church. Reformed (Calvinist) congregations often favoured unaccompanied singing because the Bible does not say that the early Christians sang to instrumental accompaniment. Old Testament worship mentions instruments but some of the reformers argued that that kind of worship had been superseded with the coming of Christ.

The Russian Orthodox churches of the seventeenth and eighteenth centuries began to Westernize their church music under influences which had reached them through Poland and the Ukraine. In the same period, the Roman Catholic Church was returning to early church music and retrieving the traditions of chant and polyphony, and also enlarging its repertoire as modern classical music emerged on the secular scene.

Among the Anglicans and Lutherans liturgical frameworks remained largely conventional. The Roman Catholic Church moved from Latin to the vernacular for worship after the Second Vatican Council in the late twentieth century.

Variation in the levels of popular participation were also bound to be noticeable, for example the late medieval move to an arrangement for saying Masses where the priest stands with his back to the congregation and celebrates a 'mystery' at the altar. Reforming practice in the sixteenth century tended to emphasize the idea that the Eucharist is an action of the whole community. Altars were removed and replaced with communion tables, behind which the priest stood and faced the congregation. The emphasis moved to 'worthy receiving' of the bread and wine by individual worshippers and away from thinking of the actions of the priest as automatically powerful and effective, so that when he consecrated the bread and wine he made them capable of 'doing something' to assist the salvation of anyone who received them. Anabaptist fellowship groups used the kiss of peace and the washing of feet as a way of emphasizing that they were a community imitating the pattern of relationship Christ encouraged among his disciples.

Then there was the question of the frequency of worship. Lutherans celebrated the Eucharist every Sunday and at every major festival. The Reformed kept to infrequent communion: four times a year at Christmas, Easter, Pentecost and harvest or autumn.

There was a move among the sixteenth-century reformers away from the elaborate penitential system of the later Middle Ages and the connected system of indulgences towards a concept of group or general confession. This could involve the congregation confessing its sins together in an act of worship, and the minister declaring absolution to them all generally. It could go further. Public confession in worship in the sixteenth-century Swedish Church Order involved the priest examining the members of the congregation on their knowledge of the catechism and discussing each individual's sins.

these runaway nuns was Katharina von Bora (1499-1552). She, or perhaps it was their families, rejected at least one student as her husband, and it emerged that she really wanted to be married to Luther. The marriage took place in 1525.

Luther and his sympathizers began to develop a critique of the sacramental system. One of the practices of the late Middle Ages which gave them most offence was the saying of private Masses. These were celebrations of the Eucharist which were not acts of community worship but solitary acts of a priest. They were paid for, and the idea was that if the Mass was said for the soul of a dead relative it would add to the credits in the account of that soul and, like the purchase of indulgences, shorten its time in purgatory. The practice rested on the belief that the celebration of a Mass somehow added to the force of what Christ had done when he died on the cross. That seemed to the Lutherans an affront to Christ, for it seemed to suggest that he had not done enough. And it imputed to the human priest a staggering personal power, which was also a distasteful idea to them.

Andreas Karlstadt (b. 1477) was one of those who began to urge like Luther that private Masses should be stopped, that communion should be celebrated as an act of shared worship, with the congregation given the wine as well as the bread, and that 'idolatry' should be discouraged by removing pictures and statues from churches. Karlstadt had trained as a Thomist (that is, in the thinking of Thomas Aquinas) in German universities and arrived at Wittenberg in 1505. In April 1517 he published 151 theses derived from and proposing an Augustinian style of theology.

Luther saw a need to rethink the doctrine of the sacraments (see pp. 106–107) as a whole. Only two appeared to have been endorsed by Jesus himself: baptism, when he was baptized by John the Baptist, and the Eucharist, which he instituted at the Last Supper. The others, which had been added to the list as of equal standing as sacraments during the Middle Ages, Luther was inclined to think were not to be regarded as equally sacraments at all. He felt particularly strongly in the case of ordination. He accepted the need for ministry, but he wanted to put the emphasis on preaching and pastoral care and not attribute to the minister any special powers to celebrate the Eucharist as a sacrifice. Lutherans did not in the end rule out the office of bishop.

Luther was an academic but he also showed concern for the needs of ordinary people. He produced catechisms in the late 1520s, a large and a small version, in which people could study the Ten Commandments, the Apostles' Creed and the Lord's Prayer, and learn about the meaning of baptism and Holy Communion, as well as confession and absolution.

One of the important questions which was now arising for the Lutherans was what form of worship they were going to approve of, and what they were going to eliminate from the liturgy. In the end they settled on a largely conventional liturgy, for Luther was well aware that a liturgy carries a theology within it, and what he was anxious to do was remove what he saw as accretions, unnecessary impositions on the faithful, not the core traditions of the life of the church which had emerged in its first generations. Within the celebration of the Eucharist he wanted to alter the emphasis on the idea that it was a sacrifice, and the danger that it might seem that the sacrifice could add something to what Christ had already done.

Lutheranism

Anti-papalism was already manifest in Germany and for many it found a welcome expression in Luther, as Gaspar Contarini, the Venetian ambassador, remarked in his letters home: 'I cannot tell you how much favour he enjoys here.' A repeating pattern in the history of movements which have been begun by a charismatic leader is that when the leader is no longer there, there comes a 'make or break' moment for the continuation of the movement. The importance of Lutheranism in the history of Christian Europe lies at least partly in the geographical extent of the influence Lutheranism now came to command, especially in Germany and the Scandinavian countries.

Lutheranism extended its influence eastwards. A marriage between Ferdinand of Hapsburg (1503–1564), who ruled provinces in Germany and Austria, and Anna of Hungary and Bohemia (1503–1547) paved the way for a union of Austria and Hungary when Anna's brother Louis II died at the battle of Mohacs in 1526. Many of the local bishops were also killed, leaving the church comparatively rudderless.

Into this enlarged realm of Austria-Hungary moved Protestant preachers and returning students from noble families who had been sent to German universities by their parents. From Swabia came Paul of Spretten, who had been ejected from Salzburg for his Lutheran opinions. Merchants brought in Lutheran publications in the ordinary course of the book trade. The heightened fear of Turkish invasion from the East may have made the people particularly receptive to new confident Christian teaching.

The Lutherans had already taken a step in the direction of becoming a movement with agreed principles before the end of Luther's life. In 1530 the emperor Charles V called an Imperial Diet at Augsburg. The Preface

LUTHERANISM IN SCANDINAVIA

The second important phase of Christian influence in Scandinavia came with the Reformation. To consolidate a reforming position in a city, a Swiss canton or even a German principality, which might be of modest size, could perhaps be achieved relatively rapidly, but the Scandinavian realms were diffuse. Reformation ideas were spread by German merchants in the 1520s in the Scandinavian ports (Riga, Stockholm, Malmö, Copenhagen and Bergen), but that did not necessarily take these opinions inland.

In Denmark, Catholic ecclesiastical order was abolished in 1536 by King Christian III (1503–1559). A new liturgical order was designed and Luther's views sought as to the best way to do this. The Elector of Saxony even sent assistance to help with the finalization of the Danish liturgical order. Patience was urged in Norway because there were no Norwegian translations of the Bible yet and Norway was not so advanced in reforming ideas. The new Danish order was resisted in Iceland, which was under Danish rule at the time.

Sweden also took things slowly, while Olavus Petri, a student at Wittenberg in 1516–1518, translated the New Testament and designed a catechism and liturgical order. In 1530 the Swedish Mass was licensed to be used in Stockholm, but it was not approved for general use in the kingdom until 1536 and even then each parish could choose.

Latvia and Estonia were influenced by Lutheranism very early (in the 1520s) but Lithuania and Poland were resistant and remained predominantly Roman Catholic. In Finland the Russian presence made Orthodoxy not Roman Catholicism the alternative.

This history formed the background to the 'Nordic-Baltic Conversations', in which the Lutheran churches of the northern borders of Europe held discussions with the Anglican churches of Great Britain and Ireland and arrived at the Porvoo Agreement of 1992:

Despite geographical separation and a wide diversity of language, culture and historical development, the Anglican and Lutheran churches in Britain and Ireland and in the Nordic and Baltic countries have much in common, including much common history. Anglo-Saxon and Celtic missionaries played a significant part in the evangelization of Northern Europe and founded some of the historic sees in the Nordic lands. The unbroken witness of successive bishops in the dioceses and the maintenance of pastoral and liturgical life in the cathedrals and churches of all our nations are an important manifestation of the continuity of Christian life across the ages, and of the unity between the churches in Britain and Ireland and in Northern Europe.

to the Augsburg Confession of 1530, addressed to the emperor, identified the two purposes of the Diet. One was to discuss 'measures against the Turk', who is described as the hereditary enemy of the Christian name and religion, so that the empire may be able to withstand the attacks from the East. The threat from the Ottoman Turks was causing understandable disquiet in central Europe; the autumn before they had laid siege to Vienna. The second was to talk through the dissensions about the Christian faith which were troubling Germany. The emperor was anxious to unify the lands over which he ruled so as to provide a stronger basis for resisting the Turks, and that included the religious differences.

Luther was not permitted to be present at the Diet but Philip Melanchthon had compiled with Luther a 'Confession of Faith', which he read before the emperor. This came to be known as the Augsburg Confession and it has remained the main confessional statement of the Lutherans. This was one of the first examples of a trend among reformers, which was to create a statement of the particular opinions of their community, commonly in the form of a series of statements or 'articles', sometimes called 'commonplaces'. These, just like the ninety-five theses, derived from the propositions (or premises) and conclusions which had formed the staple of disputations in the medieval universities.

The first twenty-one articles of the Augsburg Confession are positive statements of the doctrines of the Christian faith as Lutherans understood and accepted them. Article 10 affirms the 'real presence' in the Eucharist, that is the belief that Christ is really there once the bread and wine have been consecrated.

Articles 22 to 28 tackle what the Lutherans were claiming to be errors and abuses. The alleged abuses concerned denying the ordinary faithful the wine in the Eucharist and giving them only consecrated bread; not allowing priests to marry; selling the saying of Masses for money; requiring people to confess in detail to a priest and do penance before they can be free of their sins and the consequences; distinction of foods and other over-elaborate requirements; monasticism involving the taking of vows; and abuse of ecclesiastical power on the part of bishops when they behave as though they were secular lords.

The overall purpose was not to declare a new faith but to return to what Luther and his friends believed to be the original one in its pure form, without the accretions and 'human inventions' the reformers said were misleading the faithful and placing unnecessary burdens on them. It was all quite simple: believe and be saved. Nothing more was necessary.

Modern European universities still often have 'confessionally distinct' faculties of theology. This development thus involved a significant move away from the early Christian insistence that although there might be different ways of worship and institutional arrangements for running the church, there could be only one faith and it could never change.

ERASMUS

Desiderius Erasmus (c. 1466–1536) embodies the 'Renaissance' trends which ran alongside the Reformation and exchanged ideas with it. He was a Dutchman, who was ordained a priest in 1492 and spent a period as an Augustinian friar until he found employment as secretary to the bishop of Cambrai. The bishop permitted him to go to the University of Paris to study in 1495. He also spent time at Louvain in France, in England, in Basel in Switzerland and in Italy (1506–1509), both as a private scholar and as a student and teacher, for example becoming Lady Margaret's Professor of Divinity at Cambridge. He made important friendships in England, especially with John Colet (1467–1519), Thomas More (1478–1535), John Fisher (1469–1535), Thomas Linacre (c. 1460–1524) and William Grocyn (1446–1519).

Erasmus of Rotterdam, caught in a pose which shows him intently at work as a scholar, in the portrait by Holbein the Younger.

We are still at Louvain, kept here, as we were cast here, by the plague… The Bishop of Besançon has died, of whom I had great hopes. The lady of Veer has been snatched away by a worse than servile marriage. My English lord is cut off from me by the sea… France, Britain and Germany are all at the same time closed against me by the plague. NB I am pleased with everything at Louvain, only the living is a little coarse, and the prices high; and besides I have no means at all of making money.

This letter of Erasmus to a friend from September 1502 illustrates the mix of personal ambition, precariousness of livelihood and a sense that Europe is his oyster.

Erasmus was a keen student of Greek, though he came to the conclusion that trying to learn Hebrew at the same time might be too much. His interest was stimulated by the realization that since the Bible was not written

CHRISTIAN ART

Christianity has left its stamp on every aspect of European art and also upon utilitarian objects. Its imagery was painted on walls in frescoes, dominated the painting of pictures, shaped the illustration and binding of books, and largely determined the subjects of sculptures and the kinds of portable 'objects' that craftsmen made.

At the same time, contemporary secular culture affected the way Christians 'saw' and understood the images they made. In the late Roman period, Christ is characteristically portrayed as a teacher among his disciples, like the philosophy teachers of the day with their classes. In early medieval Byzantium he becomes the Pantocrator, the all-powerful, brooding with great dark eyes over the apses of churches. In the medieval West it is the crucified Christ in agony who appears everywhere. In the Renaissance less stylized figures of Christ and the disciples depicting the events of his life in contemporary dress begin to appear in realistic scenes with accurate perspective.

The favoured medium varied with period and place. Mosaics cover the interior of Byzantine churches. In the medieval West the pictures are frescoes. In the early modern period (Renaissance and Baroque in the West) the monumental statue detaches itself partly from the wall; its draperies appear to move, and its limbs

Christ the All-Powerful Lord (Pantocrator) in a twelfth-century mosaic in Sicily, one of the areas of Europe where both 'Greek' and 'Latin' Christians were to be found.

express ecstasy or agony or grief. The oil painting appears, reaches its high point of development and sometimes decays with the nineteenth century into sentimentality

A feature of Christian books is the 'luxury' version of a text. The book as we know it was invented in late antiquity, replacing the scroll. At first, decoration was tentative, then experimental. Books might have purple pages and small but detailed narrative pictures. In the East there was a pause in the production of ambitious volumes during the period of the iconoclastic controversy, but from about the ninth century luxurious books proliferated, involving the composition of new scenes for newly composed texts, though in East and West the usual convention was to use standard sequences of agreed pictures with an established iconography. In the West, such books were produced in the later Middle Ages for wealthy lay people. Books of Hours (beautifully illustrated volumes of prayers for different times of day) were for gazing at as much as for reading.

Iconography (see p. 39) involved a series of conventions which would enable the illiterate or semi-literate to 'read' a narrative sequence of pictures or identify a saint by his or her symbol. For example, St Christopher would be shown carrying the Christ Child on his shoulders. Moses was usually shown with horns, because of a misreading of a word in the biblical text. The Stations of the Cross, still found in churches, are a lasting remnant of this use of standard iconographical conventions.

In the early modern West most artists of note still chose Christian themes. Patrons often expected it when they commissioned a statue or a painting. But well before the eighteenth century in the West, landscapes were emerging as subject matter in their own right along with still lifes and family portraits, instead of being used as a background or element in pictures of Christian themes, with the patron at best positioned in a corner as giver of a gift.

Michelangelo's *Pietà*, in which the figures express complex emotions.

RIGHT: In this sixteenth-century Book of Hours (lavishly illustrated collection of prayers), the Virgin Mary and the infant Jesus are shown in various scenes round the opening of the Latin text of Psalm 70 (69 in Roman Catholic numbering) *Deus in adiutorium meum intende*.

Eus madiutorii
meum intende. ꝺ
omine adadiu
uandum me festina.

originally in Latin but in Greek and Hebrew, with the Greek Septuagint version of the Old Testament itself to be regarded as a key source, a serious student of the Bible ought to equip himself to read it in Greek.

He learned in 1515, while he was in England, of the grand plan to publish a multi-language ('Polyglot') version of the Bible in Greek, Hebrew and Latin which was under way in Spain, though there were delays in getting it printed while papal approval was sought. This fired him with the ambition to produce a version of his own, and he rushed it out in order to beat the Polyglot editors. He prepared it by looking at Greek manuscripts, though he did not have access to a complete set, and the result has a patchwork quality. It is also apparent that the manuscripts surviving in Erasmus' day, from the Byzantine world, were probably less reliable than some that Jerome had had available to him when he made the translation into Latin which was to become the Vulgate text and the standard version used throughout the Western church for over a thousand years before Erasmus was born. The editorial scholarship required was in its earliest infancy, and in any case Erasmus made mistakes because he worked so fast. A second edition came out in 1519, and this was used by Luther when he made his translation into German. A third edition which appeared in 1522 became the basis for two English translations: the Geneva Bible (1560, with many revisions and later editions), begun in exile in Switzerland by Protestant refugees from the reign of the Catholic Queen Mary, and the King James Version (1611), which became the accepted version until the late twentieth century and provided the text usually quoted in early modern English literature.

Erasmus added a fresh Latin translation of his own. This prompted him to review the accuracy of the Vulgate, which led to controversial claims that the latter was full of mistakes. It was in this area of his work that Erasmus came closest to the interests of contemporary Christian theologians.

For instance, his *Institution of a Christian Prince* (1516) includes in its title the reassurance that it is 'reduced to aphorisms so as to make it easier to read'. It begins with the birth and education of the prince, selecting relevant pithy sayings from classical authors. It contains sections on the arts of peace, taxes, princely generosity, how to make and amend laws, how to choose 'magistrates', how to make war and how to make treaties. He thought it important for rulers to be well educated and intellectually well rounded and cultured.

Erasmus was ambitious as a classicist. He wrote an elaborate and pretentious neoclassical Latin, in which he deliberately distanced himself from the style and vocabulary of the late medieval language. He envisaged the future publication of his collected works, including his letters, should they deserve such posterity. The first version of his *Book Against the Barbarians* was written in the period leading up to 1494, developing from a collaboration with his friend Cornelius Gerard, who was the author of an oration intended to defend classical literature before those who despised it and those who pretended to know more about it than they did. He did not lose interest in the subject and was writing a revised version as late as 1520. One of the perennial questions for Christian authors was whether it was legitimate to enjoy the writings of the pagans of ancient Rome and Greece. This was a dilemma that Jerome had found so painful that he described himself as not a Christian but a Ciceronian. It was acknowledged that good moral standards were often to be learnt from the classics, at least from certain authors. It was argued that God had allowed these works to enter the tradition of human knowledge and the earliest Christian authors had reconciled their use with their own task of writing for Christians.

Luther and Erasmus were fundamentally sympathetic to aspects of one another's work, but Erasmus was not a reformer of the same stamp as Luther. He preferred to work through the medium of scholarly writing and comment, though he could be extremely fierce and quite ruthless in what he said. He wrote satirically about Luther's ideas on free will and provoked Luther to write in riposte *On the Bondage of the Will* in 1525, condemning Erasmus as no Christian. His *Handbook of the Christian Soldier* of 1503, dealing in a homiletic style with matters of current controversy such as the veneration of saints and the proper structure for a Christian society, became a popular work. It was soon translated into English by William Tyndale (c. 1494–1536). In *The Praise of Folly* he attacked popular superstition and various current church traditions and practices, and dedicated the book to Thomas More.

Humanism, which set a new value on human beings and the writings of non-Christian writers of the ancient world, was not restricted to Reformation scholars by any means. Pope Pius II (r. 1458–1464) was himself a humanist. He had led a somewhat wild life before ascending the papal throne and his literary work was important enough for the emperor Frederick to crown him 'poet laureate' in 1442. As pope he wrote an autobiography of surprising openness about his personal opinions. One of the two Latin secretaries of Pope Leo X (r. 1513–1521) took an oath that he would use no word that did not appear in Cicero.

In other parts of Western Europe another strand of reforming influence was becoming noticeable. Huldrich Zwingli (1484–1531) studied at Berne and then went to Vienna to study in 1498, before he finished his studies at Basel. He was one of the new generation who learned Greek and Hebrew and read Erasmus. He later maintained that Luther had not been an influence, although they were contemporaries and hit on very similar ideas at the same time. He claimed he had seen the need for reform for himself.

Huldrich Zwingli.

His realization seems to have begun after 1518, when he became priest at the Great Minster church in Zürich, and a year later heard one of the travelling preachers of indulgences. He became indignant, just as Luther had. He acted conscientiously on his resulting conviction that papal policy about indulgences was an abuse. He renounced his own pension from the pope in 1520, and from January 1522 foreign services and the acceptance of foreign pensions were forbidden in Zürich wherever he had any say in the matter. He would not allow foreigners to preach in his church's pulpit. Meanwhile, he was turning out to be a good and caring pastor to his flock. He endeared himself to the local people by his work during the plague of 1520.

The themes of his new reforming zeal were familiar, seen again and again running through dissenting arguments from at least the time of the Waldensians: the rejection of 'human traditions' and 'human impositions' on the faithful, and the belief that they constituted an imposition on the faithful of unnecessary burdens, such as the observation of fasts. He began to preach that nothing was needed for the living of a good Christian life but the study of Scripture, which meant letting people read it and hear it in their own language. Zwingli's own German translation of the Bible appeared between 1524 and 1531.

He was against allowing images in church. Speedily, in the early 1520s his followers took images and pictures out of churches; instrumental music stopped. In 1525 Zwingli took the significant step of introducing a new liturgy for the Eucharist on Maundy Thursday, the occasion when

Jesus' Last Supper with his disciples is commemorated. The people, men and women on opposite sides of the table, sat down as for an ordinary meal. They were given ordinary bread and wine.

Monastic houses were closed and the forms of the religious life which were lived in them condemned. Like others among the reformers, Zwingli rejected celibacy for himself, although he was a cleric. In 1524 he married Anna Reinhard.

Reform was associated with civil unrest among Zwingli's followers as elsewhere. The support of ordinary people for reforming movements was driven partly by their own social and political resentment, for the fine theological distinctions which troubled professional theologians were naturally likely to have less immediate importance for people who lacked the education to notice them. There was nothing in the Bible about paying rents, taxes and tithes to lords, so the peasantry began to refuse to pay.

Reform has always tended to be divisive. This was not a special feature of its sixteenth-century manifestations, though it was marked. Zwingli was as vigorously opposed to those more radical than him (the Anabaptists) as to Roman Catholicism. Where he had authority to do so he persecuted and even tortured them. He was never able to reach agreement with Luther about the Eucharist, despite an attempted meeting to resolve the matter by public disputation at Marburg in 1529.

'Reforming' ideas began to pervade Switzerland, reaching Zürich, Constance (1527), Berne and St Gall (1528), Biel and Mulhausen. In 1529 Schaffhausen agreed on a list of 'Christian' civil rights. But not all of Switzerland joined the movement; the cantons of Uri, Schwyz, Unterwalden, Lucerne, Zug and Fribourg remained loyal to Rome, though not without a certain restlessness and some calls of their own for reform. An unsuccessful Concordat of Faith was proposed in 1525.

An attempt was made to set up a public disputation with Johann Eck, like the memorable ones he was holding with Luther. Zwingli did not come. For two weeks at the end of June a disputation was held at Bäden, close to Zürich, and again Zwingli did not appear, though he sent representatives and instructed them each day in what they were to say.

The dispute between the Zwinglians and their Catholic opponents even started a war. Zwingli found himself in a commanding position, an ecclesiastical and a political leader all at once, and it made him conceited and over-ambitious. He began to think it was realistic to plan to convert not only Germany but also Italy and Spain. At Zwingli's instigation, Zürich marched against the Catholic territories. The Catholic districts allied themselves with Austria in a 'Christian Union' in 1529 and answered in kind. Zwingli fell on the battlefield in October 1531.

Zwingli's successor as pastor of the Great Minster at Zürich, Heinrich Bullinger, was elected to the post on 9 December 1531 and remained there until his death in 1575. He had his own significant contribution to make to Reformation thought but not as a revolutionary; he consolidated.

CALVIN

John Calvin was born in Picardy in 1509 and sent in 1523 at the age of fourteen to study in Paris. He was living in Geneva from 1536, though he was expelled, and moved to Strasbourg to serve as a pastor from 1538 to 1541. There he came under the influence of the German reformer Martin Bucer (1491–1551). He returned to Geneva and remained there until he died in 1564. He had married in 1539, though his wife died ten years later. He began to suffer from ill-health (he lived on a restricted diet) and became so weak and ill that he sometimes had to be carried into the church so that he could preach.

Calvin's first publication was an edition of a secular classical work, Seneca's *De Clementia*, accompanied by a commentary. But his ground-breaking piece of writing was the *Institutes of the Christian Religion*, published when he was only twenty-six in 1536, first in Latin and then in 1541 in French, with revised editions appearing in 1559 (Latin) and 1560 (French). It is a book of systematic theology with the usual medieval contents, dealing with God the creator, the Trinity, revelation, man's first 'estate' (the condition of Adam and Even before they sinned) and original righteousness, the Fall of Adam and Christ the Redeemer, but then adding special emphases by moving on to topics particularly important to the reformers, such as 'justifying faith', 'election' and 'reprobation'.

These last two are of particular importance in Calvinism. Are some people specially chosen by God, through no merit of their own? Some passages, especially in Paul's letter to the Romans, seem to suggest so (for example Romans 8:29–30). This had become a topic of lively controversy in the Augustinian period, largely because of the influence of the Pelagians. Pelagius' teaching that anyone could be good by trying hard had Augustine emphasizing ever more strongly the helplessness of sinful human beings, their inability to do anything right by the exercise of their own free will and their utter dependence on God to enable them to behave even moderately well. He went further: he said that only God could make any human being acceptable to himself and that was his own free and secret choice. No one could know whether he or she was predestined for heaven (in which case nothing he or she did could make any difference) or would, despite any efforts they made, find themselves left among the majority who would get their just deserts as sinners and go to hell.

Calvin revived this controversy by saying two things Augustine had denied. The first was that those who were saved had a conviction about it. It made sense to go up to someone in the street and ask 'Are

IOANNES CALVINVS

you saved?' From this belief has developed the pattern of evangelization which calls those present at a meeting to come forward, invite Jesus into their lives and declare their certainty that they are saved. The second point on which Calvin went further than Augustine was in claiming that God not only predestined some to heaven; he also predestined others to hell. Augustine, and others in the Carolingian period, had objected that this would be to see God as the author of an evil, for going to hell was an evil. He said that God simply did not choose some people, and that left them to the inevitable consequences of their own sins.

Calvin's *Institutes* gives an outline of a 'presbyterian' idea of the way the church should be run and the nature of ministry. This was to become an important issue. Three rival ecclesiologies emerged among the reformers of the sixteenth century. The first was of the

John Calvin, in a portrait which gives him burning eyes.

type which located the visible church solely in the local worshipping community or 'gathered' church. The second was the conventional structure, in which bishops had a special responsibility for considerable areas, with priests taking local pastoral charge, and an overarching system to ensure that all were ordained on the same understanding of what it meant to be a Christian minister and within the same church. This had broken down in 1054 when East and West fell into schism, for they would not recognize one another's ministries from that point. But that did not undermine the principle, and Lutherans retained bishops in some parts of Europe, such as parts of Scandinavia (Denmark was an exception). Bishops became the subject of passionate debate in the West in the sixteenth century when reformers began to question the notion that a personal authority was inherent in what was by then held to be an episcopal 'order'.

The third mode of understanding the nature of ministry rejected bishops, and placed the emphasis on the idea of the 'elder' (*presbyteros*) described in the New Testament. Those who favoured this said that New Testament terminology made no real difference between priests and bishops and that bishops should be abolished. The 'Presbyterians' set up a new church order in which there were no bishops, only 'presbyters' or elders.

Calvin's version of this ecclesiology involved a strict discipline in the running of the church. He recognized that some learned 'doctors' had a teaching ministry, and should be responsible both for advanced theological scholarship and the training of future ministers. Pastors were to look after local congregations, preaching, administering the sacraments, admonishing and teaching, with an appropriate degree of severity. There should be deacons who would have a function similar to that which they had had in the early church, making sure that the poor and sick were cared for. The supervisory role which went to bishops in an episcopal system was to be discharged by the elders, working as a group not exercising personal powers as individuals, and acting as a strict monitory body where they saw misbehaviour. Together with the pastors they formed a Consistory, or ecclesiastical court, which kept a puritanical eye on the conduct of the people and banned dancing and singing as well as the teaching of wrong doctrine. The Consistory could impose punishments such as requiring offenders to hear sermons or to go to classes to learn more about the faith, or even floggings.

It was within this strict disciplinary framework that Calvinists and other 'Reformed' believers developed a 'work ethic' and a puritan style of life which led to prosperity. (For example, the silk industry flourished in Geneva.)

Calvinism gained ground in the Netherlands, where Lutheranism had failed to do so, particularly in Flanders. Calvinism moved into Eastern Europe too, especially Hungary, where it became known as the 'Hungarian faith' in contrast to the 'German faith' (Lutheranism) and the 'Right faith' (Roman Catholicism).

The 1581 translator's preface to the English version of Calvin's *Institutes* describes it as a gem, of immense value to the English church. It gives a lively impression of the appetite for Christian instruction in Elizabethan England and the distinctly Calvinist tone of some of the keenest:

So great a jewel was meet to be made most beneficial, that is to say, applied to most common use. Therefore, in the very beginning of the Queen's Majesty's most

SCOTLAND'S CALVINISM

Prominent among the Scottish reformers was John Knox (1514–1572), a great fulminator. He wrote a *History of the Reformation in Scotland*. John Knox does not discuss the way Christianity arrived in Scotland; the natural starting-point as far as he is concerned is the historical evidence for the first stirring of dissenting thought:

Our chronicles make mention that in the days of James the First, about the year of God 1431, was deprehended in the University of St Andrews one named Paul Craw, a Bohemian, who was accused of heresy before such as then were called Doctors of Theology [over transubstantiation].

Looking at the more recent dissent in which he had himself taken a prominent part, he reflected that though they were few, the reformers had had a considerable impact:

In how great purity God did establish amongst us his true religion, as well in doctrine as in ceremonies! To what confusion and fear were idolaters, adulterers, and all public transgressors of God's commandments within short time brought? The public order of the Church, yet by the mercy of God preserved, and the punishments executed against malefactors, can testify unto the world.

John Knox, in a nineteenth-century engraving.

He recollects that in 1561 'the Queen [Mary, Queen of Scots, mother of the future king James I of England] accused him that he had raised a part of her subjects against her mother and against herself', because he had published *Against the Monstrous Regiment of Women*. His answer was that 'if the true knowledge of God and his right worshipping be the chief causes that must move men from their heart to obey their just princes... wherein can I be reprehended?'

The Scottish reformer favoured a Calvinist approach, including an institutional framework for the church which would be Presbyterian rather than episcopal. The Scots became fierce on the subject of bishops. This became a long-standing bone of contention with the joining of the two thrones in the person of James VI of Scotland and James I of England (1566–1625), who became king of England in succession to Elizabeth I in 1603.

143

blessed reign, I translated it out of Latin into English for the commodity of the Church of Christ, at the special request of my dear friends of worthy memory, Reginald Wolfe and Edward Whitchurch, the one her Majesty's printer for the Hebrew, Greek, and Latin tongues, the other her Highness' printer of the books of Common Prayer. I performed my work in the house of my said friend, Edward Whitchurch, a man well known of upright heart and dealing, an ancient zealous gospeller, as plain and true a friend as ever I knew living, and as desirous to do anything to common good, especially by the advancement of true religion.

Calvin was admired by the preacher and writer Richard Hooker (1554–1600) as 'incomparably the wisest man that ever the French Church did enjoy'.

Reformation influences in England had at first been mainly Lutheran, and at first official opinion was hostile. In 1524 William Tyndale travelled to continental Europe to prepare an English translation of the Bible. When copies appeared in England the bishop of London publicly burned the translation and the archbishop of Canterbury tried to round up all known copies.

This was the period when Henry VIII (1491–1547, king from 1509), increasingly desperate for a male heir, dispensed with or disposed of one wife after another. He was also taking an intelligent and pious interest in the religious ferment of the time. It was convenient for him to be able to justify the removal of England from the jurisdiction of the pope so as to place it under his own as Christian Magistrate and Defender of the Faith (a title he had, ironically, been given by Pope Leo X in 1521).

He eventually had a son, the sickly Edward VI, who succeeded his father as a pious small boy in 1547. Thomas Cranmer (1489–1556), his father's Archbishop of Canterbury, continued to guide him and it was in Edward's reign that the first versions of the Church of England's Book of Common Prayer were created. This liturgy made no dramatic break with the medieval liturgical rites it replaced, but it was influenced by continental reformers such as Martin Bucer and Peter Martyr (1499–1562), whom Cranmer invited to England for discussions. A list of Articles defining the faith of the Church of England was also drawn up, forming the basis of the 'Thirty-Nine Articles' eventually settled on. This was a device analogous with the Augsburg Confession.

Edward died in 1553, and never reached adulthood. He was succeeded by his elder sister Mary (1516–1558), the daughter of Henry VIII's staunchly Roman Catholic first wife. She declared England to be

Roman Catholic once more and a period of persecution of the reformers followed. Cranmer himself was burned at the stake in Oxford in 1556 after refusing to recant.

Mary, too, died after a short reign and Henry VIII's remaining daughter, Elizabeth I, succeeded her in 1558. Under her the people of England were required to swing back again to Protestantism. How far the population as a whole followed its leaders in its heart as the Tudor monarchs moved backwards and forwards it is impossible to be sure. Ordinary people were probably better informed theologically than their modern counterparts, but they could not easily have kept up to date with developments in the continental Reformation and the Counter-Reformation.

The Act of Supremacy of 1559 re-established the principle that the English monarch not the pope was head of the Church of England. An oath of supremacy was required, which would root out those not prepared to accept this. A connected principle establishing the dominance of state over church was (and remains) the rule that Parliament must agree before one of the Church of England's laws is binding, even within the church. A further act in the same year, the Act of Uniformity, set out the form the English church would now take. There was to be a Prayer Book and Articles and a set of canons (the laws of the church). The 'Thirty-Nine Articles' were given royal assent in 1571 and after that all clergy of the Church of England had to assent to them publicly on induction into a parish. An definitive English translation of the Bible was prepared, the King James Version. The language of the Prayer Book and the King James Bible was of great beauty and had an influence on the development of the English language for many centuries.

THEOCRACY AND THE EXTREME RADICALS

Thomas Müntzer

The sixteenth-century upheaval included extreme reformers who called for the rejection of almost all the apparatus of ecclesiastical supervision. Thomas Müntzer (b. c. 1489) became one of these. He fell under the influence of Luther and Andreas Karlstadt in Wittenberg between 1517 and 1519. Müntzer then moved to Zwickau in Saxony to begin parish ministry, and his beliefs began to become more radical. He began to reject infant baptism, causing offence to the local authorities; if a local priest refused to baptize babies, that was a matter which directly affected local families. He was expelled by the Zwickau authorities in 1521 and made his way to Prague, where the Hussites had had such an impact a century earlier.

He was welcomed at first because of his known association with Luther, but he quickly wore his welcome out when it was found that he preached rather different ideas. In November 1521 he wrote his *Prague Manifesto*, of which several versions survive. It is an angry document. One of the features of the movements led by the sixteenth-century reformers and of their behaviour and that of their opponents was the fierceness of the hostility felt. This was debate characterized by vivid polemic.

Müntzer's travelling over the next two years further disseminated his radical ideas. Some were in line with a consistent pattern of dissenting notions, such as the belief that the ordinary faithful should be

A reconstruction of the first printing press, invented by Gutenberg, which made it possible to print books for the first time, using moveable type.

able to read the Bible and to worship in their own language. By December 1523 Müntzer had devised a liturgy in German. Others were personal expressions of rebellion against the conventions, such as the celibacy of the clergy and members of religious orders. Clerical celibacy had never been insisted on in the East, where local priests were usually married. But in the eleventh century in the West a problem had presented itself because many clergy had children and were often only too ready to make special arrangements to allow their sons to 'inherit' their clerical livings or other titles. It is not surprising that this happened, since the clerics in a noble family had brothers who were thoroughly pragmatic about ensuring that their own children had a right to hold property. The problem was that a cleric's pastoral duties normally went with the use of property too. Partly to try to protect the church's rights over its own property, celibacy was insisted on and simony (the buying of office) condemned, in treatise after treatise which survives from that time.

Celibacy had, however, always been a feature of the dedicated religious life, in East as well as West. In 1523 Müntzer married a former nun, and however profound and genuine his attachment to her may have been, this action was inevitably going to be perceived as a challenge to the sensibilities of a contemporary world – perhaps a little like the indignation of some modern critics at members of the clergy being practising homosexuals.

He was now bound to be perceived as a threat to the conventions of the church and society. Frederick the Wise, Elector of Saxony (1463–1525) called him in for questioning. Even Luther suggested a meeting to discuss what should be done.

Müntzer's Sermon to the German Princes of 13 July 1524 was a memorable indicator of the way his mind was going. It is apocalyptic, a sermon on Daniel 2, where the prophet Daniel becomes the king's adviser because he is able to interpret the king's dreams for him. Müntzer is the new Daniel: he will tell the princes of Germany what their dreams mean. When they hear the words of Daniel 2:44 they should understand that the Kingdom of God will swallow up all earthly kingdoms.

This was exactly the sort of talk which made religious dissent disturbing to the secular authorities. Müntzer and some of his known sympathizers from Allstedt were summoned to a hearing before the duke of Saxony about the end of July or the beginning of August 1524. Müntzer's printing press at Allstedt was shut down and he fled.

Müntzer's leading idea was that the Word of God was 'living' and 'prophetic', in the practical sense that it provided a guide to modern life and modern politics. This is an approach still familiar, in which the Bible is taken with a particular sort of literalness sometimes known as 'fundamentalism'. It had its medieval antecedents too, for example in the

ERASTIANISM

The insistence of Lutherans and Reformed that their churches' affairs should be under the protection of local 'magistrates' formed part of a continuation of the long-running wider debate about the balance of power between church and state in Christian Europe.

One approach to the question of the right way to balance the powers of church and state came to be known as Erastianism. The Erastus who gave his name to it was born Thomas Lieber or Liebler (1524–1583), though he preferred to use the Latin name in his writings. He was Swiss by birth and had some university education there, but he studied medicine in Bologna before moving to Germany to serve as a court physician and a professor of medicine at Heidelberg. That brought him into a region where Reformation controversy was at its height with disputes between reforming sects. Erastus was himself a follower of Zwingli and he became involved in the disputes with the Lutherans. Arguments involving Calvinists were also becoming heated because the Elector Frederick III (Frederick the Wise), who succeeded in 1559, began to try to force his people to embrace Calvinist views. Also in evidence in Calvin's *Institutes* was an awareness, similar to that which the Lutherans had been developing, that if the pope was not to be looked to for approval and supervision at a high level, the civil authority or 'magistrate' might make an acceptable substitute. Calvin was doing nothing new in sending his work to an important person for approval. This was a commonplace in writings of the sixteenth century and the late Middle Ages too, for it had the advantage of creating a built-in advertisement. The ordinary reader saw the prefatory dedication and was intended to be suitably impressed. So Calvin writes disingenuously in his prefatory address to King Francis of France:

When I first set my hand to this work, nothing was farther from my mind, most glorious King, than to write something that might afterward be offered to Your Majesty.

He goes further and addresses the king on the subject of proper supervision of ecclesiastical matters by secular authorities. He seeks to reassure him that not all rebels against papal authority are seditiously inclined towards the authority of the state:

That no one may think we are wrongly complaining of these things, you can be our witness, most noble King, with how many lying slanders it [this book] is daily traduced in your presence. It is as if this doctrine looked to no other end than to wrest the sceptres from the hands of kings, to cast down all courts and judgments, to subvert all orders and civil governments, to disrupt the peace and quiet of the people, to abolish all laws, to scatter all lordships and possessions – in short, to turn everything upside down!

work of Joachim of Fiore, who had tried to work out from the prophecies of Scripture at the end of the twelfth century exactly which emperor was likely to prove to be the last and when the world would end.

Müntzer now became involved in movements of political dissent.

Meanwhile no one comes forward to defend the church:

It will then be for you, most serene King, not to close your ears or your mind to such just defense, especially when a very great question is at stake: how God's glory may be kept safe on earth, how God's truth may retain its place of honor, how Christ's Kingdom may be kept in good repair among us.

A flurry of Bible quotations on rulers follows.

At a conference at the monastery of Maulbronn in 1564 Erastus was invited by the Elector to defend Zwingli's teaching. In 1568, Erastus published his *Theses*, which were attacked by Theodore Beza (1519–1605, a disciple of Calvin and a reformer) on behalf of the Calvinists, with a rejoinder from Erastus in the *Confirmatio Thesium* the following year. In 1570 at Heidelberg a presbyterian structure was introduced in the church and Erastus was excommunicated. The *Theses* and *Confirmatio Thesium* appeared in print only in 1589. The last three theses concern the relations of church and state.

Erastus argues that modern Christian magistrates should be able to exercise the authority over the nation which is entrusted to their equivalents in the Jewish nation in the Old Testament. If the magistrate is 'godly' he can be responsible for all the people need by way of rule and discipline.

Erastus' ideas had a good deal of influence in Germany and in England. Richard Hooker's *Ecclesiastical Polity* refers to the dispute between Beza and Erastus in its preface:

Whatever State has once suffer'd by a General Rebellion, like a Man that has once undergone the Fatigue and Danger of some Infectious Disease, has this Advantage above any other, as yet Free, that a Relapse into the same Condition is easily prevented, or almost impossible, but through a total Neglect... One would think, that one Tryal of the Experiment should teach us to be wiser for the future.

He arrived at Muhlhausen in Thuringia, an imperial city where there was long-standing bad feeling between the craftsmen and the city council. He and Henry Pfeiffer produced eleven Articles designed to create a new kind of city council which would be an 'eternal council', to run the city according to divine justice and under God's Word. This naïve programme of social reform now superimposed the supernatural upon the worldly realities, leading to a degree of geographical confusion. (It was not dissimilar perhaps to the confusion there seems to have been in some medieval crusaders' minds between the heavenly Jerusalem and the earthly Jerusalem they were marching to defend in this world.)

That it was indeed naïve is shown by Müntzer's failure to understand the political realities. He sent off his Articles to stir up the peasantry in the surrounding countryside, not realizing that their discontents were different from those of the bourgeois members of the craft guilds. He and Pfeiffer were expelled from Muhlhausen in September but by February he was back, and the people of the city voted the city council out and replaced it with an Eternal League of God. That seems to have awakened the peasants at last to the possibility that they too could rise up. In May 1525 nearly ten thousand peasants under Müntzer's leadership fought a battle at Frankenhausen in the misplaced confidence that God would make sure they won.

The authorities had had enough. Müntzer was captured, imprisoned, tortured and beheaded (even though he had recanted), and his body put where it could be seen by the populace as a warning against any further uprisings. The sixteenth-century authorities were slow to understand that it is not always wise to create martyrs in a cause, and that popular enthusiasm might be strengthened if they did so.

In this case, the ideas for which Müntzer died had already caught on. Others tried to set up a 'theocracy' at Münster in Westphalia in the 1530s. Müntzer himself had, it turned out, won a lasting reputation, and he was still seen as a Communist hero of the 'oppressed classes' in East Germany in its Communist period.

Anabaptism

Müntzer's legacy for the history of Christian Europe is rather different, however. His movement belonged to the type usually called 'Anabaptist'. This involved a rejection of the belief that sacraments were necessary to get a believer to heaven, particularly baptism.

Not all of those who thought this were so threatening to the good

Menno Simons, in a nineteenth-century portrait.

order of society. George Fox (1624–1691) was one of the founders of the movement known as the Quakers, or Society of Friends, who tried to live lives of quiet simplicity; their worship was so stripped of sacramental content that it had no content at all, their faith so simple that they needed no creed. They simply sat in silence, until one of them felt moved by the Holy Spirit to say something for the edification of the others. It has had little influence in Europe though there has been some expansion in the Americas.

Among this cluster of those who held radical views on the sacraments fell believers who were far from rejecting the importance of baptism in particular, so much so that they came to be known as Baptists. Their belief was, however, that baptism as practised by the institutional church had fallen into error. It concentrated on the use of water and the invocation of the name of the Trinity ('I baptize you in the name of the Father and of the Son and of the Holy Spirit'), when, they said, it was the faith of the person baptized which was the crucial thing, and that meant infants could not be baptized.

Moreover, said the Baptists, there should be enough water to

Mennonites meeting for worship in Amsterdam, from an eighteenth-century study of different kinds of religious dress.

immerse the candidate. They began a practice which had been forbidden from a very early date, which was to baptize afresh people baptized as infants because, they said, they had never really been baptized at all. To the Baptists this was not rebaptism but baptism.

The Anabaptists and their like were not looked on with universal favour by other contemporary reformers. Luther for one considered the Anabaptists to be fanatics. The part of Europe most receptive to this branch of reforming thought was the Netherlands, especially Holland and Friesland. Lutheranism did not establish a following here. But in 1578 the States-General of the Netherlands gave approval to Baptist practices as institutionally acceptable.

Menno Simons (1496–1561), from whom the Mennonites took their name, was a Dutch Anabaptist who did not accept the literal incarnation of Christ in the form in which it had been agreed in both East and West since the Nicene Creed had been accepted in AD 325. He returned to debates of the sort which had preoccupied early Christians, though probably without any clear idea that that was what he was doing. He seems to have preferred the idea that Mary had contributed no fleshly human body but had rather been like a channel through which God could enter the world in a human body he had brought with him. This had been put forward by Marcion (c. AD 110–160) among others.

This is an example of the tendency for the basic or archetypal challenges to orthodox Christian belief to reappear in generation after generation, but it was relatively unusual for the reformers of the sixteenth century to display a preoccupation with these fundamental questions about the nature of God and the mode of the Incarnation. They were much more often interested in questions touching on human lives in their own day and the way to salvation for individuals.

Were such accusations of radical unorthodoxy justified? What did Mennonites, Anabaptists and members of other popular heretical movements really believe? This may not always be easy to say, at least at the popular level. Plain, even puritan, living and a refusal to take oaths, to bear arms, to hold worldly offices or posts or to accept worldly advancement had long been recognized marks of persons holding heretical opinions. In the period of the medieval Inquisition such views were often imputed to the alleged heretics brought before the inquisitors and trick questions asked to get them to agree that they did indeed feel a reluctance to swear, so that they might be condemned.

These or similar opinions now emerged as marks of the groups which called themselves 'brethren'. These were believers who thought a Christian life could be lived outside, or independently of, the institutional framework of the church. They often worshipped in what would now be called 'house churches' with no officially recognized system of overarching ministerial oversight. Brethren were inward-looking and typically practised exclusiveness, and excommunicated from their number those who did not meet the standards they set themselves.

This 'congregational' ecclesiology, which located the visible church in a 'gathered' community, allows each community to choose its own pastor or leader, and it won favour even in reforming communities which were not so radical themselves. Such structures lend themselves to extreme positions, however, because with the institutional oversight goes the possibility of requiring that local ministers are trained, and that their orthodoxy is assured. Without that there is a danger that a natural demagogue may win the hearts of a congregation while holding beliefs which depart some way from accepted Christian basics.

6

Early Modern Expansion and Conflict

EASTERN EUROPE

Christianity and the Turkish Expansion

The fall of Byzantium in 1453 allowed the Turks to pass into Europe and expand. From the end of the fifteenth century, the Turks were moving aggressively into Europe, conquering territory and achieving dominance over the conquered peoples throughout the sixteenth century and into the seventeenth.

From 1458, Dubrovnik was paying a tribute to the Ottoman Turks and formally recognizing them as the 'great power'. It also paid taxes to the Hungarian-Croatian King. (It ceased to do both in 1526.) The Ottoman conquest of Bosnia came in 1463. From 1468 Ottomans begin to make further systematic incursions into Dalmatian and Croatian lands. In 1476 Wallachia became a vassal state of the Ottoman empire; Moldavia did so in 1512.

In 1526 the Ottomans defeated the Hungarians and seized Buda. The Croatians resisted but the Turks had conquered them too by the late 1550s. In 1565 a new wave of Turks consolidated the hold on Bosnia. Pressure continued to be felt from Western Christian political powers too, as these Balkan regions became the subject of a tug-of-war between East and West. There was a defeat of the Ottoman fleet at the Battle of Lepanto in 1571. In 1573 Cyprus was ceded to the Ottoman empire by Venice, and in 1669 the Ottomans captured Crete from the Venetians.

The gradual takeover of Europe ended only when the Ottomans were stopped at the gates of Vienna in 1683. It remained an open question for some time whether Christianity or Islam would dominate south-east Europe in the end.

East and West Fail to Unite

There had been a nearly successful attempt to mend the schism between East and West at the Council of Florence-Ferrara early in the fifteenth century. In 1439 a basis was agreed on which the two churches might be able to unite. But when the Orthodox bishops who had attended took the proposals home, they proved unacceptable to their own people.

One solution to the breakdown of this agreement was for communities of Christians in lands which were otherwise Orthodox to establish links with Rome when they themselves had loyalties to a sovereign in a country which was Roman Catholic. Such communities are known as 'Uniate' churches, and they preserve liturgical rites which derive from Orthodoxy and also sometimes practices, such as allowing married clergy, which the Roman Catholic Church forbids. For example, Ukrainians who were subjects of the king of Poland chose to submit to Rome in 1596. Each 'Eastern Rite' church has its own patriarch and these patriarchs are members of the Congregation for the Oriental Churches, which looks after the relationship of these churches with Rome.

Among the leaders to reject the mending of fences proposed by the Council of Florence was Prince Basil of Moscow. The Russian Orthodox church had gained its independence from Constantinople in 1448. In 1452, Basil, Patriarch of Constantinople, forbade the publication of the Acts of the council in Russia, and the Russian patriarch was ejected as an apostate. The fall of Constantinople to the Turks in 1453 altered the balance of power among the Orthodox churches. Russian Orthodox began to call Moscow the 'Third Rome' and to consider that it could now take over from Constantinople, with its Metropolitan bishop as a counterpart to the pope in the West. The position was consolidated as a series of synods was held in the 1540s and 1550s, which strengthened the working relationships of the local churches of Russia and helped to ensure unity of practice.

The claim to be the Third Rome was strengthened further in 1589 when the then Metropolitan of Moscow, Job (1589–1607), was recognized as Patriarch of Moscow and All Rus. From that point the Russian Orthodox church was autocephalous, one of the churches of Orthodoxy. During an ensuing period of a generation or more the tsars were relatively weak and the church authorities exercised considerable secular power.

Monasticism was as strong in Russia as in the rest of the Orthodox world, with the same characteristics of emphasis on spirituality rather than the learning which was to be found in some religious orders and houses

in the West. Monasteries were founded in the far north as well as the more hospitable south of Russia. One of the most notable was on the peninsula of Mount Athos in northern Greece, which had been regarded as the 'holy mountain' of Orthodox monasticism since perhaps the tenth century. There were upsurges of controversy, particularly about the secularization of monastic lands, and also outbreaks of frank heresy, such as a move to return to something resembling a form of Judaism, with Old Testament law reinstated.

The sixteenth-century establishment of Russian Orthodoxy was followed in the seventeenth century by a vast territorial expansion. In the 1680s, after a struggle, Constantinople reluctantly and with protest allowed Kiev to be transferred to the jurisdiction of Moscow. Russian Orthodox missionaries travelled as far as Siberia (St Innocent), Alaska (St Herman) and eventually the western coast of America.

Political control of the Russian Orthodox church followed hard on the heels of this success. In 1700, Peter the Great (1672–1725) stopped the creation of a patriarch to succeed Adrian, who had died, and two decades later he brought about the creation of a completely new structure for the church in Russia. From 1721 there was to be a Holy and Supreme Synod, an arrangement which lasted until the patriarchal system was restored in Russia after 1917.

Orthodox Intellectual Culture

Nothing quite like the Western university emerged in the Byzantine world, even though the level of intellectual culture there, especially insofar as it was associated with the court, remained high. The question can be asked why there were no 'renaissances' in the Orthodox Christian world.

Learning in the Greek-speaking half of Europe followed different paths and was acquired within a different framework. Monastic learning had a different character. Western monasticism, whose mainstream from the sixth to the twelfth centuries followed the Rule of Benedict, involved community life and regular patterns of reading and study, with readings at communal mealtimes. Each house had to run a school of sorts because until the late eleventh century, when adult converts became more numerous, it was usual for children to be given to monasteries by their families to become monks or nuns, often in infancy. So the teaching of Latin was essential, and enough education beyond that to enable the monk at least to understand the faith he professed and to take part in the *Opus Dei*, the 'work of God' or round of daily worship. In some houses

The monastery of Saint Panteleimon on Mount Athos was founded in the eleventh century though the present monastery, of Russian Orthodox monks, dates from the eighteenth century.

where there was a teacher of exceptional ability, the level of instruction could be very high indeed. Anselm of Canterbury taught the monks while he was at the monastery of Bec to a level where the chronicler Orderic Vitalis (1075–1142) says even the 'peasants' among them seemed like philosophers, and Anselm's surviving writings give a lively picture of what it was like to learn in the environment he created.

In the East, monastic life had other priorities. It was often the life of a hermit, and even where monks lived in groups they would commonly do so according to an individual pattern of life, each in his separate cell, with the 'community' meeting for meals or worship occasionally. The style of study was also individual; it tended to be conservative and respectful, involving the reflective reading of the solitary monk (if he read at all), rather than an exchange of ideas. Whereas in the West a monk like Bede could write about what he read and be quoted and debated for centuries alongside other authors and authorities such as Augustine of Hippo and Gregory the Great, there was no such growth of this tradition in the East.

Learning in the form of a high level of culture and education was available to the well-born, men and women. The Byzantine princess Anna Comnena who wrote so disparagingly of the barbarous habits of the Western crusaders at the end of the eleventh century was a cultured woman herself. But this sort of thing was a product of the culture of the court rather than the result of a formal education in a school.

The ancient pattern of master and pupils, familiar from the ancient world, persisted in the East. The Photios who made his name as Patriarch of Constantinople collected extracts from nearly three hundred classical authors, many of which are now known only through his collection, the *Myriobiblion*. He liked historical writing and was keen on theology but did not bother with poetry or the philosophy of the ancient world, so it is impossible to know what else was available in his time in such categories and has now disappeared. He concentrated on works which would be less well known to his contemporaries, and that gives a glimpse of the normal acquaintanceship of educated people with a range of earlier Greek writings. He also prepared a Lexicon to help contemporary readers make sense of words in these texts which had passed out of use. Among his original compositions is the *Amphilochia*, in which he discusses a series of questions arising from the study of the Bible, and polemical writings against Manichaeans and Paulicians, which he did not intend to be used only by specialists. He wrote to Boris of Bulgaria when he was converted to explain various theological principles to him.

So it would not be true to say that there was no active endeavour in the East going beyond humble and unquestioning reading of Scripture and approved Christian writings. But the spirit in which it was conducted remained reverential and hostile to experimental thinking. The mode was that of late Platonism, mystical and by Western standards allusive and suggestive rather than analytical and exact.

THE GREEK REVIVAL AND THE RENAISSANCE OF THE WEST

The study of Greek came alive again in the West at the end of the Middle Ages, along with the study of Hebrew. The Complutensian University in Madrid was founded in 1499 and there between 1502 and 1517 was prepared the first printed Bible to contain the text in Greek, Hebrew and Latin, with Aramaic versions of some portions.

Legend had it that after the fall of Byzantium in 1453, Greek scholars fled to the West and prompted the new classical revival of learning. The humanist and logician Peter Ramus (1515–1572) tells this tale in his oration about the study of philosophy at the University of Paris, published in 1557, naming Lascaris (1445–1535), Bessarion (1403–1472), Gaza (1398–1478) and Trapezuntius (1396–1484).

The addition of the Greek Fathers to the 'patristic' corpus, now that knowledge of classical and early Christian Greek was being recaptured in the West, was an irresistible attraction to both Reformation and Roman Catholic scholars. The leaders of the Reformation were further motivated by their conviction that the church had somehow taken a wrong turning in the Middle Ages; that it was time to reject scholasticism and everything it had brought and return to the sources, the earliest Christian writings, where, they argued, the truth was most likely to be found.

Hebrew studies in Germany were largely led by Johannes Reuchlin (1455–1522), whose relations with those of reforming sympathies were sometimes uncomfortable, but who influenced Melanchthon for a time. Also in Germany, Tübingen was founded in 1477 as a new-style university. Some institutions of the day found they were home to two kinds of course: the official, traditional one and a rival 'modern' course being delivered unofficially on the outskirts, but very popular with students. This might include study of the ancient languages and modern textual criticism. The University of Wittenberg, which became Luther's university, was founded in 1502. Melanchthon became a teacher of Greek there after studying the language at Tübingen and making a name for himself. Although he gradually became absorbed in the Lutheran project he also wrote on humanist themes, light, literary and secular.

Catholic and Orthodox in Northern and Eastern Europe

Until the fourteenth century, northern Estonia had been dominated by Denmark, although Estonia was included in the Hanseatic League from the end of the thirteenth century. The Germans sought to control the territories of Estonia but the Estonians rose up in 1342 and threw off German authority. Russia made a bid for the area in 1481 and in 1558, but without success. Estonia, which could have remained Roman Catholic or Orthodox, chose to adopt Lutheranism as early as the 1520s. The ruling classes were mainly drawn from German families of Baltic descent.

Gustavus Adolphus of Sweden.

This choice of religion did not confer political stability, however, or ensure that Estonia was not broken up again. Early in the sixteenth century Sweden began a period of aggressive behaviour against its neighbours and aggrandizement, confronting Denmark and Norway (linked at the time), and also Russia too. The Swedes and, for a short time, the Poles took control of Estonia in the late sixteenth century. It was divided into the provinces of Estonia, Livonia and Latvia until the early twentieth century. Under the Swedes a university was founded and printing of books began. Sweden exercised a relatively benevolent rule. Gustavus Adolphus (1594–1632) did not abolish serfdom but he did endeavour to ensure that the peasantry were better treated by their noble lords. Serfdom was finally abolished in Estonia only at the beginning of the nineteenth century. In the first half of the eighteenth century, Estonia was captured from Sweden by Russia as one of the outcomes of the Great Northern War.

Once serfdom ceased an Estonian nationalist movement began to emerge, to which the Estonian language was central. A published literature was created in the nineteenth century and a strong musical tradition. Intellectuals called for independence from Russia and a War of Estonian Liberation was successful in 1920, though the freedom proved precarious and lasted only a couple of decades.

Another area where Swedish influence was important for a period was Poland and Lithuania. They had formed an alliance in the sixteenth century at the Union of Lublin (1569). The two countries kept their sovereignties and institutions, currency and law. In Lithuania, this arrangement ended in 1795 and lands were lost to Austria, Prussia and (the vast majority) to Russia. Lithuania reappeared as an independent nation in 1918, with a capital in Vilnius, though there were continuing disputes over the ownership of territories between Poland, Germany and Lithuania. The Soviet Union took over Lithuania at the beginning of the Second World War. It was not until the 1980s that Lithuania began to emerge from Communist control.

In Poland, the numerous members of the 'noble' classes conducted affairs of state with proud independence and a good deal of freedom. But in the seventeenth century Sweden and Russia made invasive attempts to control the area and by the end of the eighteenth century the lands were divided among Austria, Prussia and Russia. Napoleon (1769–1821) restored a Duchy of Warsaw but the Congress of Vienna of 1815 divided Polish lands again. The Russians ruled the east of Poland and Austria had the west, including Cracow.

It was not until the twentieth century that Poland fully re-emerged and was able to determine its Christian allegiance in favour of Roman Catholicism and against Russian Orthodoxy, but at the cost of yet another redrawing of the borders and the migration of huge numbers of Ukrainians, Germans, Poles and Jews. In the 1980s, the Polish 'Solidarity' movement, essentially a trade union movement, led by Lech Walesa (b. 1943) brought about the beginning of the collapse of Communism in Eastern Europe.

During the seventeenth century Sweden became a European power to be reckoned with. Its period as a great power lasted until the early nineteenth century, by which time its empire had shrunk and even Finland had been lost. Since that time Sweden has kept out of war by being neutral, not aligning itself with other powers in peacetime.

As Russia became unified it pushed Sweden back. Finland was perhaps inevitably drawn into the power struggle because of its long union with Sweden. In the eighteenth century there were two periods when Russia occupied Finland, 1714–1721 and 1742–1743, in the name of rescuing the Finns from the 'oppression' of the Swedes. The Finns took a different view, describing these two periods as the Greater and the Lesser 'Wrath', respectively. In fact, Russian oppression of the Finnish peasants was probably worse than that of Sweden. But one of the most noticeable

PATRONAGE AND CHURCH-BUILDING

The late medieval city was characterized by a corporate ethos and run according to statutes, from guild to city council. The sixteenth-century city saw a movement towards an administrative style more appropriate to the aggrandizement of princely rulers. While Lorenzo the Magnificent (1449–1492) ruled Florence many grandiose building projects were put in hand, including a princely palace. 'These were truly worthy of a lord', commented a contemporary. Lorenzo purchased houses from the city guild, some of which his own ancestors had given to the guild to use for charitable purposes. The guild benefited from the money; he was able to rent them out profitably; and those who rented them had somewhere to live.

Lorenzo's son became Pope Leo X in 1513 and this empire-building approach began to recommend itself equally to the papacy, for this was a pope who saw himself as a Christian prince and was ambitious to build a new Rome, including an imperial palace for himself.

St Peter's was emerging as the cathedral of Rome and it made a visible link

St Peter's Square in Rome. The Basilica of St Peter was built over what was believed to be the resting-place of the bones of St Peter, between 1506 and 1626. It was funded at the outset partly from money raised by the selling of indulgences. It is a grand statement of the glories of the papal monarchy of the time.

between Peter, Jesus' disciple, whose bones lay within it, and the pomp and majesty of the contemporary papacy. Popes began to emerge into the piazza and bless the people assembled there. Pope Paul V (1562–1621) erected the façade which completed the building.

One of the effects of the Counter-Reformation was to encourage a new austerity in building in Rome. The Council of Trent had emphasized the importance of ensuring that ecclesiastical and Christian art taught the faithful and was not just a means of showing off for ambitious popes and lay patrons.

differences for the population would have been the shifts between Catholicism and Orthodoxy they were obliged to accept as political authority changed.

THE COUNTER-REFORMATION IN THE WEST

In the West, the reformers did not have it all their own way. France and much of southern Europe remained, and remains, loyal to the Roman Catholic Church. And there was what has been called by recent students of the phenomenon a 'Counter-Reformation', a concerted attempt by Rome and its allies to reassert its position. It had not failed to learn something. Indeed, the very developments Luther had criticized had had reforming intentions, and it was only a century before the reformers began to have such a startling effect that the Conciliarist movement had attempted to diminish the monarchical power of the pope and restore decision-making in the church to something closer to the process of forming a common mind which had characterized it in the first centuries.

Luther had been calling from an early stage for a great council of the church, like the ecumenical councils held in the first centuries, to consider the matters on which there was so much dissent. His wish was fulfilled in the end by the Council of Trent (1545–1663). This began during the pontificate of Paul III (r. 1534–1549) as an attempt to deal with problems such as corruption and absenteeism among the clergy and

THE NETHERLANDS

The Roman Catholic authorities had the support of the secular authorities in seeking to suppress the reformers and their followers. In the Netherlands, particularly Flanders, where Calvinism had won a following from the 1560s, Philip II of Spain joined forces with the Inquisition to eradicate it. The people reacted indignantly. Religious images were destroyed in the churches to emphasize the seriousness with which they took their change of religious affiliation. The Prince of Orange, William the Silent (1533–1584), who had himself become a Calvinist, began a war which was to last for eighty years to free the Dutch from Spanish overlordship in 1568. Holland and Zealand were captured for the Dutch in 1572. These had not been Calvinist strongholds up to that point, but now they decided to support the Prince of Orange, under the leadership of Paulus Buys (1531–1594). The people began to become Calvinist, the cities attracted Protestant immigrants from France and Germany, and a climate of religious toleration emerged in the region which has lasted ever since.

recognized financial abuses, some of them connected with the sale of indulgences. But it also confronted the reformers and took a position against what they were saying and in favour of the traditional positions which had historically been stated by the church in the West. For example, it insisted on retaining the Vulgate as the accepted text of Scripture; it upheld the doctrine of transubstantiation, which said that the consecrated bread and wine literally became the body and blood of Christ; it kept to seven sacraments. Paul IV (r. 1555–1559) instituted an inquiry into what was being said in the flood of newly-published printed books, and censored and prohibited those deemed to conflict with Catholic doctrine. This represented an authoritarian crackdown in response to the awkward questions the reformers had been asking and it was, of its nature, a high-risk strategy.

BETTER MUTUAL UNDERSTANDING

One of the most important realizations to arrive in Europe as a consequence of its expansion was that Christianity was going to have to arrive at a rapprochement or arrangement of some sort with the peoples of the new lands where Europeans were making positive missionary expeditions, and sometimes settling permanently.

The English traveller Thomas Cavendish (1560–1592), on his own voyage round the world (1586–1588), landed on the American coast on 16 December 1586 and described the 'Indians' he found there:

They seldom or never see any Christians; they are as wild as ever was a buck or any other wild beast; for we followed them and they ran from us.

To speak thus or to think in terms of 'discovering' another land, when there were people there already, says a good deal about the attitude of superiority with which the Europeans went out into the world. Part of this sense of superiority derived from a belief that as Christian peoples the Europeans were entitled to regard themselves as emissaries of God and carriers-forward of his purposes, even where they went not as missionaries or as conquerors, but simply to enquire what the world was like or to engage in trade. In the tale of the recovery of the prize ship *Exchange* in 1621, God's support for the Christians is not left in doubt: 'When all was done, and the ship cleared of the dead bodies, John Rawlins assembled his men together, and with one consent gave the praise unto God.'

One of the most notable figures in creating the tradition that all these motives could be mixed and the enterprise still thought of as God's work was Richard Hakluyt (1552/3–1616). He was a cleric, who became archdeacon of Westminster in 1603. He published his first collection of contemporary travellers' tales in 1589 under the title of *The Principal Navigations, Voyages and Discoveries of the English Nation*. He dedicated this volume to Sir Francis Walsingham (1532–1590), who had taken a

The Jesuits

One way of countering what had happened was by missionary effort and persuasion. The Jesuits were probably the most important group of 'professional' missionaries to emerge in the Counter-Reformation. Their founder was Ignatius Loyola (1491–1556). He called them 'The Company of Jesus' because Jesus was to be their leader; from this they came to be known as 'Jesuits', though the epithet was not of their choosing.

The origin of the order lay in a group of Christian friends. Ignatius brought together Peter Faber, Francis Xavier, James Lainez, Alonso Sameron, Nicolas Bobadilla, Simon Rodriquez, Claude Le Jay, Jean Codure and Paschase Brouet and filled them with enthusiasm for the idea of living in the Holy Land in imitation of Christ. They took vows of poverty and chastity in 1536 and swore an oath at the same time that they would go to

constructive interest from within court circles.

In the dedicatory letter Hakluyt describes how when he was young he visited the rooms of his cousin and namesake Richard Hakluyt in the Middle Temple in London and found a great map spread out. His cousin had a robust commercial view of matters as well as a religious one; he had his connections with the merchant venturers, and his sympathies with the notion that the purchasers of traded goods would benefit by the transaction and have their needs met. He explained to young Richard how the world had conventionally been divided into three parts but how it could now be more accurately divided into many more:

From the Mappe he brought me to the Bible, and turning to the 107 Psalme, directed mee to the 23 & 24 verses, where I read, that they which go downe to the sea in ships, and occupy by the great waters, they see the works of the Lord, and his wonders in the deepe.

This so struck him that his life's work lay before him from that moment. He did little travelling on his own account (only to Paris) but a great deal of studying.

There could be a surprising degree of 'recognition' and fellow-feeling with European travellers on such voyages, if not quite a sense of having a common cause. Thomas Cavendish records the pleasure with which his party encountered some Portuguese on 12 March 1588 in Java, on his trip round the world. Their common Christianity seems to have been more important to them than the divisions of the Reformation:

These Portugals were in no small joy unto our general and all the rest of our company, for we had not seen any Christian that was our friend for a year and a half before.

Ignatius Loyola.

the Holy Land two years later. It proved impossible to fulfil this promise so instead they offered themselves to the pope for his service.

The order was approved by the pope in 1540. It was to take the form of a 'mendicant' community, which lived on alms and according to a Rule, so it was of the same broad type as the Franciscan and Dominican orders, which had been founded in the early thirteenth century. Loyola's vision was of a life lived in 'imitation of Christ', and at first he had no formal plan to found an order. But the pope saw a use for him and his followers as missionaries.

Ignatius was encouraged to draw up a constitution. He did this by trying things out first and adjusting the Rule. The constitutions were not adopted in their final form until 1558. Their theme is charity moderated by wisdom and they place an emphasis on the living of a community life, but also strongly on personal spirituality. Ignatius' spiritual exercises are a required discipline and taken to constitute a test of vocation (a purpose for which they are used more widely, for example by some Anglican ordinands). The continual reform of the inner self is central to the Jesuit life. All those who are fully professed as Jesuits are priests. They take vows of poverty, chastity and obedience, with a special vow of obedience to the pope to undertake missions as he may instruct.

The Jesuits share with the Dominicans a consciousness that effective missionary endeavour requires an appropriate level of education. They are an order dedicated to teaching as well as to preaching.

The main objective of the missionary endeavour as it was first conceived was to convert the Moslems, and it was only a secondary thought that the Jesuits might prove useful as missionaries in Protestant lands. The Imperial Ambassador from Germany was probably the first serious promoter of that idea. The predominant Roman Catholicism of southern and western modern Germany and of Austria owe a good deal to the Jesuits' work in this period. Jesuits were active in Eastern Europe, too, establishing themselves in Dubrovnik in 1560 and taking over the former Dominican house in the Zagrebois quarter of Gradec in 1606.

Jesuit missionaries took the colour of their activities partly from the political complexion of the areas to which they were seeking to bring the

Christian faith, making such adjustments as sensitivity required and orthodoxy of faith and practice did not seem to forbid. In Portugal, for example, they found a commercial dimension to the Christian life acceptable and put no objections in the way of the slave trade. In the Netherlands they put on attractive 'performances' with liturgical and other celebrations and educational exercises, which succeeded – especially in rural areas – in drawing people back to familiar patterns of the Christian life to which they had been accustomed as Catholics.

Meanwhile, Jesuit missionaries were working in Japan and China, where Europeans did not achieve political control, as they did on much of the Indian subcontinent and in the Americas. In India, Jesuit missionaries had behaved a little like the late Roman syncretists. They endeavoured to 'inculturate' Christian teaching so that it could be assimilated by the Hindus. In China, some Jesuits tried to argue that the Chinese had had a revelation of Christian truth in ancient times, which had not been part of the history known to the Western Church but which should now enable them to accept Christianity with ease. In Japan there were rival communities of Christian converts, those who owed their faith to the Jesuits and those who had been approached by Franciscan missionaries.

EXPANSION AND COMMERCE IN EAST AND WEST

Looked at in close-up Europe is a cluttered corner into which history has thrown a great many languages, and peoples of numerous races. Europe has been extremely busy over many centuries. Its culture is the product of a great deal of activity in writing and the arts, which has benefited from the exchange of ideas. And Europe has sent feelers out into the rest of the world, through trade, exploration and conquest. In these ways it has probably had a more extensive influence on the world as it is today than any other geographical area. To take an obvious example, English, a European language formed in a tiny offshore island from the roots of the languages spoken by invading tribes (Angles and Saxons, and other, later invaders from Normandy, who themselves spoke a debased form of the Latin of the Roman Empire), has become the default language of communication throughout the world.

This cannot all be put down to the effect of the adoption of Christianity throughout Europe. Part of the motivation of this outgoing activity was political, part economic. But in the self-justification of writers engaged in, or commenting on, what was happening, there repeatedly rings a note of Christian conviction that the process is God's will for the world. This is important because it encouraged a conflation of territorial discovery, the conquest of new lands and the extension of trading activities, with mission, pilgrimage and even crusade.

First Portugal, sailing west, then Spain, going south round the point of Africa and up its eastern coast, tried to find a direct sea route to India. There was a competitive desire to test in the process whether the world would turn out to be round. The Iberian peninsula dominated the missionary endeavour of the Roman Catholic part of Europe but France was actively involved too. French settlements in the north American continent still leave their mark on Canada. The Portuguese, along with Europe's more northern explorers, the French and English, discovered not India but the Americas, north and south. This became known as the 'New World' to distinguish it from the 'Old World' with its familiar three continents.

Père Joseph (1577–1638), a Capuchin friar who was in the confidence of Cardinal Richelieu (1585–1642), encouraged him in a dream of mounting one last great crusade. The moment when the Turkish advance was stopped at Vienna in the reign of Louis XIV (1643–1715) brought an end to this plan, for it was no longer so urgently needed, but it is a reminder that the expansion of Europe was looking east as well as west, and not only by seeking out sea routes to the desirable trading available with India and China.

Once bigger ships were available, partly as a result of the building of vessels capable of engaging in the explorations which led to the discovery of the New World, trade in bulk became possible, for example of grain from the Baltic regions. From South America came gold and silver. The medieval merchant associations developed into arrangements more like modern businesses, with shareholders owning a ship or its cargo. That meant that a trader could avoid putting all his enterprise at risk on one voyage and divide his investment among a number of different ships. These flexible arrangements eventually led, from the sixteenth century, to the chartered trading companies, which were in private ownership but under state supervision.

Two porcelain Chinese figures laughing, in a style unlike anything to be found in Europe until such objects began to find their way there as a consequence of the trade of the seventeenth and eighteenth centuries.

But the balance between what the European merchants had to offer and what they wanted to buy remained somewhat unequal until the Industrial Revolution gave Europe manufactured goods to sell to the East, and now the New World, south-east Asia and Australasia, in return for commodities which most of Europe could not supply for itself. The scale of trade grew enormously, and with it the incentive for the state to treat the enterprise as an opportunity for colonization.

There was also a new awareness of Eastern religions arising out of contact, through trade and commerce and the importation into Europe of beautiful and precious artefacts, with the belief-systems of China and Japan, as well as a closer engagement with Islamic thought.

For Rome, consolidating Europe's faith, both in areas affected by the Protestant reformers and on the eastern borders, was important too. National Colleges to train Jesuits coming from different parts of Europe were founded or expanded in Rome, incuding a German College (1552) and a Hungarian College (1578), which merged with the German one in 1580. A Greek College was founded in 1577 and an English one in 1578.

Speaking of the confrontation observed between the Orthodox Russians and the Tartars, one English voyager observed that some of the Tartars came to the Russians for help, though they were their enemies, because they were dying of hunger:

At that time it had been an easy thing to have converted that wicked nation to the Christian faith, if the Russes themselves had been good Christians: but how should they show compassion unto other nations, when they are not merciful unto their own?

7

Christianity and the European Scientific Revolution

CHURCH–STATE RELATIONS AND THE TOLERATION OF PRIVATE RELIGIOUS OPINION

In his *On Toleration* (1689), the English thinker John Locke (1632–1704) took a fresh look at the question of the purpose of society. He moved decisively away from the notions of a unified political hegemony, the argument that whoever headed a state should determine its religion, which had been developed in various forms in Lutheran, Reformed and Erastian thinking.

This also presented a challenge to the Establishment of the Church of England as it had emerged in England after the Reformation there. Establishment had become controversial during the seventeenth century and it had had to survive the challenge of England's Civil War. From his accession in 1603, King James I had sought to strengthen the position of the monarchy, claiming a 'divine right of kings'. Parliament wanted to keep the monarchy under control so that it remained a constitutional monarchy. The behaviour of James's son Charles I (1600–1649), who succeeded him in 1625, exacerbated the bad feeling. Between 1642 and 1649 the Royalists ('Cavaliers') fought the Parliamentarians ('Roundheads'). The two sides got their nicknames partly from their appearance. The Roundheads were puritan in dress and attitude.

William Walwyn (1600–1681), a 'Leveller' (a member of a group with proto-communist ideals that wanted to iron out social inequalities), had an interest in the debates of the seventeenth century about toleration. *Tolleration Justified, and Persecution Condemned* (January 1645/6), of which he is almost certainly the author, set forth a series of rejoinders to the arguments of a 'Letter of the London Ministers'. He wanted to argue that all opinions, even those of atheists, ought to be tolerated, and the coexistence of differences of opinion is no reason for division of communion.

Charles I was beheaded in 1649 and during the 1650s England was run as a Commonwealth, headed by a Protector, Oliver Cromwell (1599–1658). Puritanism ruled. Cromwell's followers went about defacing the medieval treasures of English churches. This was the period when much of England's medieval stained glass was smashed in the churches and statues defaced, to render them plain and unadorned as places of worship. The Church of England was displaced as the Established Church for a time.

On Cromwell's death in 1658 a couple of uncertain years followed in which his son Richard (1626–1712) failed to maintain the precarious Commonwealth, and in 1660 Charles II (1630–1685), the son of the previous king, was restored to the throne, and with him the Church of England. This was to remain the Established Church except for a brief period in the reign of the Roman Catholic James II (r. 1685–1688).

Locke wanted to return to the older separation of temporal and spiritual jurisdictions so as to withdraw the interfering fingers of the state from people's religious lives. 'The commonwealth seems to me to be a society of men constituted only for the procuring, preserving, and advancing their own civil interests,' he wrote. He made a list of 'civil interests', in which he considered it was proper for the state to interfere, distinguishing them from spiritual and religious interests: 'Civil interests I call life, liberty, health, and indolency of body; and the possession of outward things, such as money, lands, houses, furniture, and the like.'

The duty of the 'civil magistrate' ought, in his view, to be confined to such matters. The magistrate is:

... by the impartial execution of equal laws, to secure unto all the people in general and to every one of his subjects in particular the just possession of these things belonging to this life. If anyone presume to violate the laws of public justice and equity, established for the preservation of those things, his presumption is to be checked by the fear of punishment, consisting of the deprivation or diminution of those civil interests, or goods, which otherwise he might and ought to enjoy. But seeing no man does willingly suffer himself to be punished by the deprivation of any part of his goods, and much less of his liberty or life, therefore, is the magistrate armed with the force and strength of all his subjects, in order to the punishment of those that violate any other man's rights.

The state, then, has a duty to protect people from one another's intrusive and greedy behaviour. But that is a very different thing from interfering with the liberties of individuals when they are not doing any harm to anyone else, especially when those liberties concern a person's beliefs:

Now that the whole jurisdiction of the magistrate reaches only to these civil concernments, and that all civil power, right and dominion, is bounded and confined to the only care of promoting these things; and that it neither can nor ought in any manner to be extended to the salvation of souls, these following considerations seem unto me abundantly to demonstrate.

Locke gives a list of reasons in which he explores the idea of liberty of conscience:

First, because the care of souls is not committed to the civil magistrate, any more than to other men. It is not committed unto him, I say, by God; because it appears not that God has ever given any such authority to one man over another as to compel anyone to his religion. Nor can any such power be vested in the magistrate by the consent of the people... For no man can, if he would, conform his faith to the dictates of another. All the life and power of true religion consist in the inward and full persuasion of the mind; and faith is not faith without believing.

But if the individual is to enjoy this liberty he must accord it to others too. And so, Locke argues, must the state. But that was not the practice. Requirements such as those imposed in the Test Acts of 1672 and 1678 were designed to ensure that no one could hold an official position or even obtain a university degree who was not a practising member of the Church of England.

In 1689 some English clergy refused to take the oath of allegiance to William and Mary (r. 1689–1702), who succeeded James II. These were known as 'non-jurors' and included a number of bishops, who were subsequently deprived of their sees. Behind the resistance were objections not dissimilar from those which had created the Donatist schism in north Africa in Augustine's time. The question was, after all the upsets of preceding decades, with whom the true succession of ministry lay, and what right the state had to interfere in this fundamentally ecclesiastical question.

These 'civil disabilities' have progressively been removed in England. Nonconformists and Roman Catholics were freed of these social disadvantages with the repeal of the Test Acts in the nineteenth century. Modern developments towards state interference in religious freedom of worship, especially for Moslems, in the interests of resisting terrorism are a reminder that such interference is a recurring danger in European societies.

THE DISCOVERY OF EXPERIMENTAL METHOD AND THE CHALLENGE TO CHRISTIAN CERTAINTIES

We have seen Europe going out into the world, first in ships from the sixteenth century, and then increasingly in its people's thoughts and ideas as contact grew with the religious ideas of other peoples. One of the most important consequences of this new world view for Christian Europe was that it forced it out of its complacency. Trade and commerce brought back objects, pictures, fabrics and customs, as well as languages and books and even people, which inescapably opened up the view of the world Christian Europe had formed in its first fifteen centuries. From among the German merchant settlers in the Baltic came thinkers who were important in encouraging the revolution in assumptions which was beginning. Holland was also often accused of being a ringleader.

From the sixteenth century a revolution in intellectual attitudes began to take place, resulting in a new freedom of thought and the beginnings of fresh speculations. It cannot be overemphasized that this was restricted at first almost entirely to Western Europe. It was not to reach into the Eastern, Orthodox world for some generations. One of the drivers of this change was the Reformation, which had taken the monopoly of advanced study out of the hands of the clergy and made it easier for a wider range of people to benefit from a university education, and to do so at least partly in their own languages, though the official language of scholarship in the West was still Latin. Young men of good family all over Europe began to spend time at university as well as to travel to complete their education.

This began to affect the syllabus within the universities of Europe. Logic had become central during the later Middle Ages but it had also become demanding and complicated as some of the best minds of the day worked to develop its possibilities. The logic course had become extremely onerous by the end of the Middle Ages. Peter Ramus in sixteenth-century France offered a simplified version. It was not very good, but it had the attraction of being much easier.

The real revolution was brought about as a result of the suggestion that traditional Aristotelian logic had been reasoning in the wrong direction, deductively and not inductively. The English philosopher Francis Bacon (1561–1626) suggested that at least when it came to understanding the natural world, valid conclusions which were also truths might best be arrived at inductively.

This was revolutionary. From the ancient world, the medieval West of Europe (as well as the Greek-speaking East and the Arabic-speaking translators of Greek philosophers) had inherited a fixed conviction that, essentially, truth and certainty lay in ideas which were intuitively known and also identifiable by their beauty. The 'Platonic' view of the universe had been absorbed into Christian thought at an early stage. It took it as axiomatic that every thing which had physical existence was merely an exemplification of an 'idea' which was also an 'ideal'. Because physical being was inherently changeable and uncertain, testing things by physical experiments could never disprove the rightness of a theory. If an idea was beautiful and intuitively convincing, experiments could lead to acceptable results only if they confirmed it.

Francis Bacon was suggesting that this was wrong. To learn about elephants, cabbages or anything else in the natural world and discover the laws by which they lived, one must be prepared to test hypotheses to destruction by experiment and observation. If those suggest that the hypotheses were wrong one must change them until, by induction from the study, one arrives at an explanation which fits the perceived realities.

The Baconian method gained support from other parts of Europe, where similar challenges were arising. For example, the calendar still in use in the early sixteenth century (the Julian calendar) was now notably out of step with the actual progress of the seasons, by as much as ten days. Copernicus (1473–1543) was one of the scholars interested in astronomy who had been asked to find a solution. His *On the Revolutions of the Heavenly Bodies* of 1543 reminded its readers that the Fifth Lateran Council (1512–1517) had proposed reform of the calendar. He realized that the first task was to achieve accurate measurement of the length of the year. He challenged the old model in which everything in the heavens was thought to revolve round the earth with a model in which the sun was the centre of the system.

The new calendar (the Gregorian calendar) was eventually begun in 1582, but by then interest had shifted to the implications of these alarming new ideas about the shape and operation of the physical universe. The problem was that the Christian tradition had made a huge investment over many centuries in a certain way of looking at things and had based its position on a mode of interpretation of the Bible, and a certain understanding of the way God had intended it to be read. So change based on fresh scientific thinking could not be risked without a sense that much was at stake. Moreover, recent experience with the consequences of reforming movements had made the Roman Catholic Church particularly sensitive when it came to being open to change.

The Italian philosopher and natural scientist Galileo (1564–1642) began to collect evidence and it seemed to him that Copernicus was right. Sympathizers with Copernicus had argued that it had never been God's intention as he 'dictated' Scripture to include instruction in science. Galileo agreed. The Jesuit Giovanni Battista Riccioli (1598–1671) also tried to emphasize a distinction. The Bible contains teaching on physics and astronomy. Is what it says really about faith and not about science?

Galileo, in a contemporary portrait.

The Council of Trent's strictures on the Bible in its Session IV represented an official attempt to stop the dam from bursting under the pressure of these challenges by insisting that everyone kept to the church's official interpretation of the Bible:

Furthermore, in order to restrain petulant spirits, It decrees, that no one, relying on his own skill, shall… in matters of faith, and of morals pertaining to the edification of Christian doctrine… wresting the sacred Scripture to his own senses, presume to interpret the said sacred Scripture contrary to that sense which holy mother Church… whose it is to judge of the true sense and interpretation of the holy Scriptures… hath held and doth hold; or even contrary to the unanimous consent of the Fathers.

The 'petulant spirits' were not put off. This approach transformed the way the natural world was studied. It caused a radical rethinking of the way the boundary between natural and supernatural was understood. By definition the 'super-' natural was 'above' nature, but it had been accepted throughout Christian history up to this point that chains of causation could pass down from the supernatural world to the natural, the spiritual to the physical. The 'down' is important; the physical realities were seen as inherently inferior to the supernatural. To begin to rely on what could be perceived by the senses as hard evidence, even to dare to reason from such evidence to conclusions about higher realities, was new indeed.

One of the last conceptual barriers to move was this belief that the intellectual universe formed a continuum in which supernatural passed into natural, and the scientific and philosophical were faces or aspects of the same area of study. The modern understanding that science stops at the point where it can verify its conclusions by experiment did not arrive all at once. It seemed to interested and anxious Christian thinkers that the new ideas about the natural world and its place in the universe might threaten Christian orthodoxy.

This, as it turned out, was the beginning of modern science. It is not that there had not been an interest in the subject matter now thought of as 'scientific' in earlier centuries. Aristotle, Latin authors such as Seneca, early Christian commentators on the creation story in Genesis and medieval authors had written about such matters as the nature of heaviness and lightness, falling, motion, elements, cosmos, macrocosm and microcosm. There was a tradition of writing about the six days of creation, to which Robert Grosseteste (c. 1175–1253) contributed in the thirteenth century and Henry of Langenstein (c. 1325–1397) in the fourteenth century. The idea was to hang a number of scientific topics on the exegesis of the scriptural text. The creation of light invited a discussion of optics, for example.

The Bible is manifestly deficient as a scientific textbook; that was growing more and more obvious with the advancement of early modern science. The uncovering of the fossil record was causing disquiet as early as the sixteenth century, with its obvious incompatibility with the story of the creation in Genesis, for it indicates a different sequence of events, occurring on a different timescale. Charles Lyell (1797–1875), in his *Principles of Geology* (published 1830–1833) pointed out that the earth's history could not be as Genesis said.

It was argued in defence, a little desperately, that God could have created a fossil record apparently at odds with the story in Genesis for his own mysterious purposes. But this did not seem such an absurd notion when it came to trying to explain 'God's design in the contrivance of Scripture'. The urge to do this was consciously linked with contemporary enthusiasm for 'design' as an indication that God created the world.

A number of conceptual barriers which stood in the way of initiating the kinds of approach which were now going to make such a difference were beginning to be put aside, though not without some false moves. Exciting hares were started, such as the idea that far from there being only one world, saved by the death of Christ, there might be many worlds.

Could There Be Many Worlds?

It had been fundamental to the Christian faith that the world whose creation is described in Genesis was central to God's plan and the future of the human race on that one world essential to his scheme for the universe. The argument that God could have made more than one world therefore went against the fundamental supposition of the Christian centuries. But daring thinkers were toying with it now.

Bernard de Fontenelle (1657–1757) published his *Entretiens sur la pluralité des mondes* in 1686. It was soon being read outside France and it continued to be popular. The English translation of Jerome de Lande (1732–1807) of the French Academy was published in London in 1803. Fontenelle begins by explaining that he has tried to write in a way even a woman could understand, thus providing a valuable glimpse of the extent to which these new ways of doing science remained a male preserve, though there can be no doubt that they were the subject of general discussion in social conversation involving both sexes. He has, he says:

… represented a woman receiving information on things with which she was entirely unacquainted. I thought this fiction would enable me to give the subject more ornament, and would encourage the female sex in the pursuit of knowledge, by the example of a woman who though ignorant of the sciences, is capable of understanding all she is told, and arranging in her ideas the worlds and vertices.

Fontenelle feels free to be radical, because, he maintains, the old fixed framework is no more:

At the appearance of a certain German named Copernicus, astronomy became simplified… he dislodged the earth from the central situation which had been assigned to it, and in its room placed the sun.

The English review *The Spectator* in 1711 comments on this possibility that there is more than one world, that on one or more of the heavenly bodies which are strewn across the sky may be other peoples with minds and religious beliefs, and conjures with the idea that each may have its own valid ways of understanding the universe and its situation within it. How wasteful it would have been, after all, for God to leave all those worlds empty:

The Author of the Plurality of Worlds draws a very good argument from this Consideration, for the peopling of every Planet, as indeed it seems very probable from the Analogy of Reason, that if no part of Matter, which we are acquainted with, lies waste and useless, those great Bodies which are at such a Distance from us should not be desart and unpeopled, but rather that they should be furnished with Beings adapted to their respective situations.

Sometimes the religious interests which accompanied a taste for science were of a kind which now seem to sit very oddly with the instincts of a scientist. For example, the English mathematician and physicist Isaac Newton (1643–1727) took an active interest in what would now be regarded as at best fringe subjects, such as alchemy and prophetical literature, without any apparent sense that these might be incompatible with the rigours of serious sciences. All sorts of boundaries had yet to be defined and science had to determine its limits and decide where the 'natural' ended and the 'supernatural' began within this new universe of modern scientific discourse. Yet Newton's *Mathematical Principles of Natural Philosophy* (1687) shows a remote God ordering the cosmos, not a daily intervener in the details of life. The philosopher and scientist Robert Boyle (1627–1691), too, toyed with ideas between the chemical and the mechanical, such as 'dregs' and 'denseness'; some contemporary alchemical studies were testing the boundary between natural and supernatural, physical and metaphysical. Boyle identified 'mechanical' laws as superior to the Aristotelian explanations. He liked this approach partly because it allowed for God's acting or operating in the world according to the laws of nature he had himself built into it.

Isaac Newton.

New Kinds of Problem with the Bible

One of the biggest areas of emerging concern was the apparent challenge to the truth of the Bible. Concerns were expressed that respect for the Bible was going to be challenged by scientific enquiries which led to conclusions in conflict with what the Bible seems to say if read in its obvious sense. It had been recognized for centuries that some of the things the Bible says have to be taken metaphorically or figuratively, or it contradicts itself. But this method of dealing with its apparent anomalies had gone out of fashion under the pressure of reforming insistences that the church's interpretations were of merely human origin and 'Scripture alone' was to be trusted, taken at its face meaning.

The challenges which were now emerging were, however, something new. They went beyond pointing out that the Bible did not always agree with itself, to suggesting that it did not always agree with the observable facts about the world. One way of dealing with this was to try to identify a difference between things which the new science (with its inferences from experiments) could conclude by the use of reason, and things which can be known only because God chooses to make them available by 'revelation'.

One distinction had been familiar from the very beginning of Christian thought. Some things (the existence of God, the nature of God: was he good, merciful, just, powerful, immortal?) could be approached with the aid of human reason alone. These had been the subject of discussion in classical philosophy. Other things (the story of Jesus' life and death and the difference this was believed to have made to the eternal future of sinful human beings) were 'known about' only from what the Bible said, and from subsequent discussion by Christian authors. The evidence for these was historical rather than rational, although once accepted this evidence could be analysed by reason.

Boyle writes that the Bible tells us things we could not discover by reason alone:

Revelation gratifys and obliges Reason by discloseing to it divers excellent, desireable and to us important, Truths that Reason of it selfe could never have discover'd, such as are the Order and Time of the Creation [of the world, and of] the first Man & Woman; the certain History of Adams Fall, & the other Transactions that preceded the Universal Deluge; divers Particulars about the Creation, Immortality, Employments and Performances of good Angels; the Decrees that God has made about the destruction of this World or of [this] Vortex of ours, and the State of Mens Souls and Bodys after Death; the Way of worshipping him that is most pleasing to him; the Mystery of the Blessed Trinity; the Incarnation of the Son of God; his satisfaction for the sins of Men; and in summe the Oeconomy of Mans Salvation in which are divers Mysterys so noble and so abstruse, that not only we Men must owe them to Revelation, but the holy Scripture teaches us, that the Angels themselves desire to looke into them, & do receive Informations about them by the Intervention of the Church [1 Peter 1:12].

The Bible with its 'Divine Light' is also clearer, says Boyle, about things we can glimpse by reasoning, but only 'very dimly, incogently & defectively'. They are so blurred when seen in this way that the famous philosophers of the past could not get very far and disagreed:

That the World had a Beginning, and that some Intelligent Being was the Author of it, is a Truth not unattainable by Reason, but yet not so manifest to it but that Aristotle and all his numerous sect held the world to be Eternal; and the Epicureans & other Atomists, who denied that, yet affirmd it to have been made not by God or any Intelligent Cause, but by the casual Concourse of Atoms.

On providence it is pointed out that:

Aristotle and divers others are acknowledged to have confind it to Heaven; & he seems to have denied, that God takes Care of particulars by denying that he knows them.

Boyle was seeking for a 'lodging' in the intellectual life of the Christian believer for new kinds of scientific interest, in a way that need not disrupt his Christian belief. The first enquirers of this sort had no intention of turning the faith on its head.

The method of argument from analogy, which had been popular in the Middle Ages, had a period of revival during the eighteenth and at the beginning of the nineteenth century. A passage from a 1711 edition of *The Spectator* illustrates the way thinkers looked for patterns so as to infer that what worked on a small and observable scale might be true for the universe at large:

Every part of Matter is peopled: Every green Leaf swarms with Inhabitants. There is scarce a single Humour in the Body of a Man, or of any other Animal, in which our Glasses do not discover Myriads of living Creatures. The surface of Animals is also covered with other Animals... nay, we find in the most solid Bodies, as in Marble it selfe, innumerable Cells and Cavities that are crowded with such imperceptible Inhabitants, as are too little for the naked Eye to discover.

Joseph Butler (1692–1752) wrote an influential book, *Analogy of Religion Natural and Revealed* (1736), in which he pursued this method further and tried to show in detail how divine lordship of the world accorded with the behaviour of the natural world. Despite all these efforts at getting round the newly recognized problems, it was obvious that some explanation of Scripture's 'unsatisfactory' form and content was needed if the new scientifically minded generation was not to be put off reading it altogether.

Boyle said he had heard criticisms about 'the seemingly Disjoyned Method of that Book [the Bible]'. Ironically, this was a version of the problem with which Augustine of Hippo had grappled in the fourth and fifth centuries and Gregory the Great in the sixth. Confronted by critics with the evident grammatical and stylistic oddities in the text of Scripture, Gregory had argued that God cannot be constrained by 'the laws of Donatus', one of the principal authorities on Latin grammar. The Word of God has its own laws, indeed it makes the rules of language. Similarly, Boyle seems to suggest, neither the laws of nature nor those which determine the form and content of Scripture are to be understood in their completeness in human terms. He responds to critics with the argument that:

The Book of Grace doth but therein resemble the Book of Nature; wherein the Stars… are not more Nicely nor Methodically plac'd than the Passages of Scripture… That it became not the Majesty of God to suffer himself to be fetter'd to Humane Laws of Method.

It remained a problem that the Bible had to be accepted as a source of reliable historical information if it was to stand beside the new challenge from reason and these scientific insights and proposals. 'The Christian religion has very strong evidences. It, indeed, appears in some degree strange to reason; but in History we have undoubted facts,' insisted James Boswell (1740–1795), the biographer of Johnson, in 1763.

MIRACLES AND PROPHECY

One notable aspect of the boundary-defining exercise of the new scientific method was the discussion of miracles and prophecy, and the ways they could be used as evidence by serious thinkers. In the early church and the Middle Ages this had not been seen as a methodological difficulty, for the supernatural powers of God could be taken to be more than capable of acting outside the laws which created nature usually followed, and God, being eternal, knew the future and could inspire his prophets to tell his people about it. Questions about futurity were in themselves a familiar stamping ground of Aristotle and later of early Christian and medieval debate. They go directly to the problem of God's foreknowledge and predestination of events and the possibility of human free choice. A great deal of thought had been expended on this complex of problems, which Anselm of Canterbury described as 'a most famous question'.

But in the new climate, David Hume (1711–1776) in his *Essay on Miracles* (1748) pointed out that it is impossible to prove a miracle has occurred. Miracles are simply not experimentally verifiable. Similarly, prophecy is inherently uncertain as long as the events prophesied remain in the future.

A New Kind of Bible Study

In the nineteenth century it began to be asked whether the Bible could still be taken as the Word of God in the medieval way, that is, as dictated by the Holy Spirit to its human authors so that every word was to be weighed with the respect that it required. Or was it possible to see it as an ancient text which had come into being in the way other ancient texts had done, and was subject to study in a similar way? The intellectual movement which is often described as German Romanticism, though its effects were felt far outside Germany, was hugely influential here. Samuel Taylor Coleridge (1772–1834) in England, for example, explored its ideas.

One of the most important works in transforming attitudes was *The Life of Jesus* by Friedrich Schleiermacher (1768–1834). He had been born into a Reformed family and educated in a Moravian school, but as he studied further his ideas became more and more radical. His great contribution to the future of Bible study was to argue that the techniques scholarship uses to establish whether a piece of writing is authentic (that is, was written when it was claimed and by the author claimed for it) could be used in the study of Scripture too. Insofar as it was the work of human authors it should be subjected to the same sort of textual criticism and analysis. Such ideas were taken forward in the course of the nineteenth century by David Strauss (1808–1874), whose *Life of Jesus* (1835) saw the gospels as mythological, and Ludwig Feuerbach (1804–1872). Ernest Renan (1823–1892) in his *Vie de Jésus* (1863) suggested that Jesus was not a theologian and had perhaps been merely a human leader of great personal charisma.

The Evidences for the Christian faith are Questioned

The effect of the shift to evidence-based reasoning was, then, having a number of substantial effects, some of them threatening to the comfortable Christian certainties which had scarcely featured in the recent debates of the Reformation in the West. With the emergence of the idea that it was important to seek to rely on evidence came questions about the evidence for Christian beliefs. Many of those actively involved in the 'scientific revolution' also discussed these matters.

What exactly were the 'evidences' of Christianity once one looked behind the account in the Bible? The idea that the very design of the universe is evidence that it had a creator is there in Romans 1:18–20. It was developed by Aquinas in the thirteenth century at the beginning of the *Summa Theologiae*, as he set out his arguments for the existence of God. The same 'argument from design' can be taken to indicate what

Friedrich Schleiermacher.

CHARLES DARWIN AND *THE ORIGIN OF SPECIES*

Charles Darwin (1809–1882) began as a student of medicine before turning to biology. He spent five years voyaging on the ship the *Beagle* and keeping a journal, which he subsequently published. His observations and collection of fossils and geological and other specimens had raised questions for him, which he began to discuss privately with friends. In 1859 he published *On the Origin of Species*, in which he set out a theory that explained the phenomena he had observed. This theory, the theory of 'evolution', postulates that variations of form and function in the natural world can be explained by a process of adjustment of creatures to their local environmental needs, as the less well-adapted die and the better-adapted survive to pass on their genes to their offspring, until by 'natural selection' a new 'species' is established.

Darwin's arguments aroused hostility, not only from those who said that they were

A contemporary watercolour depicting the *Beagle* on its voyage.

incompatible with a literal reading of the description of the process of creation in the Book of Genesis, but also from rival scientists who had competing ideas of their own.

Darwin's own religious faith (he had been brought up in a Nonconformist family but when he planned to become a clergyman it was to have been in the Church of England) was shaken by the illness and death of his daughter Annie. He had in any case grown up with a father and brother and also a grandfather who were 'Freethinkers' (the term seems to have crept into view at the end of the seventeenth century). He had some sympathy with William Paley's 'proof' from the design of the world that it must have had a creator. It took the slow process of reaching his conclusions about the origin of species, however, for him to abandon his belief in the literal truth of the Bible's account, at least so far as to treat it as historical, although he did not necessarily distance himself from its moral teaching. He was not supported by the Church of England's more senior figures, but soon a younger generation of clerics began to publish in cautious approval.

kind of God the creator is (powerful, good, beautiful and so on). William Paley (1743–1805) was the author of *A View of the Evidences of Christianity* (1794), in which he discussed the external evidences which seem to support the historical accuracy of the account given in Scripture or which open it to question. More influential still was the vivid picture he drew in his *Natural Theology* (1802). On a walk we may see rocks lying about and find ourselves able to believe the landscape took its shape by chance. But find a watch lying on the ground and study its construction, and it is impossible to believe that so complex and refined a design did not have an intelligent and purposeful creator.

But would such a God 'care'? Was he not a mere machine-operator? Did he even make the machine? Here were laid the foundations of the modern debate as to whether a biblical Creationism is compatible with a scientific account of the way the world began. As Boyle remarked, 'Whereas the Scripture assures us, that Gods Care extends to Sparrows themselves, & that not only good or bad Actions, but Thoughts too are by him punish'd and rewarded.'

Deism: Simplifying God and Creation

One way of dealing with these unsettling questions was to strip Christianity of the complexities of doctrine which had developed over the centuries. Emmanuel Kant's (1724–1804) *Critique of Pure Reason* (1781) and David Hume's *Dialogues on Natural Religion* (published after his death, in 1779) are particularly influential examples, among many throughout Europe, of a growing literature of discussion of the limits and possibilities of pursuing theological questions by 'reason' alone.

Some thinkers were ready to assert a plain 'Deism'. In France Jean Bodin (c. 1530–1596) was already exploring the idea that the most that could be clear to a reasonable person was that there was one supreme being. Much of the strength of arguments of a Deist sort lay in their apparent self-evidency, their appeal to the notion that everyone must agree with them as soon as they heard them.

Then there were the Unitarians, who did not see how the doctrine of the Trinity could be sustained and who argued that if there was a God he was simply one God. Such ideas were first seriously floated in modern Europe by the sixteenth-century uncle (1525–1562) and nephew (1539–1604) who shared the surname Sozini, and whose theories became known via a Latinized version of their name as Socinianism. Their thinking had some popularity among the educated classes of Poland and other parts of Eastern Europe.

An eighteenth-century engraving of Emmanuel Kant.

Atheism and Scepticism

It tended to be assumed that atheism must go with moral corruption, until this was challenged, especially by the French philosopher Pierre Bayle (1647–1706), a Calvinist turned Roman Catholic who had returned to Calvinism. The truth was that the new, wider range of ways of thinking about Christianity and the accompanying challenge to its claims of monopoly had opened the way to making atheism socially acceptable in some parts of Europe, especially where intellectuals prided themselves on advanced ideas.

Robert Southey (1774–1843) wrote to John Estlin (1747–1817), a Unitarian minister at Bristol, who had sent him one of his writings about atheism:

I see many Atheists and Sceptics, and, as I never decline controversy, seldom see them without an argument. Your discourse does not touch upon what appears to me the principal cause of Atheism: the existence of physical and moral evil and the difficulty of reconciling its existence with that of a God, powerful and benevolent. The system of optimism, to which I assent and which I, therefore, profess is not without its difficulties, great and many; but every other system appears to me to have more and greater; and I therefore assent to this. To have used the word believe would have been perhaps expressing myself too strongly.

Southey did not altogether like what he saw, commenting that 'those who are decidedly Atheistical… are in general self-satisfied'. It seemed to him that there were two 'camps' of Christians: 'those who allow everything, or nothing, to authority'.

EARLY MODERN MISSION MOVES ON

The way Christians thought about mission began to be transformed by the opening up of new understandings about the way other peoples thought, both within and outside Europe. The Moravians emerged from the tradition launched by John Hus. They were Protestants of a fairly radical sort, and pacifists. In 1722 Moravians took refuge on the estate of Count Nicholas von Zinzendorf (1700–1760), where, together with a number of like-minded 'Pietists', they formed a community which they called 'God's house'. The style of their lives was quiet and industrious and they were productive.

At first they were concentrated geographically in Moravia, but in due course the Moravians sent missionaries as far as Greenland, Africa and

A Moravian mission in South Africa in the early nineteenth century.

the Americas and there are still communities in parts of the world far from Europe. These were not colonialists or colonizers. They simply wanted to spread the gospel. At the same time, they were beginning to see mission less as the bringing of a faith already complete and perfect to a benighted people who lacked the true religion, and more as a conversation in which the missionary might learn something and modify his approach accordingly.

The Moravians had an influence on John Wesley (1703–1791), the founder of Methodism. The story, as Wesley eventually told it, concerned 'four young gentlemen of Oxford... Mr. John Wesley, Fellow of Lincoln College; Mr. Charles Wesley, Student of Christ Church; Mr. Morgan, Commoner of Christ Church; and Mr. Kirkham, of Merton College' who, in 1729, 'began to spend some evenings in a week together, in reading, chiefly, the Greek Testament. The next year two or three of Mr. John Wesley's pupils desired the liberty of meeting with them; and afterwards one of Mr. Charles Wesley's pupils. It was in 1732, that Mr. Ingham, of Queen's College, and Mr. Broughton, of Exeter, were added to their number. To these, in April, was joined Mr. Clayton, of Brazen-nose [Brasenose], with two or three of his pupils. About the same time Mr.

THE SLAVE TRADE

Christians had been implicated in the acceptance of slavery from the beginning. The advice to those who were slaves was to accept their lot patiently and concentrate on serving their masters well. It was not suggested that those who owned slaves should work for the abolition of the system. Contemporary society's arrangements could not have survived such a change.

After the fall of the Roman empire much of northern Europe began to develop the land-tenure system known as feudalism, which also depended on the bonded labour of serfs if it was to work. French feudalism came to an end with the French Revolution at the end of the eighteenth century. Feudalism was slow to die out in Russia and other parts of eastern and northern Europe, particularly in Austria, Hungary, Prussia and Poland. Polish serfdom was still alive in 1768, when a lord's right of life or death over his serfs was ended. The abolition of serfdom took place in Romania only in 1864. In Russia it ended with the revolution of 1917.

A new sort of slavery had begun with the discovery of the New World and the growth of a trade in captured Africans, who were sold to the plantation owners in the southern states of America and the Caribbean islands. The English politician William Beckford (1709–1770), father of the William Beckford (1760–1844) who built Fonthill Abbey, published *Remarks upon the Situation of Negroes in Jamaica* (1788). He restricted his remarks to the observations he had himself as a plantation owner been able to make of slaves on the plantations, touching only in passing upon their much greater sufferings in the process of their seizure, shipping across the Atlantic and waiting to be sold on to their future owners. He wrote his book in the belief that 'political and national advantage will be the consequence of a system directed to the alleviation of their general sufferings; if it can be done without infringing upon the rights of individuals'.

William Wilberforce (1759–1833), who became a Methodist, was drawn into the movement to abolish this slave trade at a meeting in 1787 and began to campaign in the English parliament, of which he was a member. The problem was that there were powerful vested interests anxious not to have their businesses disrupted. It took him until 1807 to achieve abolition by the passing of an Act of Parliament, and in the meantime he had become interested in other needs of social reform, particularly the eradication of 'vice' (by which he meant sexual immorality). He had, however, done enough to ensure that endorsement of slavery would no longer be tolerable to the Christian conscience in Europe.

James Hervey was permitted to meet with them; and in 1735, Mr. Whitfield.' They began to be known as 'Methodists' because of their methodical approach to the Christian life.

On 14 October 1735, with his brother Charles (1707–1778) and two friends, John Wesley 'took boat for Gravesend, in order to embark for Georgia. Our end in leaving our native country was not to avoid want (God having given us plenty of temporal blessings), not to gain the dung or dross of riches or honour; but singly this – to save our souls, to live wholly to the glory of God'.

There is a faint echo here of the 'mission by coracle' of the early Celtic saints, who similarly cast themselves on the water to see where God would take them, leaving all that they knew at home and abandoning all thought of material advancement.

'Believing the denying ourselves... might by the blessing of God be helpful to us, we wholly left off the use of flesh and wine and confined ourselves to vegetable food, chiefly rice and biscuit,' Wesley remembers.

The Wesleys were in like-minded company. On 17 October, John Wesley records, 'I began to learn German, in order to converse with the Moravians, six and twenty of whom we had on board.' On 20 October, David Nitschmann (1676–1758), bishop of the Moravians, and two others began to learn English.

The group saw the spontaneous formation of a religious community:

We now began to be a little regular. Our common way of living was this: from four in the morning till five each of us used private prayer. From five to seven, we read the Bible together, carefully comparing it (that we might not lean to our own understandings) with the writings of the earliest ages. At seven we breakfasted.

The day was then spent in study, particularly learning languages, prayer, instructing the children on board and reading to the adult passengers.

The interest in the Moravians did not end with the crossing of the Atlantic. On 28 February 1736, two weeks after the party had landed in America, John Wesley went to a meeting of the Moravian brethren. He was able to observe an approach to church-planting quite different from that of the Church of England, with its historic and territorially fixed parish boundaries, livings and land-tenure arrangement. It seemed to him much closer to the simplicities of the early church than anything he had known before:

John Wesley.

They met to consult concerning the affairs of their church… After several hours spent in conference and prayer, they proceeded to the election and ordination of a bishop. The great simplicity as well as solemnity of the whole almost made me forget the seventeen hundred years between, and imagine myself in one of those assemblies where form and state were not, but Paul the tent-maker or Peter the fisherman presided; yet with the demonstration of the Spirit and of power.

But John Wesley was to find as his own movement began that such departures from the ordinary patterns were readily misunderstood. From the late 1730s he was back in England, putting his principles into practice in preaching and in the encouragement of greater holiness and strictness in local Christian life.

Wesley's achievement from this point is significant as an illustration of an important face of modern mission: the realization that there is a place for 'mission' to those who are already nominally Christian, and within the territories of Christendom, to awaken a more lively faith. This had already struck Bernard of Clairvaux in the twelfth century as a significant choice to be made when he resisted the call to preach the Second Crusade at first, in favour of concentrating on mission to the people of God in Western Europe.

8

Christian Europe in the Modern World

ORTHODOX THEOLOGY AND COMMUNISM

A significant strand in the social upheaval which accompanied and followed the Reformation in the West was the stirring of ideas which in a later age would be described as 'Communist'. Sixteenth-century precedents already hint at something which looks very like an early form of Communism. For example, in the 1520s, Joss Fritz (fl. 1502–1519), who was a serf of the bishop of Speyer, made several attempts to rouse the local peasantry to call for the reform of society and the abolition of the ruling classes.

The German political economist Karl Marx (1818–1883) began modern Communism. He revolutionized the understanding of the way society works in ways which affected the Christian history of Eastern Europe for more than a century, and whose effects still linger in the various forms of European socialism and the economic aftermath of Communist control in the societies of Eastern Europe.

In the *Communist Manifesto* he published in 1848, Marx began with the claim that the history of all societies up to that point had been a story of class struggle. He argued that the class enemies of the proletariat, the oppressed ordinary working people, were not the nobility, but the bourgeoisie. He believed that their overthrow and replacement by rule of 'the people' was inevitable everywhere.

These views were not greatly influential in Marx's own time but once they were taken up by political activists they were to have a huge impact. Partly as a result of the influence of these ideas in Russia and other parts of Eastern Europe, Christian theologians trained within the churches of Eastern Orthodoxy began to write and speak out more loudly than had been usual since the schism of 1054.

Nicolas Berdyaev (1874–1948) became a Marxist as a student at Kiev and was ejected from the university in 1898 in consequence, after a student demonstration. He grew into an Orthodox believer but a critical article about the Holy Synod got him sent to Siberia for life for heresy in

1913. The revolution and the First World War allowed him to continue to write and teach until he was expelled in 1922 with other intellectuals who were causing concern to the authorities, on the 'philosophers' ship'. He first tried to settle in Germany but then moved to Paris, where he was able to found an academy and live relatively comfortably among French intellectuals until his death. He was particularly interested in the

REVOLUTIONARY RUSSIA

Russia saw something of a revival of Orthodox faith at the end of the nineteenth and the beginning of the twentieth century. Religious and philosophical meetings were held in St Petersburg between 1901 and 1903, and charismatic enthusiasms and mystical trends emerged. The 'professional' religious were still numerous. Before the revolution of 1917 there were, it is estimated, more than 55,000 churches and over 500 monasteries and an almost equal number of convents, containing nearly 100,000 monks and nuns.

Lenin making a speech in St Petersburg, a photograph taken in 1917.

But the revolution decisively separated church and state, and privileges which had proceeded from the patronage of the tsars naturally ceased. Soviet rule was militantly atheist, despite an official claim to religious toleration. Orthodoxy went underground and survived quietly among the people. After the death of the patriarch in 1925 the Soviet authorities would not allow a successor to be elected. Seminaries were closed to prevent the training of more priests. Young people who joined the Communist Party were encouraged to torment worshippers and to vandalize churches.

importance of protecting individual creativity against the oppressive effects of social structures of a mechanistic sort.

Pavel Florensky (1882–1937) was the son of an Orthodox priest who began his studies at Moscow University and founded a society with a group of friends which was to dedicate itself to 'Christian struggle'. This led to his arrest in 1906 and he gradually lost his youthful interest in Christian socialism. His first important work was *An Essay in Orthodox Theodicy*, written in the form of letters to Christ as an archetypal Friend and exploring the theology of Christian friendship. He was also interested in the Holy Wisdom. His theological work was interrupted after the revolution, when he was obliged to work on the State Plan for the Electrification of Russia, at the instigation of Trotsky. He went on writing on Christian theological topics and Russian art, however, as well as making an ambitious attempt at a Christian interpretation of Einstein's theory of relativity. More than once he was sent into exile and sentenced to years in labour camps. He seems to have been executed in 1937.

Sergei Bulgakov (1871–1944), also the son of an Orthodox priest, became interested in Marxism but he rapidly became disillusioned and began to write critically on the subject, partly under the influence of Leo Tolstoy (1828–1910) and Fyodor Dostoevsky (1821–1881). He became a Christian socialist and adopted some of the ideas of Florensky on the Holy Wisdom. In 1922 he was among the leading intellectuals sent away on the 'philosophers' ship' by the Bolshevik government. Arriving in Prague, he began to teach church law and theology at the university. In 1925 he founded an Institute of Orthodox Theology. He was an enthusiast for the ecumenical unification of Orthodox and Anglican churches and helped to found the Fellowship of SS Alban and Sergius as an Anglican-Orthodox ecumenical fellowship.

CHRISTIANITY AND SOCIAL RESPONSIBILITY

The Industrial Revolution and Christianity

Although the Industrial Revolution was to bring great prosperity to Western, and later to Eastern Christian Europe, in those countries where it began the social changes it brought about were harmful to working people at first. Workers moved in from the countryside to work in factories in the towns. Parents and even quite small children alike worked long hours, often in degrading and exploitative conditions. The miserable lives of workers and their families, and the way small children worked in conditions which often led to their deformity and early death, prompted men of conscience to begin to raise concerns. Henry Mayhew (1812–1887) made the effort to meet and talk to the labouring poor, and wrote *London Labour and the London Poor* (1851), adding a new volume ten years later when he had interviewed thieves and prostitutes too. There arose a desire in Christian minds to emphasize the 'dignity of labour'. Holman Hunt's (1827–1910) picture of the carpenter's shop in which Jesus was brought up is an example. There was also concern that such an idea must be meaningless where labouring life so obviously lacked any dignity.

This was an early counterpart to the Marxist approach, which was also eager to dignify labour, but at the cost of destroying a society in

In Holman Hunt's picture, the figure of Jesus is throwing a shadow on the wall, which 'foretells' his own future crucifixion.

which privilege could flourish. Many of its leading apologists were from the British Isles, where the Industrial Revolution was more advanced than almost everywhere else and its drawbacks became apparent soonest.

Thomas Carlyle (1795–1881) deplored the way, as it seemed to him, the Industrial Revolution had made everything mechanical and limited the possibilities for the individual to make a difference:

In former times the wise men, the enlightened lovers of their kind [i.e., philanthropists], who appeared generally as Moralists, Poets or Priests [applied] themselves chiefly to regulate, increase and purify the inward primary powers of man... the wise men, who now appear as Political Philosophers, deal exclusively with the Mechanical province; and occupying themselves in counting-up and estimating men's motives, strive by curious checking and balancing, and other adjustments of profit and loss, to guide them to their advantage.

CHRISTIAN MYSTICISM AND SPIRITUALITY

Christian mysticism has gone through several phases. In the West it concentrated at first on the idea that a few individuals experience a 'rapture' in which they seem to be carried out of themselves into a brief ecstatic union with God. Paul describes something like this in the New Testament.

Pseudo-Dionysius, a fifth-century author writing in Greek, who gained a high reputation from the myth that he was the first-century Dionysius the Areopagite, had described a celestial hierarchy stretching unimaginably above ordinary earthly human experience and suggested that even the names of God are beyond our understanding. This was a way of thinking congenial to the mystics of Greek-speaking Christianity, because it chimed with the Platonism they had adopted and modified to fit Christian teachings.

In the later Middle Ages in the West, a 'negative' mysticism became fashionable, in which thinkers such as the German Meister Eckhart (1260–1328) began to argue that the only thing we can know about God is that we cannot really know him. This was a revival of the ideas of Pseudo-Dionysius.

Mysticism was consciously revived and made intellectually respectable in the modern Orthodox world by Vladimir Lossky (1903–1958), born in Germany to Russian exiles, in his book on the mystical theology of the Eastern church.

Mysticism has always been closely associated with devotion to, or the sense of a special relationship with, the Holy Spirit, and even in periods and places where mysticism has not been widely practised or revered there have been outbreaks of 'Spirit-led' enthusiasm, such as occurred in early Methodism and can be seen among the Pentecostalist churches of the present day.

This age is:

… not an Heroical, Devotional, Philosophical, or Moral Age, but, above all other, the Mechanical Age. It is the Age of Machinery, in every outward and inward sense of that word; the age which, with its whole undivided might, forwards, teaches and practises the great art of adapting means to ends… On every hand, the living artisan is driven from his workshop, to make room for a speedier inanimate one.

Carlyle deplored how in the modern age:

Nothing follows its spontaneous course, nothing is left to be accomplished by old natural methods. Everything has its cunningly devised implements… it is not done by hand.

The grimness and intellectual as well as bodily poverty of peasant life was being replaced in industrialized societies by a new kind of grinding poverty and misery for working people.

The emergence of a sense of Christian global responsibility has followed on from these nineteenth-century attempts to take responsibility for society's ills and try to mend them. It now has new dimensions and fresh anxieties as the developing world begins to catch up with industrialized Western Europe and the United States and challenges their commercial supremacy. The economic balance is shifting and with it the balance of power in the world. At the same time as the threat of 'global warming' is making it politically necessary for the developed world to be seen to exercise restraint in many of the activities associated with prosperity, large populations in emerging economies are wanting to claim their own share and are bound to ask why they too should exercise restraint when they have not yet enjoyed the benefits of industrialization for themselves and enjoyed the resulting prosperity.

The Social Gospel

It was a long-standing early tradition that one of the acceptable 'penitential acts' Christians might do in order to make up for sins they had committed was alms-giving. But the main purpose of giving alms was to benefit the sinner and the help given to the needy was thought of as secondary and almost incidental.

The needs of the poor and helpless had been carefully catered for in early Christianity when they were members of the Christian community, but the idea that there was a general Christian responsibility to ease want and suffering was slow to emerge. There was a strong feeling for many centuries that a distinction was to be drawn between the 'deserving' poor and those who were in need because they had been feckless or idle and had not done what they could to earn a living. Under the Elizabethan Poor Law in England, for example, the poor were to be assisted only if they were known to be local people, so that vagabonds could not wander into a parish and expect to be helped. Something of the same punitive approach lingered into the early modern and Victorian period in England, when the workhouse was a house of correction as much as a shelter and place of work for the destitute.

The twentieth century saw the beginnings of a more generous awareness that the roots of poverty may be complex. William Temple

(1881–1944) launched a 'social Anglicanism' with his book *Christianity and Social Order* (1942). Catholic Action was at work in many countries, especially in the nineteenth century, forming groups of lay people striving to ensure that Christian principles left their mark on society, including the relief of the needy. In these ways a traditional Christian preoccupation has acquired a 'new look' in the modern world in the area of social responsibility.

Albert Schweitzer (1875–1965) began life as a musician and then moved to a medical career. He became a Christian missionary, setting up a hospital in modern Gabon (then French Equatorial Africa) and treating major diseases of the area such as sleeping sickness and leprosy. He won the Nobel Peace Prize in 1952. He lived in Africa from 1913 and cut himself off from Europe except for periodic visits to raise funds for his work. He was also a

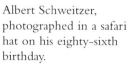

Albert Schweitzer, photographed in a safari hat on his eighty-sixth birthday.

writer and thinker, emphasizing the role of the 'historical' Jesus as a complement to the example he was trying to set of practical Christianity.

'Liberation theology' is a Roman Catholic movement of 'Christian socialism' which had its main focus in South America after the Second Vatican Council, under the influence of the Jesuits. It saw Jesus as the liberator of oppressed peoples. It was condemned by the Vatican in the 1980s; the future Pope Benedict XVI (r. 2005–present) was among those who made his disapproval known.

Modern Theologies

We have seen Christian influence on the development of thought in Europe radically challenged in the period of rational and scientific challenge now known as the Enlightenment. It has been questioned further in the modern world, but with differences.

One of the most notable of these differences has been the arrival of a new generation of 'leaders' of thought in Europe, individuals who have changed the way society sees things, launching words and ideas which have entered the general consciousness. This seems to be a different phenomenon from the emergence of the Fathers of early Christian Europe. They were not formally identified as 'Fathers' until about the sixteenth century, though they had undoubtedly been influential and specially respected for a thousand years. The question Christians asked about their writings was not how original or influential their ideas were, but how faithfully they transmitted the one faith and how satisfactorily they resolved heretical suggestions which appeared to challenge it. Members of the new, modern generation of leaders of thought have felt free to think what they like and to propose what seems to them to be true. They have gained respect (or condemnation) by saying something new rather than by defending established positions. And the result has been major changes of direction for Christian thought.

Søren Kierkegaard, in a drawing made in 1838.

Rethinking the Study of the Bible and Christian Theology

The Dane Søren Kierkegaard (1813–1855) wrote partly in response to what the German philosopher Georg Hegel had said a generation earlier. Hegel (1770–1831) had had an enormous impact throughout Europe by arguing that it was no longer necessary to accept that philosophy would always go round and round, never resolving the great perennial questions, but that it could now be applied in practical ways to resolve contemporary problems; he suggested that this process could even be made comprehensible to non-philosophers and therefore popular. Kierkegaard was hostile to the inadequacies of the church of his day as he saw it in Denmark. His writings were susceptible of a wide range of interpretation – which is what he intended – and were taken as a starting-point for a good deal of radical speculation in succeeding generations. He had dared to ask awkward questions and that encouraged others.

Alfred Loisy (1857–1940), a professor of Hebrew, boldly led a trend in Roman Catholic theology towards a fundamental review of the methods and purposes of Bible study. For example, it no longer seemed to him acceptable to remain enslaved to the expectation that the Bible's account of creation was to be taken literally. Nor could he go on teaching that Moses was the author of the Pentateuch. He argued that the quality and historical reliability of the books of Scripture was variable and that they must be read on that understanding. Pope Leo XIII (r. 1878–1903) and Pope Pius X (r. 1903–1914) both condemned him and he lost his

PSYCHOLOGY AND THE SOUL

Psychology has altered the understanding of the relation between the 'inner', spiritual person and the 'outer', bodily person. When Guibert of Nogent spoke of his 'inner man' in the late eleventh century he meant his soul. He thought the most important thing he could do with his life was to learn to regulate this 'inner man' so as to fit himself for heaven. The word 'psychology' is derived from the Greek *psyche*, 'soul' (Latin *anima*), but it has been primarily concerned with the mind (Latin *animus*) and the way it affects the body. Sigmund Freud (1856–1939), as an Austrian neurologist, perceived something of the complexity of the relationship of the brain as a physical organ to the mind, but he did not include the concept of the soul in his explanations of the clinical manifestations of psychiatric illness. He developed a theory of the 'unconscious mind', as a powerful force in human conduct of whose activities the individual might not be fully aware, but which was actively working out its own agenda of repression and displacement of desires. Here was a 'scientific' replacement for the Christian tradition that the effect of original sin is to make us behave in ways we neither approve nor seem able fully to control. Freudian ideas found their way into other influential explanations of the world, including Marxism and feminism.

Carl Jung (1875–1961) broke through other conventional boundaries. He included religious explanations in his psychological theories, but in a rather broad and sweeping way. He suggested that the old Christian certainties about the absolute individuality of each person as a soul to be saved or lost might be misplaced; there might even be a 'collective unconscious'. He blurred the lines between the contributions of the world religions, including elements of the oriental religions, in his theories and he did not rule out areas of study Christianity had long rejected as dangerous or unsound. For example, he was ready to dabble in astrology and alchemy. The main thrust of his rebalancing of assumptions was to be critical of too much reliance on hard science and logic and to call for a revival of 'spirituality'.

Carl Jung.

position at the Catholic Institute of Paris in 1893. The Vatican condemned his writings, and he was excommunicated in 1908.

Adolph von Harnack (1851–1930) came from the German-speaking community in the Baltic lands. He was born in Livonia, under Russian domination at the time but now part of Estonia, into an academic family. He was a church historian as well as a theologian, and was therefore well aware how far what he proposed conformed with or departed from the Christian tradition. One of his main scholarly interests lay in working out how late antique philosophy had entered into early Christian traditions. This led him to ask awkward questions about the way the early church had identified its key doctrines. His controversial early lectures on such subjects as Gnosticism soon brought him to notice as a young teacher at the University of Leipzig.

He realized how inadequate were the available editions of many of the texts of early Christianity and of contemporary texts which had interacted with them. With some of his colleagues he set about making an edition of the *Apostolic Fathers*, a small group of key texts, some of which were once candidates for inclusion in the Bible.

He conceived the idea of writing a comprehensive history of Christian dogma, published in three volumes between 1885 and 1898. This was a quite different concept from that which had produced the series of summas of theology (systematic treatments of all the main doctrinal questions in an approved order), running from the twelfth-century *Sentences* of Peter Lombard (c. 1100–1160) and the thirteenth-century *Summa Theologiae* of Thomas Aquinas. Their purpose had been to organize Christian theology under headings and provide the student with a list of authoritative opinions drawn from key early Christian writers supporting the orthodox view and arguments from the same sources with which to rebut unorthodox suggestions. Harnack was asking a different question. How had these doctrines emerged and how had it been agreed that they were 'right'? He went on in the 1890s to publish a history of early Christian writings and studies of the early missions.

Harnack's conclusion was that Protestant Christians ought to feel free to distance themselves from some of the teachings of the church as they had been consolidated in the Roman Catholic West and to return to a 'pure' early faith, which he believed himself to be unearthing from underneath the later accretions. In saying this kind of thing he was doing nothing new. The notion that 'true' Christianity had been buried under additions and impositions on the faithful had been actively pressed by dissidents in the West at least from the time of Wyclif. Although he became a controversial figure and his appointment was opposed by conservative theologians, Harnack was appointed to posts at the universities of Marburg and Berlin and was made a member of the Academy of Sciences. He attracted criticism for saying that the Apostles' Creed would no longer do as a basic statement of the Christian faith to which all Christians, especially ordinands, ought to be prepared to subscribe. He was conscious of the special contemporary circumstances in which it had emerged, and the failure to cover a number of topics which had been the focus of official doctrinal decision-making only in later centuries (notably many aspects of the doctrine of the church and the sacraments). He insisted that the Bible should be treated for the purposes of study just like any other ancient text and subjected to the same critical demands.

His *Essays on the Social Gospel* appeared in 1907. Nevertheless, Harnack blotted his reputation as a fearless critic independent of social expectations by approving the actions of Germany at the outset of the First World War with his signature (together with that of ninety-three professors of theology and other intellectuals in Germany). Their 'Manifesto to the Civilized World' of 1914 claimed divine support for a war to be waged in support of a 'culture'.

Not all these ground-breaking theologians with German links supported the First and Second World Wars. Karl Barth (1886–1968) was a theologian of the next generation to whom this proved repugnant. Barth grew up in Switzerland and became a Reformed (Calvinist) pastor and a professor of theology in a series of German universities (Göttingen, Münster and then Bonn). He was involved with the Christian socialist movement of Germany and Switzerland. His own writing began to reflect his distaste for the philosophy of the 'Manifesto to the Civilized World' and to express (for example in his commentary on Romans of 1922) a view of the death of Jesus which frees it from all cultural contextualization and resists attempts to tie it to any particular cultural theme.

The practical implications of this stand became significant in the 1930s, when the Nazi movement was gaining ground in Germany. Barth played a leading part in writing the Barmen Declaration, which sought to separate the church decisively from any link with Hitler. Barth was made to leave his post at Bonn because he would not swear an oath of allegiance to Hitler. He was able to move to Basel and continue to teach there.

After the Second World War he turned his attention to encouraging overtures of reconciliation and repentance from German churches towards Christians in other countries, for example collaborating in the writing of the Darmstadt Statement of 1947. He argued that it was the loss of contact

Karl Barth, photographed in the 1950s.

with socialist and social gospel imperatives which had made it possible for the German Christian leaders to align themselves with Nazism.

Like Harnack he was attracted to the idea of writing a systematic account of the whole conspectus of Christian theology. His *Church Dogmatics* appeared in thirteen volumes between 1932 and 1968. The approach was chronological and responsive to the questions which were presenting themselves throughout the period in which he was writing, including questions raised by students. His attitude to the Bible was far from the traditional extreme evangelical Protestant view of its inerrancy.

MISSION, ECUMENISM AND INTERFAITH DIALOGUE

The Modern Missionary Revolution

A World Missionary Conference was held in the Assembly Hall of the United Free Church of Scotland in Edinburgh in 1910. This was the largest gathering ever of representatives of Christian missions going out to convert the world, chiefly from Protestant churches. There were 1,200 delegates and only 170 were from the non-English-speaking 'missionary societies' of continental Europe. Seventeen were from Africa and the East and they were present as representatives of the churches which had been 'planted' there, mainly in the course of colonial expansion. All the rest were British or American and their numerical dominance reflected the importance of a polarity stretching across the Atlantic between the UK and the USA, rather than between Europe and the rest of the world.

John R. Mott gave the closing address, in which there was a note of the old triumphalism of the colonial age of missionary endeavour: 'The end of the conference is the beginning of the conquest'. Africa, claimed Mott, was, as a result of the work of missionaries, 'in the beginnings of transformation from ignorance, barbarism, and superstition, into the light of modern civilization.'

But there is awareness in some of the reports of the conference that the times had other tides, and that the future prospects of success of Christian missions were going to depend in part on world events in which the outreach of European Christianity was no longer going to be possible from a position of dominance. Japan was emerging as an industrialized nation. The situation in Asia was changing, especially in China and Korea. There was growing understanding of the potential for conflicts between Islam and Christianity, especially in some parts of the world. There was also some acknowledgment of a trend towards secularism in lands which had formerly been definitively Christian.

Christian Attitudes to Modern War

The new way of thinking about the missionary task also reflected the severance of the old link between 'mission' and 'conquest'. European wars in the twentieth century became World Wars. Both sides in the First World War saw themselves rather as though they had been crusaders, as defenders of a Christian civilization against those who would destroy it.

Conscientious objectors were at first reviled, but the tide of popular opinion began to swing against the war as it became clear that the casualty figures were enormous, and there were mutterings against the church leaders who had not spoken out against it. For church leaders to speak against violence was novel and disturbing, as much in the Orthodox lands as in the West. The First World War regiments from Russia set off with icons which the Orthodox clergy were happy to bless, as they did the troops themselves. Memorials to the dead of the First and Second World Wars are still to be found in churches, often with inscriptions speaking of the sacrifice of the soldiers.

Soldiers in the trenches in the First World War.

The Second World War was still widely perceived among Christians as a necessary response to the dangerous ambitions of Nazi Germany, a war which had to be fought to defend the freedom and independence of threatened nations. It was not apparent until afterwards how extensive what we would now call the 'ethnic cleansing' of the Jews had been, as the full horrors of the Holocaust emerged. But even if Nazism had not had this agenda of racial purification, it was a real enough threat to the independence of peoples which faced invasion. The history of Europe had repeatedly taught the lesson that no one's boundaries were secure and no nation's culture was safe.

The Second World War spread, however, far beyond Europe, and extended outside the mainly Christian lands of Europe itself. The traumatic consequences of lengthy imprisonment in Japanese prisoner-of-war camps came back to Europe with the survivors. The determination to ensure that there was no Third World War kept Europe at peace for half a century.

The Cold War was undoubtedly a protective factor here. The invention of nuclear weapons at the end of the Second World War and the balancing of power between the Communist bloc and the West 'froze' situations which were potentially capable of starting fresh wars. The consequences were too terrible to contemplate when a new war could lay waste huge areas of the earth under a cloud of radioactivity for generations.

The collapse of Communism in the 1990s removed this check. The new 'enemy' which emerged in the minds of the Western powers was Islamic terrorism. Though there were apparent moves by Islamic countries to develop nuclear weapons, the situation was not a re-creation of the opposing 'Great Power' blocs, but the confrontation of a 'Great Power' with the guerilla warfare of terrorism, real or imagined. Europe was sandwiched in the middle, geographically and culturally, and was helpless to prevent the escalation of Moslem hatred of the West on its eastern borders and within its own communities, where by now considerable numbers of Moslem immigrants were living.

The two World Wars helped to transform relations and aspirations both inside Christianity (prompting the 'ecumenical movement') and between Christianity and other faiths.

ANGLICANISM AS A WORLD COMMUNION

The Church of England grew into a worldwide Anglican Communion, reaching far beyond Europe. Though it has never had more than a toehold in mainland Europe its global reach makes it an important factor in the history of European Christianity.

The colonial expansion of Britain up to the nineteenth century resulted in outposts of the Church of England, which gradually became provinces of the Anglican Church. Each had a relationship with the local government which was peculiar to the political circumstances of the locality and no attempt was made to recreate in other parts of the world the special relationship set up under Elizabeth I between the Church of England and the English state.

The first serious test of this diversity came with the calling of the first Lambeth Conference in 1867, when it was formally recognized that the Anglican provinces must remain autonomous and the Conference could not make decisions which would be binding on any of its members. The Lambeth Conference has met once every ten years since, on the same basis.

A characteristic of Anglicanism, perhaps deriving from this structural feature, has been its readiness to embrace diversity. There are informal 'parties', such as evangelical conservatives, liberals and Catholics, leaning to one end or the other of the spectrum between extreme Reformation and conventional Roman Catholic ideas, but they all coexist within Anglicanism, and have not so far proved divisive to the point of fragmenting the Communion.

Ecumenism

The World Council of Churches began in 1937, although its formal inauguration was delayed by the Second World War until 1948. At the outset 147 churches joined, and now there are more than 300, including many of the Orthodox and most of the Protestant churches, although the Roman Catholic Church has never been a member. Nevertheless, the Vatican appoints working members to join in its activities.

The ecumenical movement of the mid- and late twentieth century grew out of the Faith and Order process of the earlier twentieth century and the founding of the World Council of Churches. It has had a particular piquancy in Europe because of the need to repair relationships among Christians which had been strained for centuries: between 'Roman' and Orthodox; between Protestant and Roman Catholic; and between different sorts of Protestant, each with different geographical distributions, sometimes involving rivalries within a small area.

The Second World War had involved widespread mutual destruction, which included historic monuments of Christendom. Britain bombed Dresden in Germany; the Germans bombed Coventry. Christians responded as early as 1945 by forming links, notably between these two cities as Coventry set about building a new cathedral. It was conceived not as a rebuilding of the old but as something which was to be wholly new and send a different message to the world.

The ecumenical movement was given a considerable stimulus by the Second Vatican Council (1962–1965), and there followed several decades at the end of the twentieth century when committees were formed between the divided churches to discuss how they might be united and report back. Conversations began between the Evangelical church in Germany and the Church of England as early as 1964. The topics chosen were ambitious. The final report of the first Anglican-Roman Catholic International Commission, for example, deals with 'Eucharist, Ministry and Authority'.

The bilateral agreements were typically arrived at as a consequence of a process of mutual rapprochement, and even swapping over the participants in the dialogue, as they met once or twice a year and spent a week or two living, eating and working closely together. The difficulty of keeping an eye on the rapprochements which were taking place in other bilaterals involving a given communion led to some anomalies.

The problem of language also proved important. At the time when most of the divisions had taken place, in the sixteenth century, theology in the West was still 'done' in Latin, at least by the 'professionals'. Now

Coventry Cathedral after
it had been bombed, and
the rebuilt cathedral with
Graham Sutherland's
tapestry.

agreement had to be reached by subtle adjustments of understanding in a variety of European languages, though in the case of the Anglican-Methodist conversations English served for both partners. In the case of Anglican-Roman Catholic dialogues it was agreed to work in English and make English the authoritative language of publication.

The shock came when the agreed statements had to be referred to the participating communions for ratification. Each bilateral dialogue (and most were bilateral) naturally focused on the most painful points at issue between the two churches concerned. It turned out that they were still painful. It emerged that 'decision-making' was not the same or understood in the same way everywhere. This was particularly evident in the case of the agreed text

YVES CONGAR, JEAN TILLARD AND HANS KÜNG

Yves Congar.

Hans Küng.

Yves Congar (1904–1995) was a French Dominican who had grown up in an area of northern France occupied by the Germans during the First World War and kept diaries of what he saw. During the Second World War he was a prisoner of war for some years. He became one of the leading theologians of the Roman Catholic Church to develop a doctrine of the church which would help to take ecumenism forward by making it possible for Christians of different persuasions to stop 'unchurching' one another.

A further leading figure in Roman Catholic ecumenical theology in the twentieth century was another Dominican priest, Jean Tillard (d. 2000). He, like Ratzinger and Küng, was appointed an official expert at the Second Vatican Council. He became a member of several of the commissions which worked on bilateral dialogues and produced ecumenical statements and reports in the decades which followed. He was a member of the first Anglican-Roman Catholic International Commissions (1968–2000), the dialogue with the Disciples of Christ (1977–2000), the Orthodox-Roman Catholic Commission (1980–2000), and the Faith and Order Commission of the World Council of Churches (1975–2000).

Hans Küng (b. 1928) is a Swiss theologian and Roman Catholic priest. He was a colleague of Joseph Ratzinger (later Pope Benedict XVI) at the University of Tübingen in Germany in the 1960s and, like Ratzinger, he was appointed as an official expert (*peritus*) to advise the bishops in their discussions at the Second Vatican Council. In 1979 he had his licence to teach Roman Catholic theology removed by the Vatican because he too concluded that the doctrine of papal infallibility is not acceptable. His book *Infallible: An Inquiry* was published in 1971.

Küng was able to continue to make a name as a theologian and to teach at Tübingen as a professor of ecumenical theology. In this capacity he began to explore the idea of a global and universal set of ethical principles and to tackle the problem of the relations of science and religion in its modern forms.

on 'Baptism, Eucharist and Ministry' of the World Council of Churches.

The resulting uncertain 'agreements' have led to some tentative experiments in shared worship, but so far the big dividing factors of the past have not really been removed as continuing causes of division, particularly the disagreements about the nature of ministry in the church and the ways in which ministers should be appointed or ordained. Until those are resolved, the visible structures of the church cannot be unified. Growth towards full, visible unity remains a distant ambition. Meanwhile new divisive effects have made themselves apparent in the late twentieth century, with the ordination of women in some communions to the priesthood and to the episcopate, and more recently with the ordination of practising homosexuals.

Among the most successful rapprochements have been those between Lutherans and Anglicans (resulting in the Meissen Agreement of 1991) and those between the Lutherans of the Nordic–Baltic countries and the Anglicans of Britain and Ireland (the Porvoo Agreement of 1996).

Multicultural and Interfaith Situations

A 'world' context for Christian belief has inescapably established itself in Europe with the immigration of recent generations, often from regions of the world where a part of Europe expanded by sending settlements there

THE OLD CATHOLICS

The first of the 'Old Catholics' appeared in the Netherlands in the eighteenth century following disagreements with the Roman papal court or Curia. The Declaration of Utrecht of 1889 defined their position and they formed a Union of Utrecht, a federation of Old Catholic churches. Similar movements began in Germany and in Switzerland after the First Vatican Council in 1869. The Old Catholics as a group seceded from the Roman Catholic Church in the nineteenth century because its members refused to accept the doctrine of papal infallibility. They are therefore not in communion (able to join together in the celebration of the Eucharist) with Rome. The question which prompted the Old Catholics to take their stand has not gone away.

The Old Catholics made the first ecumenical agreement in 1931, with the Anglicans. They are also in communion with the Philippine Independent Church. In recent times the Old Catholics have shown a tendency to be liberal, for example over the ordination of women and the acceptance of unions of persons of the same sex, which has occurred in Old Catholic communities in the Netherlands, Germany, Austria and Switzerland, though there have been recent secessions over such points.

in earlier centuries. For example, Spain has many immigrants from Spanish-speaking South America; France has immigrants from Morocco. Britain has immigrants from India and Pakistan, Africa and the Caribbean. Some of these are Christians; many are not. The Netherlands have Islamic immigrants from Surinam ('Dutch Guiana') and Indonesia, former colonies, and migrant workers from Turkey and Morocco. Others have arrived as refugees as a result of recent upheavals in their own countries of Afghanistan, Iraq, Iran and Bosnia. The proportion of Moslems has risen, causing some tensions, especially after the murder of the film director, actor and social commentator Theo van Gogh in the Netherlands by a Moroccan Moslem, Mohammed Bouyeri, in 2004. A new wave of migration has been encouraged by the expansion of the European Union, so that Roman Catholics from Poland or Orthodox from Romania may arrive to work for a time or to settle.

All this requires sensitivities not envisaged in earlier European generations. Among the Christian immigrants there may be lingering resentments. For example, some Caribbean Methodists will say that they now feel that the spirit in which the missionaries brought the faith to their islands was imperialist. In an attempt to avoid repeating such attitudes, now repented of and looked on with horror, the world-wide Christian communions have been anxious to avoid imposing European approaches on Christians from Africa and Asia. This has been apparent, for example, at recent ten-yearly Lambeth Conferences of bishops from all over the Anglican world.

However, the history of Christianity for many centuries was European and it cannot easily be separated completely from the European traditions in which it was formed. This is proving a real difficulty when it comes to the training of those who are to be ordained. A generation ago a ministerial training course, like a theology degree which it frequently required, would consist of the study of the Bible in Greek and Hebrew as well as in translation; the study of the writings of the Fathers; perhaps a course in church history and something on systematic theology, including the more revolutionary ideas of modern theology; and a grounding in liturgy and the theory and practice of pastoral care. The early Christian tradition, with its deep roots in European civilization, is now likely to be an increasingly problematic and perhaps optional area of study.

This can lead to a dangerous ignorance about the reasons for established practices. A case in point is the way the ordination of practising homosexuals to the priesthood and episcopate has led some parishes in the USA to leave the Anglican Communion and place themselves under the oversight of a Nigerian bishop. Not long before, a similar solution of departing from the ancient idea that 'local' churches are local in a territorial sense had been proposed to help those who would not accept the ordination of women. The question was – and remains – whether the ecclesiology involved undermines an important rule or whether a metaphorical local church is an acceptable alternative to a geographical one.

In Europe at large a variety of solutions is emerging to the problem of retreating from behaviour which could look like Christian triumphalism or imperialism. The danger did not disappear with the nineteenth century. When Communism collapsed in the 1990s and Orthodoxy began to reassert itself in the lands of the former Soviet Union, some Evangelical Christian missions from the USA arrived in apparent ignorance that they were bringing Christianity to communities where it had been for many centuries, in a form which would not be receptive to their approach.

Some countries are still predominantly Roman Catholic (such as Belgium, France, Ireland, Italy, Portugal and Spain). In France religious broadcasting is dealt with by the public service channel, giving much of Sunday morning to Christian religious broadcasting, though it allows certain religious minorities access in a way it seeks to ensure is proportional to their numbers in the country: Jewish, Moslem, Protestant and now Buddhist.

Some countries have a mixture of Roman Catholic and Protestant Christians (Great Britain, the Netherlands, Northern Ireland and western Germany). Into Germany have come numerous Turkish immigrant workers bringing the Islamic faith. Other countries are predominantly Lutheran (Denmark, Finland, Iceland, Norway and Sweden). Eastern Europe contains complex juxtapositions of Moslem, Orthodox and Roman Catholic Christianity.

This lends a new complexion to the relations between the faiths in Europe. Interfaith dialogue must now be conducted in an atmosphere of mutual respect. Talk of a 'War on Terror' has added an alarming dimension to interfaith relations, since the 'terrorism' has been imputed to Islamic extremism.

The Uneasy Modern Compromise in the Balkans

Meanwhile, from the end of the seventeenth century in the regions of Europe where things had been unsettled for centuries, the borderlands between Eastern and Western Christianity where Islamic invasions had repeatedly created additional strains, there were continuing uncertainties.

'The Turks are fleeing before the Christians, the Bulgarians before the Greeks and the Turks, the Greeks and Turks before the Bulgarians, the Albanians before the Serbians,' said the Carnegie Commission, in its Report of the International Commission to Inquire into the Causes and Conduct of the Balkan Wars in 1914. 'The Serbs, as you know, have reason to feel tense. If Germany and its vassal Hungary attacked her from the north, Italy attacked her through Albania from the south and by sea from the west, and Bulgaria attacked her from the East, she would be quickly finished. Her only chance would lie in the Russians outflanking the Germans and Hungarians with an attack launched through Rumania along the Bukovina railway,' commented Eric Ambler in *The Mask of Dimitrios* in 1939.

The Ottoman Moslems had fallen back before the Hapsburg conquest of Hungary and Croatia at the end of the seventeenth century, and afterwards traces of Islamic life and monuments in south-eastern Europe were energetically removed, though there are still stylistic reminders in the architecture of Hungary, for example. The Russo-Austrian war against the Turks held the position in the eighteenth century. But there was always uneasiness. A Serbian uprising of 1804 against the Ottoman Turks was followed by another in 1815. In 1826 it was agreed between Greek and Turkish authorities in certain areas that Greeks should purchase the property of Turks where the communities had been living in the same area.

The nation-states of the Balkans drove out the Ottoman empire late in the nineteenth century, but it was by no means clear that the 'nationalities' and 'states' would be able to remain stable. Some of these new states behaved like colonial powers, sending agents to remote areas where they imposed the new régime on the locals, who were often hostile to find themselves 'colonized'. They have been described as 'A panoply of small, unviable, mutually antagonistic and internally intolerant states'.

The First Balkan War of 1912 was followed by the Second Balkan War of 1913. In 1918 a kingdom of Serbs, Croats and Slovenes was established (Yugoslavia in the making). From 1919 to 1922 there was a Greco-Turkish war in Anatolia. Arrangements had to be agreed where Christianity and Christian powers triumphed, such as those under which Turks moved out of Greece and Greeks moved out of Asia Minor under the Treaty of Lausanne between Greece and Turkey in 1923. Still all was not calm. In 1939 there was an Italian invasion of Albania.

The Mosque Church, originally a mosque but now a Roman Catholic church, in Széchenyi Square, Pécs, Hungary.

Communism collapsed in Eastern Europe in 1989, but the shift of power and influence made for new instabilities and revived old ones. In Bosnia, the period from 1992 to 1995 saw wars. We have already seen that 'ethnic cleansing' was not new in the south-east of Europe when it received so much press attention with the collapse of the former Yugoslavia.

Yugoslavia had two periods of existence. The first ran from after the First World War (which had been started by a Serb), from 1918 to 1941, when it formed a kingdom of Serbs, Croats and Slovenes. The second lasted from near the end of the Second World War, from 1943 to 1991, and took the form of a 'federal' Socialist Republic, until it disintegrated in the warfare of the 1990s.

Border-crossing has happened a good deal in the Balkans. Sometimes it has been for refugee purposes (running away from a dangerous situation), sometimes for immigration (where the place the would-be immigrants were running to was, from their point of view, not only a safer but an economically and culturally better place). For example, Serbian expansionism had Moslems leaving in some numbers the territories the Serbians were beginning to dominate from 1877.

Hungarian Christians were slow in achieving a balance of freedoms for Protestants and Roman Catholics. In 1790 a Diet granted Protestants control over the conduct of their churches, schools and religious affairs.

Roman Catholics, by contrast, were battling for equivalent control of their own affairs during the nineteenth century, latterly through the efforts of the Catholic Autonomy Association.

The first institution of higher education in Bulgaria was opened in 1888, first as a teacher training college. Within three months it was being given a wider brief, and the ministry of education was planning the governance and appointing the teaching staff. This happened only ten years after the Russo-Turkish war of 1877–1878 had secured independence for Bulgaria after 500 years of Turkish rule, when it was a matter of urgency to establish a Bulgarian 'identity' and to recruit a qualified civil service. But the problems were obvious enough. The standards in secondary schools were not adequate to provide a preparation for students and there was a shortage of native Bulgarians able to teach in the new university at an appropriate level. Moreover, no one had thought through the necessary purposes and principles for a university; it was even feared it might fail altogether. On the other hand the public benefits of having graduates in the community were obvious.

Modern Romania was formed in 1859 by joining the principalities of Moldavia and Wallachia. From 1872 the former metropolitanates of these two provinces agreed to unite to form the Romanian Orthodox church. It was not until 1885 that the Patriarch of Constantinople recognized the autocephaly of this church, and it did not become a patriarchate until 1925. There are 400 monasteries in Romanian Orthodoxy. In the nineteenth century the new Romanian constitution tried to exclude the Jews from normal membership of society, by conducting boycotts and restricting Jews from becoming students at the universities.

Why is it that Russia, much of which stretches into Asia, is still thought of as essentially 'European' while Turkey is not? This may have something to do with the fact that Russia is perceived as a Christian country, whose character was not radically altered in that respect by its period under Communism. But it is undoubtedly also in part a legacy of this still unresolved power struggle in the Balkans involving Eastern and Western churches and Islamic ambitions.

SECULARISM

In the Western parts of Europe a decisive current of the twentieth century was the drift towards secularism. The word 'secularism' first seems to have been used in the nineteenth century to describe the trend to put Christian religious belief in a less central context in the organization of

European society and arrange social expectations according to other considerations.

Secularism can have positive benefits when it comes to ensuring peace and security. It can take some of the tension out of the old passionate struggles of Christian Europe. It can provide a neutral framework within which people with different religious beliefs, or none, can live and work together. For such reasons, some European states have tried to ensure a clear separation between the requirements of the state and the expectations of religious communities. One of the unanswered questions left over from the long history of striving to find a balance between church and state is whether the state should be entirely secular. Turkey, for example, is a secular state, but in most Islamic states there is a difficult balance to be struck between religious and secular law.

England still has an Established Church, descended from the Protestant settlement of Elizabeth I in the late sixteenth century. In 1660 the English were obliged to go to church on Sunday on pain of having to pay a fine of one shilling. The English Toleration Act of 1689 allowed freedom of worship to Christians who did not belong to the Church of England but were Nonconformists, though it did not allow the same freedom to Roman Catholics (or to Unitarians, because they were deemed not to be Christians at all). The oath of allegiance to the sovereign was still required, but those who proved in this way that they were not seditious or treasonable in their intentions were allowed their own places of worship. It was not until the nineteenth century that the civil disabilities were also removed, for only members of the Church of England were allowed to hold office in the state.

The loss of the historic tensions within European Christianity can also take away the excitement and the interest which kept the affairs of Christian Europe at fever pitch for so long. It appears to be the case that a smaller proportion of many European populations are now regular churchgoers, thought there is considerable variation across Europe and expectations are changing rapidly as the European Union enlarges itself and new populations are exposed to the expectations which seem normal elsewhere. There is also a leaching away of general knowledge about the teachings of the Christian faith. It is apparent in modern Britain, for example, that relatively few of the population have a basic knowledge of Christian theology, even those who go to church, but that is as much a reflection of the national school curriculum and the adequacy of what is routinely taught at school. In schools where the children are from mixed ethnic backgrounds, with a variety of religions or none, the norm is now

Harvest festival at the
Celestial Church of
Christ, South London.

to teach comparative religion or religious studies, except perhaps in those specialist schools which are run by religious communities themselves, such as church schools. Fashions in syllabus content also affect the training and consequently the basic knowledge of the faith of those who enter the Christian ministry. Where religious thinking is comparatively uninstructed, minds may be the more easily seduced by banal substitutes such as horoscopes in newspapers, or the more dangerous preaching of various kinds of fundamentalism.

'Fundamentalism' is a modern word for a phenomenon which has existed throughout the history of Christianity. It was coined early in the twentieth century to describe a 'back to basics' movement to try to counter the tendency to liberal and 'modern' ways of explaining away Christian difficulties. It has come to be used for Evangelicals who claim that the Bible can and must be interpreted literally and – by transference – for equivalent attitudes in other religions, for example 'fundamentalist' Islam, where the Koran is taken literally.

Nazism succeeded in Germany in the 1930s partly because it was possible for a demagogue to persuade a people still smarting from losing the First World War that it could have a glorious future if it performed an 'ethnic cleansing'. The British National Party and its counterparts in other European countries at the present time play on a similar susceptibility to persuasion where the parameters of older Christian 'certainties' are less strongly felt. The present panic about Islamic fundamentalism may be heightened by the general ignorance of the teachings of Christianity and Islam in the population at large, because it adds the fear of the unknown to mutual hostilities which already have complex causes.

Alongside this leaching away of the Christian context and its replacement with secular ideas may go a positive pressure. Secularism and secularization can be ideological too. Marxist–Leninism was very keen to proselytize. In 1918 the new Soviet constitution permitted freedom in anti-religious propaganda (while maintaining a dictum of religious freedom) and banned Bibles, removed from the Orthodox church its right to own property and closed churches so that services could not be held in them.

The challenge posed by modern conceptions of secularism is what is to be done with the inveterate tendency of people to look beyond this life and wonder what will happen to them next. For most of the Christian centuries in Europe this question has been answered in terms which were also a social pacifier. However unpleasant the conditions in which you live now, the world to come will make up for it.

Conclusion

In today's world Europe is still a recognizable entity. The advent of the European Community, now the European Union, has greatly strengthened its position and its attraction as something many countries wish to join. Yet its impact cannot readily be identified now as 'Christian'.

The once more or less predictable effects of Christian belief and practice in Europe have become blurred and complicated by other factors and contrasting influences. For example, the European Union has 'overridden' the teaching of the Roman Catholic Church on contraception, which has led to a drop in the birth rate in Roman Catholic countries, and it can no longer be assumed that family size reflects the predominant religious preference or loyalty in a given region. The statistical distribution of proportions of Protestants and Roman Catholics, once clearly the outcome of the historical developments we have been sketching, can now change dramatically even if only temporarily in a period of migration. For instance, when Poland became a member of the EU, Polish workers arrived in Britain in considerable numbers, not necessarily intending to immigrate permanently, but visibly swelling the congregations of Roman Catholic churches.

The more obvious markers of a Christian Europe, such as visible Christian observance, with large congregations attending churches, are no longer socially expected everywhere in Europe. Where people once went to church every week they may now go once a month or a few times a year, or only for weddings and funerals, looking to the churches for rites of passage rather than the steady assurance of a background to their lives. In some countries, where once it took a bold individual to admit that he or she was not a convinced Christian, people are now shy of publicly calling themselves Christians and expect to be mocked for naivety and thought unfashionable if they do so.

There is often today a dearth of sophisticated theological knowledge where once it could be taken for granted that every child would be systematically catechized, even if not given much of a more general education. This can extend even to the 'professionals'. Training for the ministry varies enormously throughout Europe, in the academic level expected and the balance struck in seminaries and theological colleges between pastoral and theological preparation for the work, and in the general 'formation' of the priest or minister to ensure that he or she can be trusted for a lifetime with the heavy responsibility of supporting others in the Christian faith.

In some areas, such as parts of Britain, where immigration from the Caribbean has produced clusters of Black churches, a lively revivalist style of worship recreates a pattern more typical of some non-European styles, for example transatlantic church life, with a ministry in which the capacity to fire a congregation to strong, warm feeling may be more important than academic training, and where the congregation expects to choose and appoint its own ministers.

The question with which we must leave this study is whether these modern manifestations and changes represent the end of this long story or merely a further staging-post. For that old, deep interpenetration of Christianity and culture which formed Europe and sent its peoples out into the rest of the world is perhaps scarcely touched by these superficial contemporary adjustments.

Bibliography and Works Cited

Augustine, *De Doctrina Christiana*, ed. and tr. R. O. H. Green, Oxford: Oxford University Press, 1995.

Bede, *Ecclesiastical History of the English People*, eds B. Colgrave and R. A. B. Mynors, Oxford: Oxford University Press, 1969.

Donald F. Bond (ed.), *The Spectator*, 518, 16 October 1711, Oxford: Clarendon Press, 1965.

Robert Boyle, 'A letter to Mr. H[enry] O[ldenburg]', *The Works of Robert Boyle*, eds. Michael Hunter and Edward B. Davis, vol. 14. London: Pickering & Chatto, 2000.

John Calvin, tr. H. Bettenson, *Institutes of the Christian Religion*, Documents of the Christian Church, London: 1967.

E. Cameron, *The European Reformation*, Oxford: Oxford University Press, 1991.

Thomas Carlyle, 'Signs of the Times', *Critical and Miscellaneous Essays*, London: Chapman & Hall, 1899, vol. II.

Henry Chadwick, *East and West: The Making of a Rift in the Church*, Oxford: Oxford University Press, 2003.

Owen Chadwick, *The Early Reformation on the Continent*, Oxford: Oxford University Press, 2001.

Norman Daniel, *Islam and the West*, Oxford: One World, 1960, 1993.

Grace Davie, *Religion in Modern Europe*, Oxford: Oxford University Press, 2000.

Norman Davies, *Europe: East and West*, London: Jonathan Cape, 2006.

Erasmus, tr. Francis Morgan Nichols, *The Epistles of Erasmus*, London: Longman, 1901, vol. I.

Bernard de Fontenelle, tr. Jerome de Lande, *Entretiens sur la pluralité des mondes* (1686), London: 1803.

Misha Glenny, *The Balkans* (1804–1999), London: Granta Books, 1999.

George Holmes, *The Oxford History of Medieval Europe*, Oxford: Oxford University Press, 1988, reissued in paperback 2001.

Jonathan I. Israel, *Enlightenment Contested: Philosophy, Modernity, and the Emancipation of Man*, Oxford: Oxford University Press, 2006.

B. J. Kidd (ed.), *Documents Illustrative of the Continental Reformation*, Oxford: Clarendon Press, 1911.

John Knox, *History of the Reformation in Scotland*, ed. William Croft Dickinson, Edinburgh: Thomas Nelson, 1949, vol. I.

John Locke, *A Letter Concerning Toleration* (1689), ed. I Shapiro, New Haven: Yale University Press, 2003.

Diarmaid MacCullough, *Reformation: Europe's House Divided*, Harmondsworth: Penguin, 2003.

Mark Mazower, *The Balkans: From the End of Byzantium to the Present Day*, London: Phoenix, 2000.

John R. Mott, *The Decisive Hour of Christian Mission*, London: CMS, 1910.

John Julius Norwich, *The Middle Sea: A History of the Mediterranean*, London: Chatto and Windus, 2006.

J. M. Roberts, *The Penguin History of Europe*, Harmondsworth: Penguin, 1996.

Frank C. Senn, *The People's Work: A Social History of the Liturgy*, Minneapolis: Fortress Press, 2006.

Robert Southey, *New Letters of Robert Southey*, 9 April 1797, ed. Kenneth Curry, New York and London: Columbia University Press, 1965, vol. I.

E. E. Speight (ed.), *The Romance of the Merchant Venturers*, London: Hodder and Stoughton, 1906.

Strabo, *The Geography*, ed. H. L. Jones, London: Loeb, 1917.

Manfredo Tafuri, tr. K. Michael Hays, *Interpreting the Renaissance: Princes, Cities, Architects*, New Haven: Yale University Press, 2006.

Victor-L. Tapié, *The Age of Grandeur: Baroque Art and Architecture*, New York: Grove Press, 1957, English translation published 1960.

A. J. P. Taylor, *The Struggle for Mastery in Europe (1848–1918)*, Oxford: Clarendon Press, 1954, paperback edition 1971.

Walter Ullmann, *A Short History of the Papacy in the Middle Ages*, London: University Paperbacks, 1974.

John Wesley, *The Works of John Wesley: Journal and Diaries*, ed. W. Reginald Ward, Nashville: Abingdon Press, 1988, vol. I.

Derek Wilson, *Charlemagne: Barbarian and Emperor*, London: Pimlico, 2006.

A. D. Wright, *The Counter-Reformation: Catholic Europe and the Non-Christian World*, London: Weidenfeld and Nicolson, 1982.

Index